Remembering America's Heroes is a 501(c)(3) non-profit organization based in Milwaukie, Oregon. RAH's mission is to educate our youth and the community about the high cost of freedom and the sacrifices made by our country's military veterans.

Under the leadership of Executive Director Ken Buckles, Remembering America's Heroes (RAH) provides education to youth and the community so they can understand and appreciate the value of freedom and its cost.

www.rahusa.us

REMEMBRANCE

BY

KENNETH BUCKLES

BENJAMIN BLAIR

To Doc,

Ken Buckles

This book is dedicated to one veteran and one mother.

First, William Forrest Chisholm, Army, Korean War, Chosin Few, as he represents just one of the millions of veterans who suffer silently among us. Bill not only became a close friend, but I look at him as a father figure. It took twenty-one years before Bill would open up and share his experiences with me. It is my hope that his story and the many other veterans' stories in this book will help other veterans to open up or get help.

Second, to the amazing Holocaust Survivor Gizella Goldstein Soltesz, Eva Aigner's mother, as she represents just one of the millions of mothers who did everything in their power to protect their children from the horrors of war. Even though I never met Gizella, her story will always inspire me, and I believe she will inspire you the reader as well.

"We who have seen war, will never stop seeing it. In the silence of the night, we will always hear the screams. So this is our story, for we were soldiers once, and young."

~Joseph L. Galloway
We Were Soldiers Once, and Young

CONTENTS

I have walked these Korean hills before, crossed these rivers
I have passed through these fields, heavy with the odor of growth
My presence is here... and elsewhere
In the pages of a letter, yellow with age
At the edge of a photograph, on a torn dance program
I am by love begotten
I am not forgotten

I am here in the hearts of those who were with me
On the perimeter, at Inchon, at the Reservoir and the River
And in the hearts of those who waited
In their thoughts I walk again
And I wait at the curb in my car on a soft summer evening
The sound of crickets, of passing automobiles
And the muted sounds of the city are near
I am a tear in the eyes of mothers, sisters, fathers,
Brothers, wives, friends, lovers
I am by love begotten
I am not forgotten

I am black, white, Jewish, Gentile, red, yellow
I speak English, Korean, Chinese, Turkish, Greek, Spanish
I am known in many countries and by many people
I have heard the rush of summer seas and the fist of thunder
I have known a distant star on a cold December night
And I have known the love of a friend who would die for me
And I for him
I am by love begotten
I am never forgotten

~Richard L. (Dick) Kirk
Lt. Col. Richard Kirk, 2nd Inf. Div., U.S. Army

We're the Battling Bastards of Bataan,
No Mama, No Papa, No Uncle Sam,
No aunts, no uncles, no cousins, no nieces,
No pills, no planes, no artillery pieces,
And nobody gives a damn!

~Frank Hewlett, 1942
war correspondent and poet

Preface

"The Forgotten War" is what they called it. Most Americans know nothing about this war, and all Korean War veterans deserve better. It is shocking to learn that among all the books written about American Wars, at the very bottom of the lists is usually the Korean War. I hope *Remembrance II* will help many of us not forget those brave men who fought and many who died serving our country.

I am incredibly happy that readers of this book will learn about the men of The Chosin Few Oregon Chapter. The Battle at the Chosin Reservoir in North Korea is considered one of the US military's greatest achievements, even with so many American KIAs and casualties, plus suffering through the coldest weather North Korea had seen on record, the outcome was a miracle.

All parts of this book are important; however, I am most excited about the part on "The Most Grateful Country in the World, South Korea" and Pastor Kang Suk So, Admiral Kim, and all the adult and teenage volunteers, and the entire congregation of the Sae Eden Presbyterian Church in Seoul, Korea, whom I was able to meet personally on my travels to Korea both with veterans and in a personal capacity.

During my visits there, I have never in my life seen American veterans so respected, honored, loved, and appreciated with such heartfelt gratitude. Words cannot express what my wife and I personally experienced at the Sae Eden Church and everywhere else we went during our trips to South Korea.

To witness the love given to our veterans and how emotional and healing it was to them all, is something I shall never forget. And until the day I die, I will tell people about the Sae Eden Presbyterian Church's gratitude in Seoul, Korea.

Volume II of *REMEMBRANCE* also continues with the stories of more veteran heroes who served in World War II. I hope you will find this to be a unique book about many American veterans' personal stories, including African American, Native American, and Mexican American veterans, some of which even their spouses, children, or grandchildren have never heard. Until now.

Included in this volume are the experiences of Holocaust survivors Les and Eva Aigner, which are so helpful and inspirational for today. In addition, you will also read about the personal story of the only Tuskegee Airman, Roger Terry, and how he had to pay an unjust price for his role in the 1945 Freeman Field Mutiny. Roger deserves his place in history as well.

I am also happy that many readers will learn about the Defenders of Bataan & Corregidor -Ex-POWs of the Japanese, who survived the infamous Bataan Death March, the surrender at Corregidor, the prison camps, the nightmarish 'Hell Ships', and being slave laborers.

For twenty-four years, I brought American veterans from all over the United States to high schools in Oregon to share their military experiences during times of war with students. Over the years, as I became friends with many of these veterans, they began to open up and share their stories with me.

Many veterans refused to talk for years but reached out to me as they became older because they wanted their stories remembered. This book is also unique as it includes chapters from American veterans of many races, all of whom have served their country with great pride. We must not forget all these men and women's stories, lest we forget the cost they gave for our freedom.

Ken Buckles

★

Introduction

Every day on average 22 veterans take their lives, and it is the family that is left behind to deal with all the pain. Nationally, almost 45,000 American families go through losing a loved one every year to suicide, with the highest suicide rates being among whites and Native Americans.

Over a million Americans think seriously about suicide every year, and the ripple effect of all this is unbelievable. Many families do not like to acknowledge or even talk about losing a loved one to suicide.

I strongly feel it is particularly important to acknowledge and to share my family's painful day of learning about my father, a Korean War veteran's suicide. His death changed my life forever and hurt me greatly, however it was the major spark that eventually led me to start Living History Day.

In *REMEMBRANCE Volume I*, in the Prologue and the Introduction, I wrote about my father, Gordon W. Buckles, a Marine and Korean War veteran. He, like all veterans of combat, dealt with what is now commonly known today as PTSD (Post Traumatic Stress Disorder), and at the age of 54 years old, took his life.

What I find amazing is for almost 40 years, I never talked about Tuesday, September 19, 1984 -the day my father committed suicide. Not even with my brother and sister. That all changed when I was being interviewed and filmed by Sae Eden Presbyterian Church in Seoul, South Korea, and the interviewer asked me, "How did you find out about your father's suicide?"

I immediately responded without even thinking and never paused until I finished telling my entire story of that day. It was never my intention to do this, and I still cannot answer why I did. It was the first time I had even talked about it.

It was towards the end of seventh period, about 1:50 p.m. in strength training in Milwaukie High School's weight room, when one of the main office secretaries came into the room and told me, "The Milwaukie Police just called and ordered you to go immediately to your parents' home."

I said, "Ok, I'll call my parents at the end of the period," without even giving it a second thought. She left and came back about ten minutes later, visibly shaken and in a raised voice said, "The police said if you don't go to your parents' home now, they will come to get you and personally take you there."

That got my attention. I ran to my office and got my car keys out of my locker and told one of the PE teachers who was also an assistant football coach, "Tell Coach Harn the Milwaukie Police have ordered me to my parents' home, but I will still be at practice."

Practice always started at 2:40, and it was an unwritten law in coaching football that coaches can never be late or miss a practice. It is a sin.

At the time I owned an old 1951 Dodge pick-up and raced as fast as that truck could go the entire two-mile drive to my childhood home. I remember driving through two stop signs and a red light. My mind was racing the entire time.

All I could think of was: What in the hell could have happened? Did the house burn down? Was our home broken into? Were my parents robbed? What if they were murdered?

As I drove down the small hill to our house in the cul-de-sac, there were several police cars in the street with their lights flashing, and an ambulance was in the driveway.

From that moment on, everything happened in slow motion. I parked my truck in the middle of the street, and a Clackamas County Deputy Sheriff walked up to me and said, "Are you Ken Buckles? I'm so sorry, your father has taken his life and your mother needs you."

Just then, my mother ran out of the front door screaming, holding her head with both hands, and then she started running in circles in the front yard. I could not understand anything she was saying because she was hysterical. I grabbed her and hugged her, she started crying and wailing and said repeatedly, "He did it. He did it."

The sheriff said, "Why don't you both go into the house for a while and try to calm down?" After about twenty minutes or so, I told my mom I needed to ask the police some questions. I left the room and walked down the hallway into the living room towards the family room where my father's body lay.

Before I could get there, I was physically stopped by two policemen who told me, "You don't want to see your father like this." I was very upset and said, "I need to see my father, now." The Deputy sheriff then came into the room and repeated what the officers had just told me, but also included, "Please trust us, Ken. You do not want this to be your last memory of your dad."

After his time in Korea, my father told my mom, "There will never be guns in this house as I've seen what guns can do to humans." Even though he grew up hunting and was a Marine, he never owned a gun as an adult. Until September 19, 1984. I later found out he went to the local G.I. JOE'S store and bought a 30-06 (thirty-ought-six) deer rifle, went home, sat on the couch in the family room, put the rifle under his chin, and pulled the trigger.

I will never forget the last time I saw my father's body. The memory is seared into my memory. As I turned around to walk back to my mother, I heard a voice yell from the family room that they were moving the body out, as if they were warning the other officers to get me out of the living room. I did not move and soon saw someone pulling the rolling gurney out of the family room towards the door to the garage.

I saw a black body bag on the gurney, which of course held my father's body inside. That was all I saw, but it was still so disturbing that I will never forget it.

I got my mother to leave the house and go to a neighbor's next door. They were very gracious and shocked. I remember the two women comforting my mother.

Going through my mom's black personal phone book, I started calling my brother and sister and relatives. My grandmother (my mom's mom) and her two younger brothers all drove down from Seattle and arrived that evening. My first wife, Lorraine, was working, so I left her a message to meet me at my parents' home as soon as she could. No cell phones or voice messages back then.

I will never forget when Lorraine pulled up and got out of her car. I approached her and said, "I have some horrible news. My father committed suicide." She collapsed on the cement driveway and started wailing and saying over and over, "No! No! No!" Then, "Why? Why? Why?"

Then it hit me: I had missed football practice. The only thing I could think of was, Oh my God, what will the players think of me? And about Benjamin, my stepson who was a junior on the team and was still at practice for I had totally forgotten about him.

I learned later that night from our head coach, Jerry Harn, that it was the worst practice he had ever been a part of. He eventually stopped practice to gather the team around to talk about the tragic news.

My mom forced me to continue teaching and coaching. "Your father would expect you to do your job, and so do I." She said, "I'm ordering you to teach and to coach in the upcoming Friday night's game."

I went to our practice and gathered the team around, and I told them everything. It was very emotional with a lot of tears. This went on for over an hour. One of our great team leaders stood up and yelled that the players were dedicating the game to my father and mother.

That Friday, we solidly beat a particularly good team, but with all due respect to the team we played, the game was already won before the first kickoff.

I will never forget the last couple of minutes of the game. I was standing next to my stepson Benjamin and put my arm around him. I noticed he had tears running down his face. That got me all emotional and we both hugged. Then the rest of the teammates started joining the group hug. Many of us were crying.

Then one of the players points to the sunset and yells, "Look Coach, your father is sending us a message!"

It was an unbelievable sight. It was a cloudy evening with dark gray and black clouds and was forecast to rain. However, it did nothing of the sort, for just as the sun was close to setting, the clouds parted with beautiful rays of light shooting out across the sky reaching out to us on the sideline. It was surreal and it stayed that way for only a few minutes before the clouds covered up the sun. I will never forget it.

Back to the interview in Seoul. This is where I stopped talking and looked away from the camera. It was silent in the room. Several of the Sae Eden Church volunteers as well as the adults and teenagers, had tears in their eyes.

I looked to my left where my beautiful wife Malinda was standing and she was crying, and our personal Sae Eden chaperone Esther, a high school student, was also crying. They both hugged each other. The camera crew and interviewer were just staring at me. Then she told me, "Wow, I think that's good enough."

I still do not know why I opened up and told them the story, but I felt at that very moment that it was very healing.

But why am I telling you this? Well, it was at that moment that I also remembered, the number one word used by veterans of many wars is HEALING!

This book not only starts out continuing with the stories of World War II veterans, but also leads into the Korean War and those veterans sharing their own personal stories. With it is my hope that you will learn about all these wonderful people who gave so much for their country as well as give them the opportunity for the continuance of the healing.

It is also my hope that the readers will be inspired by these experiences as they offer hope and learning, in that all these veterans endured not only tragedy and loss but survived. For me personally, they have really helped me get through the Covid-19 pandemic of 2020-2021, and I have been comforted and inspired by all of them, many I now call my dear friends…

* ★ *

PART I : WORLD WAR II

We're the Battling Bastards of Bataan,
No Mama, No Papa, No Uncle Sam,
No aunts, no uncles, no cousins, no nieces,
No pills, no planes, no artillery pieces,
And nobody gives a damn!

~Frank Hewlett, 1942
war correspondent and poet

DEFENDERS OF BATAAN & CORREGIDOR

I was probably eight years old when, one evening, my father came home with a friend who entered our house very slowly using metal crutches. It seemed to take him forever to walk through our living room into the kitchen, where he carefully took a chair at the kitchen table.

I must have been staring because my father came up to me and said in a low voice, "Stop staring. That man is a survivor of the Bataan Death March. You're too young to learn about it, but when you do, you must never forget about them."

Since that day, I have been fascinated with things associated with the subjects of Corregidor, Hell Ships, slave labor, and Japanese atrocities in POW Camps. Having read many books on the tragic events of Bataan and Corregidor, my father was right. We should never forget about them.

AMERICAN DEFENDERS OF BATAAN AND CORREGIDOR NATIONAL REUNIONS

When working as the Veterans Outreach Coordinator at the Evergreen Aviation & Space Museum in McMinnville, Oregon, during 2012-2013, I was given the opportunity to attend two veteran national reunions of my choosing. The number-one choice on my request list was the American Defenders of Bataan and Corregidor.

As a football coach, I was in awe of these Ex-POWs because of their will and determination to live and their ability to survive over three and a half years of brutality, starvation, disease, and unbelievable atrocities. These men were incredible humans who could teach me a lot so I could inspire my players.

I reached out and spoke to the president of American Defenders of Bataan and Corregidor, Jan Thompson, the daughter of a deceased veteran of Bataan and Corregidor. I asked if I could speak at their upcoming 2013 reunion. Also, I told her that Malinda had offered to sing at their event. Jan graciously agreed.

Malinda and I traveled to Norfolk, Virginia, in May 2013 for the American Defenders of Bataan and Corregidor National Reunion. There were ten Ex-POWs in attendance at the reunion, all in their mid-nineties. The majority in attendance were the adult children of deceased Ex-POWs.

These families have done an incredible job of keeping their parents' memories alive, men who were real heroes to me. They were beyond inspirational. I hardly have the words to say how much being able to meet them meant to me.

Included in the program were question-and-answer sessions with the Ex-POWs seated at the front of the room. Earlier, we submitted a question, and if chosen, the question would be asked during the Q&A time. Jan told us to offer only softball questions.

I smiled and said, "I hope you mean slow-pitch softball because a pitch in fast-pitch softball is hard to hit."

"You know what I mean," Jan replied. "No atrocity-type questions allowed."

My question was one of those chosen. As a football coach, I was curious to hear their answers. "To survive over three years as POWs in such horrific conditions would require tremendous mental toughness, a never-quit attitude. To what do you attribute your mental toughness and never-quit attitude?"

I wish I had written their names in my notes. The first man to answer said, "My playing high school football."

The second replied, "I'd have to say playing high school football helped me, too."

The third man laughed and said, "Well, I was too small to play football, but I wrestled and played baseball."

The fourth answered, "Football and my head coach."

I was pleasantly surprised but not shocked at the Ex-POWs answers to my question. Over the years, as I got to know Ex-POWs, I learned that the majority grew up on farms during the Great Depression and learned the value of hard work at very young ages.

All of them were mentally tough and had a never-quit attitude. Back then, large numbers of boys played high school football, wrestled, and boxed, and all of these were considered rites of passage to becoming a man. On top of that, not just the Ex-POWs but most combat veterans had early morning chores before school and then after practice, evening chores back at home. As a former high school varsity football and wrestling coach, I'm deeply in awe and inspired by these Ex-POWs.

During my opportunity to speak, I told the Ex-POWs about our Living History Days and how we honor veterans, and I invited them to join us in November for our next event. In addition, I explained they did not have to pay for anything because all expenses were paid for everyone, including their spouses.

Earlier, I had told Jan that I was offering this to the veterans and their wives. She responded by saying, "For the majority of these Ex-POWs, this reunion is their last because it is just too difficult to travel anymore. So don't be disappointed if nobody takes you up on your offer."

At the end of my talk, I asked for a show of hands of anyone interested in coming to Oregon to share their stories with high school students. All ten veterans raised their hands.

The next week I received phone calls from six different Ex-POWs interested in coming to Oregon for our Living History Day celebration. All sixteen who committed in June came to Oregon in November from all over the United States. Every one of them told me he was grateful to be alive and would travel and live life until the day they died.

They had such positive attitudes about life. One said to me as he committed to come to Oregon, "Ken, I'll be there, and if I die on the plane, so be it."

It is so remarkable that all these veterans and their spouses, who were in their mid-nineties, some of them in wheelchairs, would make this effort.

THE SIXTEEN EX-POWS WHO CAME TO OREGON IN 2013

The majority of the Ex-POWs spoke to students who were field tripped from twenty-two different high schools around Oregon to Evergreen Aviation & Space Museum. The schools were divided into groups with each being assigned to a day, Monday through Friday, when the students could participate in the event.

Over the entire week, every student learned so much about heroism, courage, and sacrifice from these veterans. Each one had a story to tell that kept the students in awe.

These are their stories.

BEN STEELE   U.S. ARMY AIR CORPS
                              EX-POW

In November 2013, Ben Steele and his wife Shirley flew to Portland from Billings, Montana, for our week of Living History Days, joining the other fifteen Ex-POWs. What was remarkable about this feat was that even though Ben was an invalid confined to a wheelchair and needed help with almost everything, he still attended.

When I had first called to invite him, he graciously declined saying he was unable to travel anymore. After speaking to him for about thirty minutes or so, I found him to be the most upbeat, positive person I had ever talked to on the phone. He constantly laughed throughout our conversation, and I found it to be quite infectious.

I was mesmerized by Ben and called him several times during the summer of 2013 just to chat and to try and learn why he was so upbeat all the time. You see, I knew that Ben was a Bataan Death March survivor. In October, I received a call from Ben.

"Ken," he said, "I've decided to travel one last time and want to come to Portland in November. Is the invitation still open?" He laughed as he asked me this. "My wife will be coming to help, but I will need a lot more help than she can manage."

I was ecstatic. "We'll do whatever it takes," I replied.

For the flight to Portland, Ben had help from friends in Billings. They wheeled him onto the plane and made sure he and his wife were seated. In Portland, Malinda worked out all the arrangements for his arrival at the airport. She met them as they got off the plane, got their luggage, and drove them to the hotel where we were all staying.

Ben was loved by everyone who knew him. If you spent five minutes with him, odds are you would love him too. All the Ex-POWs of the Defenders of Bataan & Corregidor who came to attend the event were so happy to see Ben again. Watching them greet and hug each other in the hotel lobby with such joy and happiness was a very emotional scene. I think everyone had tears in their eyes.

Ben Steele's life story is beyond remarkable. It should be made into a movie. When I first met Ben, he recommended I read *Tears in the Darkness*. This New York Times best seller was written by Michael and Elizabeth M. Norman.

This book is about Ben from his childhood to adulthood. It is one of my favorite books. Whenever I begin to feel sorry for myself, I think about this book and Ben Steele, and I stop and realize how fortunate I am.

I actually called him once to get his advice on how to deal with some tough problems I was having in 2015. After I had finished explaining the difficulties I was having, he laughed and said, "Ken, I promise you that you're going to be alright. Everything will be okay." Then he laughed again.

I cannot recommend this book enough. It covers Ben's childhood growing up as a real cowboy on the ranch at his parents' homestead in Montana. It was this tough, hard-working childhood that gave Ben the strength to withstand the atrocities he would see and experience as a prisoner on the Bataan Death March: the beatings, the deaths by bayonet, and other senseless killing, as well as his own being tortured, starved, and even being pierced with a bayonet.

That upbringing gave him the toughness he would use to survive for over the more than three years that followed the Death March, followed by the Japanese Hell Ships, and forced slave labor.

Twice he was put in the camp hospital's 'Death Area', a storage area for the dead, a place where terminal prisoners were left to die. And once he was even given last rites by a POW priest, but he refused to give up.

Even though he was there supposedly to die from a combination of malaria and dysentery, as well as jaundice and beriberi, he slowly recovered. While there to pass the time, Ben began sketching on the hospital's concrete hospital floor with a stolen piece of charcoal from the nearby stove.

A fellow POW who was an art teacher before the war saw what Ben was doing and offered to teach him how to draw. Ben quickly became exceptionally good, and the POWs who were officers ordered him to draw scenes of the atrocities on the Bataan Death March and in the prison camp.

Ben was given smuggled pencils and paper, and then using his memory of the March and the more recent scenes in the camp, he began documenting the atrocities.

Sadly, all the drawings were lost when one of the hell ships was sunk by American torpedoes. After his liberation at the end of the war, while recuperating in a hospital, Ben created the lost drawings over the course of a year.

Following his recovery, he enrolled in the Cleveland Institute of Art in Ohio, where he earned his degree. It was in Ohio that Ben and Shirley met and fell in love. After receiving his teaching credentials from Kent State and a Master of Art degree from the University of Denver in 1955, Ben became a professor of art at Montana State University Billings. He was a very popular professor at the university.

"Everybody who met Ben loved him," Shirley told me. "The first several years of our marriage, he was obsessed with oil painting on very large canvases, and all his drawings of POW atrocities. These paintings are on display along with many of his drawings at the Montana Museum of Art and Culture."

When Ben and Shirley came to Oregon in 2013, we were able to arrange with the Museum of Art and Culture to bring his paintings for display at the Evergreen Aviation & Space Museum. They are amazing.

What is remarkable is that Ben continued to draw and paint until he passed away in 2016 at age ninety-eight. The year before, he sent me a beautiful watercolor painting of a cowboy riding a horse. That same year, the Billings School District School Board voted to honor Ben Steele by naming a new middle school after him.

Barbara Koostra, The Director of the Montana Museum of Art and Culture, had nothing but praise for Ben, who taught and mentored generations of young artists at Montana State University. Here is a quote from her that sums up what everyone felt about him:

> Ben is a tremendously amazing person who has lived through more torment than anyone I have ever met yet has come out an absolutely incredible human being on the other side. His sense of humor is unbelievable, and his love for Montana and the power of art brought him home alive. He is a man of forgiveness, and his story is one of unfathomable survival.

Ben's wife Shirley was a very sweet, kind, considerate lady. They were a perfect couple, and their love for each other was impressive. Malinda and I are so grateful to have had the pleasure of knowing Ben and Shirley Steele.

Ben Steele passed away at the age of 98 in September of 2016.

OSCAR LEONARD

IDAHO NATIONAL GUARD
U.S. ARMY AIR CORPS
OSS
EX-POW

Oscar Leonard and his wife Mary came up from California to Oregon five years in a row, from 2013 to 2017. Due to health issues, they were unable to travel in 2018. Oscar turned one hundred years old in May of 2019.

I heard Oscar talk to students a couple of times. He was a fascinating speaker. In addition, I had the good fortune of visiting with Oscar's son-in-law George Gonzales, who has written on his computer a compilation of Oscar's experiences for his family, both present and future. He was of great help in sharing details with me. I am using this wealth of material to augment the stories I have personally heard from Oscar.

Oscar's parents divorced when he was growing up, and his mother remarried while Oscar was still in school. He moved out because he did not get along with his stepfather. He was taken in by a family who were friends with Oscar's parents.

The family owned a logging business. During the day, Oscar attended school, and after school, he worked in a logging camp as a cook's helper. It was there that Oscar saw a man cut in half by a chainsaw.

In 1939, Oscar enlisted in the 116th Cavalry Regiment of the Idaho National Guard. In doing so, he followed in the footsteps of his father, who served in the 11th Volunteer Cavalry, when they fought in the Philippines against the Moros on the island of Mindanao.

In July 1940, Oscar enlisted in the Army Air Corps. He was assigned duty on Corregidor with the 60th Coastal Artillery, where he manned an anti-aircraft gun. At a shooting range where Oscar beat the range record, a man in a business suit ordered Oscar to follow him into a building.

He found himself in a group of about sixty men who were told to go into another room, look around, and remember what they saw. Afterward, they were given pencils and paper and told to write down everything they had seen. Because of Oscar's shooting marksmanship and ability to remember many things, he was asked to attend an intelligence school known as Counter Intelligence Corps (Army CIC).

After attending CIC, Oscar was assigned to the 28th Bomber Squadron. Flying in a B-10 Bomber, he took pictures of the Japanese ships. Then he would go into Manila and find out what he could about the ship captains.

On one of his trips seeking information, Oscar was walking near a village when he stepped over what he thought was a log, but then, realizing it was a huge snake, he shot and killed it. The villagers were happy because the snake had been killing and eating their pigs. They later ate the snake, inviting Oscar to join them as a guest.

On the morning of December 8, 1941, Oscar received a telephone call telling him that the Japanese had bombed Pearl Harbor and the Philippines would be next. The B-10s were readied to fly to safety, but the commander of the base would not allow them to leave until they had the okay from General MacArthur, who was still sleeping.

A bomber group of B-17s was sent to the Philippines. They had landed and refueled, and the crews were sitting down to lunch when Japanese bombers came over and bombed the airfield, destroying most of the planes.

What wasn't hit by the bombers were later hit by Zeros. The World War I era anti-aircraft guns couldn't hit the bombers as they flew out of range, nor could they turn quickly enough to hit the fast Zeros.

Clark Field was bombed on a regular basis, and then the Japanese invaded the Philippines. The majority of men were ordered to retreat, but Oscar and some others were ordered to stay behind to repair a couple of the B-10s at Clark Field. This was dangerous work. Both the planes drew fire and were damaged trying to take off.

Oscar noticed that the Japanese planes would go up to a hill and from there attack the airfield. He asked if he could go up the hill and see what was up there. When he reached the top of the hill, he found a hut where a man was transmitting information to the Japanese. "When the man saw me," Oscar said, "he turned and fired his gun at me, but I was a better shot and took the top of his head off."

Oscar found the bullet and put it in his pocket. He also found two large bags full of money, one American money and the other Filipino money. He turned the two bags over to the commanding officer and kept the bullet as a souvenir.

The Rangers, under First Lieutenant Edin Ramsey, were holding back the Japanese so that everyone at Clark Field could be evacuated to Corregidor, but a few Japanese tanks almost reached Clark Field. Oscar and another man were in that area and saw a tank before the tank saw them. Oscar could see a slot in the tank.

When the tank stopped, he started shooting at the slot. The other man ran up and threw an explosive into the slot. Just then a second tank came at them, killing the other man. Oscar turned and ran. As he did, he was hit in the foot and went down. Another group of men attacked the tank. Using dynamite, they rushed up and destroyed the tank.

Oscar received first aid from one of the men. He told Oscar that the wound was not as bad as it could have been because the bullet had passed through his foot rather than lodging in it. Oscar never talked about being shot. He feels that his being shot while running away was not something he wanted other men to know. That was why he never requested the Purple Heart for having been shot in combat.

After Ramsey and the Rangers could no longer hold back the Japanese, Oscar was part of the team that set explosives at Clark Field. Oscar had the explosives and charges put in a room in the weapons armory. That way the Japanese would think the Americans didn't have time to set the explosives. When retreating to Bataan, they could hear the explosives going off. Oscar always wondered how many Japanese were killed because they were inside the armory.

Once on Bataan, their officers left and did not return. Oscar and the other men of the 28th could not understand why they were there. Soon they learned that they were to surrender to the Japanese.

Oscar and many men from the 28th made their way to the beach to escape to Corregidor. Most of the boats had already left. One man was able to run out into the water and hold onto the back of a boat.

That night, Oscar and a nurse held onto a log in the water for the three miles to Corregidor. She had told him that she knew the tides and they could make it. Oscar listened to her even though he was apprehensive because he did not know how to swim. This was the first of several times a woman saved Oscar's life.

Having reached Corregidor, Oscar once again became part of Corregidor's defense. He was assigned to one of the coastal anti-aircraft guns. He helped change an anti-aircraft gun so that it could be used against the Japanese invaders coming across the water. The crews of the other anti-aircraft guns did the same thing. These guns were able to stop the first assault by killing most of the invading force.

Oscar volunteered to go with a group of men to collect explosives from mines on Luzon. They loaded the explosives on a ship and were taken to Mindanao. To avoid being spotted by Japanese planes, they hid by day and sailed by night.

At Mindanao, Oscar was assigned to help support a defensive line on one side of a river. "We were to hold off the Japanese troops attempting to cross," Oscar said. "We would wait until the Japanese were halfway across the water and then open fire. I was ordered to take out the officers with a rifle."

During the question-and-answer time with students, Oscar was asked, "Did you ever eat anything gross?" He stunned us all with this story:

"I was reassigned with another American soldier to do night raids with the Moro tribesmen against the Japanese. The Moro head chief, who spoke seven languages, said to me, 'I hate Americans, but hate the Japs more.

"The other American and I would keep watch with our forty-fives while the Moro tribesmen went in and killed the Japanese while they were asleep. On one raid, the Moros forced a Japanese cook back to camp. They turned the Japanese cook over to the women.

The first day, they gave him only water. The second day, they gave him rice and vegetables. The third day, they cooked and ate him.

"The Moro chiefs each ate a special part of the man's body and offered some to the other American and me. We told them we couldn't accept it because it was against our religion." Oscar's father had told him that when he was fighting the Moros in the Philippine-American War (Moro Rebellion 1899-1913) sometimes a cook would come up missing. Now Oscar knew why.

When Corregidor surrendered on May 6, 1942, Major General Sharp's men on Mindanao were ordered to surrender by 10:00 a.m. If they did not, the Japanese would start killing the American POWs on Corregidor. Oscar and the other Americans turned themselves in before 10:00 a.m. The Moros never surrendered and fought the Japanese until the end of the war.

Oscar was taken to his first POW camp on Mindanao, where he shared a room with General Sharp because the General wanted to keep him out of the main POW population. Later, Oscar was sent to the Los Banos POW camp in Manila.

With pride, Oscar said to me, "The first man I met in the camp was Frank Buckles, who ended up being America's last World War I veteran."

From there he was shipped to Japan in a Hell Ship and was forced to work as a slave laborer in six different camps. Two of the companies, who used POWs as slave laborers, Kawasaki and Hitachi are still in business.

"Daily I witnessed POWs beaten or killed for looking the wrong way, for not moving fast enough, or for many different reasons," Oscar said. "One guard enjoyed beating me with a stick every day. I was also interrogated. They pulled out my fingernails trying to get me to talk. Another time they put my feet in a bucket of water until the water froze."

Oscar ended up in the camp hospital. "A nurse sneaked an egg in for me to eat," he said. "I believe my health improved and it saved my life."

That was the second time a woman saved Oscar's life. Later he was told that when the Japanese officer in charge found out about the woman giving him the egg, and that the officer had her transferred to China to be a 'comfort woman'.

Later, another nurse moved him to a different bed, and that same day, a Japanese officer killed the man in the bed Oscar had occupied before the nurse moved him. That was the third time a woman saved his life.

After Nagasaki was bombed, Oscar and many other POWs were forced to clean up the city. "We were happy," Oscar said, "for we knew America was winning the war."

When he was speaking at McMinnville High School, a student asked, "Can you tell us about your liberation?"

"At the end of the war, the guards had fled the prison camp, and some of the POWs were doing their best to find the guards and kill them even though we had been ordered to stay in the camp until the surrender was complete.

"I was awakened in the middle of the night, given a new uniform, and taken to the USS Missouri to witness the surrender of the Japanese. They wanted the ceremony witnessed by a member of the OSS (Office of Strategic Services) who had been living 'under cover' in Japan. When they discovered that I was in the POW camp, rather than living undercover, I was ordered off the ship and flown to Australia.

"From there, I was put on a hospital ship and taken to the state of Washington. My parents and my sisters lived in Washington, so when I was given leave, I visited them. My mother showed me my death certificate that she had received during the war."

Oscar went on to become a pharmacist. He married Mary Lemmon, who also became a pharmacist. For over 60 years, they lived and raised their three children in Paradise, California. Due to age and health issues, Oscar and Mary moved in with their oldest daughter and son-in-law George Gonzalez in Antioch, California.

In the summer of 2018, Oscar and Mary's home was one of fourteen thousand homes destroyed by the 'Camp Fire', the deadliest wildfire in the United States since 1918. The bullet Oscar put in his pocket during the war was lost in the fire. It has never been found.

Oscar had not talked about his experiences until his son-in-law started asking questions. George told me, "Oscar will never get over being a POW, and to this day, he wakes up many mornings and tells me about a nightmare he had. The memory is still there. It will never be gone."

Thanks, George, for sharing parts of Oscar's story with me.

Oscar Leonard passed away at the age of 100 in November of 2020.

* ★ *

WILLIAM OVERMIER — NEW MEXICO NATIONAL GUARD EX-POW

I know I sound like a broken record when I say that Bill and his wife Mary are such wonderful, kind, and loving people because I can say that about almost all the veterans and spouses I have met over the years. Nevertheless, I will say it again. Bill and Mary are great people.

With the help of their son Allen, Bill and Mary have been coming to Oregon every year since November of 2013. They live in Albuquerque, New Mexico, and were planning on flying up again in 2018, but Bill, at 99 years old, was unable to travel anymore. They loved being part of our annual events. It also helped that their daughter Trina lives in Portland, so they could visit her as well.

Bill served with the 226th Anti-Aircraft Artillery stationed at Clark Air Field in the Philippines. Speaking to McMinnville High School students, Bill said, "All our weapons were those of World War I, and sometimes they didn't work. Our anti-aircraft guns did not have the range to reach the height required to hit the Jap planes, so the Japanese flew above our flax explosions and dropped their bombs.

"There was nothing we could do about it. We knew the end was coming. At night, when the Japs were firing at Corregidor and the Americans were firing back, I saw the biggest Fourth of July ever. It was unbelievable."

Bill escaped to Corregidor, where a month later, our troops surrendered to the Japanese after running out of food, water, medicine, and ammunition.

"All of us Americans were taken to Camp Cabanatuan," Bill said. "There, a Jap guard asked me to write down the kind of work I did before the war. I wrote that I was a carpenter. That note took me to Japan, where I worked as a ship's carpenter at the Mitsubishi Factory in Tokyo.

"We worked nine days in a row, with the tenth day off. It was frustrating because the Japs demanded that all work be done the way they wanted it done. Once I tried to show them a better way. The Japanese boss got very angry with me and struck my back with a steel chisel.

"It cut me, and I started to bleed. I turned and grabbed his hand, holding onto the chisel to stop him, and another guard saw this and ran over to us. I realized that I had made a mistake. I let go and just stood there. I was punched in the face and knocked down. Then they walked away."

In the winter of 2016, Bill's wife Mary called me. "Bill doesn't want to go to the National Convention this spring," she said. "But he said he would go if you and Malinda are going. Are you guys coming to San Antonio?"

"Yes," I replied. "We are. Jan Thompson says I will have an opportunity to speak at one of the sessions."

"They're going to San Antonio!" Mary yelled to Bill.

I heard Bill shout back, "Okay, I'll go then!"

That sure made us feel good. As I said, they are great people.

William Overmier passed away at the age of 101 in August of 2021.

---⭐---

JAMES COLLIER

U.S. ARMY
EX-POW

Jim traveled to Oregon from San Jose, California, with the help of his daughters. At age sixteen, with his father's permission, James lied about his age and joined the Army. Two years later at the age of eighteen, he was a member of the U.S. Army 59th Coast Artillery Battery D 'Cheney' on Corregidor Island. After the surrender, Jim was taken to the Cabanatuan prison camp.

Jim had a favorite story he enjoyed telling the students. "One of the POWs rescued a puppy from a stream and smuggled it back to camp. He named it Sea Chow. Shockingly, the Japanese guards were okay with it. Sea Chow survived by catching mice to eat.

"Many of us POWs loved that dog, but we had to protect him from the other POWs. You see, all of us were starving with meager rations. Even so, those of us who loved Sea Chow would share a bite of our food with him. But the other starving prisoners wanted to kill and eat him."

Jim credited his survival to that same group of POWs who protected Sea Chow. "When one of us became sick, we would take turns feeding the sick POW our own small portions of rice."

Sea Chow survived the war and was brought to the States where he was stationed at Camp Pendleton, California. Eventually, he retired from the Marine Corps with medals.

I remember a story Jim told the students. "Because I was tall, I was punched or slapped in the face every day I was in captivity, mostly by the same guard. This was probably because he was only about five foot, three inches tall.

"For a couple of weeks, I got a break because I told him he looked like a Hollywood movie star. I named him Mickey after the star's first name. When he found out the Hollywood star was Mickey Mouse, my life became a nightmare for the worse. He hated my guts after that."

In August 1944, Jim was shipped to Japan on the Hell Ship Noto Maru, where in Japan, he was again a slave laborer at the Nagoya-6B-Nomachi Takaoka camp for the Hokkai Denka Company, which was involved in ferroalloy smelting. Jim told one of his stories to a group of students on one of his visits that I will never forget:

"Everyone worked hard, especially on the furnace crew. We would sweat until wet and then cool down from the chilly winds that blew in from the Asian mainland. On one day, I felt bad, having recently recovered from the flu and was still feeling listless.

"That was enough to attract the attention of a guard who turned me into the captain. I never knew why, but he didn't need a reason.

"The Japanese captain who he called over was wounded in China and had only one arm. We gave him the nickname 'One-Armed Bandit'. He only had one arm, but he was good at swordplay. And we often saw it in practice.

"He ordered me to stand at attention in front of him and of course I obeyed. I remember at that moment, noticing how chilly it was, I began to shake. Things were moving so fast that I had no time for things to register. Had I thought about it, I would have fouled myself or gone to my knees for mercy. But seeing him reach for his saber, I saw in my mind's eye, my head separate from my body and fly off into space.

"Instead, I heard a crack and a thud and felt pain in my left cheekbone and then a gush of blood. Another crack, then another thud followed, and another gush of blood on the other cheek.

"It was then that I realized he had left the scabbard on the blade! My head still belonged to me! I was alive! I had two black eyes and was shaken for days after."

Jim was liberated after the surrender of Japan on August 15, 1945. He told me that he enlisted in the Army at 150 pounds and when he was finally liberated, he weighed 110 pounds.

Years later, in 1985, Jim and his wife were in San Francisco visiting a museum. On one of the walls was a picture of POWs carrying the bodies of the dead out of the prison camp to be buried. When Jim saw it, he fell to his knees.

For these Ex-POWs, the nightmares never really go away.

Jim was the only one of the sixteen Ex-POWs who was a retired teacher. He taught English and then became a counselor for many years at North Salinas High. In addition, at Hartnell College, Jim did counseling for many of the returning Vietnam veterans.

James Collier passed away at the age of 90 in June of 2014.

WILLIAM ELDRIDGE   ARMY
                          EX-POW

Bill Eldridge, who drove himself from Northern California to join us, was an impressive, stern, tough-looking man. My first impression of him was that he never smiled.

Bill was a machine gunner for the 31st Infantry Regiment, 'M' Company, 3rd Battalion stationed in the Philippines. "I was 17 when I went in," Bill told the students. "I enlisted during the Depression because my parents weren't getting by too well. There wasn't much work around, so I decided to enlist. I had to get my mother's signature, and she said if she had known where I was going, she would have never signed it."

He was in the Philippines when he was wounded by shrapnel from a Japanese mortar shell explosion. "My buddy and me were captured and taken to an area where other POWs were being brought in, and that was the starting point for the Bataan Death March," he told the students.

The students were mesmerized when Bill answered a question about the March. "For two to three days, they would make a group of two to three hundred men start marching. I didn't start marching until about the third day. As we were marching, we didn't get any food or water. I'll never forget walking over the flattened dead bodies of POWs run over by Japanese tanks and trucks. They were flat as pancakes.

"When we got to where we were going, we tried to clear an area to lay down, but we couldn't because the ground was covered in feces and bodies. The next night, we were forced into a large tin storage shed and there was one tap of water there. Some were lucky enough to get water, but we couldn't all get it. There was barely enough room in there so some people were standing through the night.

"I saw a lot of bodies on the ground that never got up. When we got out, there was a group of Japanese soldiers in the middle of the road that had a big drum full of rice balls about the size of a baseball. We each got a rice ball, which was the first food I had eaten in about three days.

"Then they put us on a train -what they called a '40 and 8 Boxcar' which was supposed to hold forty men or eight horses. They crowded us in there more than a hundred at a time. They kept us in there and it was boiling hot because it was in the middle of summer.

"When we finally got to where we were going and they unloaded us, a lot of people had died in the boxcar. We were put into boxcars packed tight like sardines. Those who died didn't fall down. They were stuck standing up because we were packed so tight.

"When we got to the camp, the interpreter was a Japanese American born in the U.S.A., a graduate of the University of California. Can you believe that?"

A student asked, "How did you survive? How did you not give in?"

"It was tough because our survival rate was low. Everyone was sick all the time. I had malaria and dysentery and received a little rice and sometimes no water. When I got weak from dysentery, I started sleeping under the barracks. I don't know who it was to this day, but somebody used to drag me out and feed me. I was even put into 'zero ward', where prisoners they figured to be too sick to live went.

"When I woke up there, someone had cleaned me up a little bit and I could see bodies stacked up beside the building. It was then that somehow, I got the strength to get better. Every day was bad, but I never gave up hope. I knew this war couldn't last forever. After the bomb dropped on Nagasaki, the Japanese cleared the camp, and we were on our own from there on out.

"I'll never forget the day American soldiers walked into our camp. The first soldier who greeted me was a friend from back home. He used to serve me milkshakes at the drugstore. What a small world. He contacted my parents to let them know I was still alive."

I was able to attend the Ex-POWs' American Defenders of Bataan and Corregidor National Reunion, and after the Saturday annual banquet, there was a dance with a live band. My beautiful wife Malinda, who attended with me, loves to dance, and joined right in with the women who filled the dance floor doing line dances.

Of course, I was required to dance a few times with my wife. And while I was sitting out between dancing, Bill joined me in watching everyone dance. I asked him, "Did you dance back in the day?"

He got tears in his eyes and said, "My wife and I danced all the time. We loved it, and I miss dancing with her."

While Malinda and I danced to the next song, I whispered to her what Bill had told me. After the song was over, Malinda approached Bill and asked him to dance.

For the first time, I saw him smile. "I'd be honored," he said. He stood up, gently took her arm, and escorted her to the dance floor. He was a gentleman and a smooth dancer.

They danced several songs in a row, and the man I thought never smiled now had a big smile on his face the entire time.

William Eldridge passed away at the age of 93 in April of 2016.

★

HAROLD BERGBOWER — U.S. ARMY AIR CORPS EX-POW

Harold Bergbower still fit in his uniform. He wore it to both reunions as well as when he flew to Oregon from Phoenix, Arizona. He was a very distinguished gentleman.

Harold said that he and a friend joined the Army Air Corp and that following his training as an aircraft mechanic, he was shipped to the Philippines with the 28th Bomb Squadron.

I heard Harold tell this story three different times, and every time he became very emotional:

"I was on my motorcycle and was struck by bomb shrapnel. It ruined my bike, and I got knocked out in the process. They took me to a hospital where I was pronounced dead. But when I came to, I realized I was in a morgue, so I got up and put my shoes on and walked back to my squadron."

Because his squadron thought he was dead, the war department was notified of his death. "My folks got a telegram saying I had died December 8, 1941.

"No one knew I was still alive until my dad heard it over the radio that I was still alive in Japan. The Japanese gave a list to the Americans of prisoners they had that were alive, and my name was one of them. The war department even said it was a mistake because they confirmed that I was killed December 8, 1941.

"My family thought I was dead until I sent them a telegram after the war. It was delivered to our house by regular mail. My mother was home alone at the time when she saw the letter and didn't think anything of it at first, but eventually, she finally opened it.

"When she read it, she went into shock. My dad called home and when no one answered he called our neighbor to go check on her, and they found her in shock at the kitchen table holding my telegram."

Before being captured, Harold helped defend the Philippines by joining up with a Filipino Cavalry unit when he became separated from his squadron. This happened because he had returned to Mindanao to retrieve some of his belongings, but the driver who was supposed to take him back to his squadron never returned. The cavalry unit told him that he should join them because Japanese troops were closing in.

"I went with three Filipino scouts on an outrigger to join back up with my outfit on Mindanao. I was with them for about 30 days or so and was on patrol when I ran into a Japanese unit where we ended up in a skirmish. A Japanese officer kept saying that we had surrendered, and I told him, 'No, we haven't.' That's when he said my squadron had, but I didn't know."

By escaping to Mindanao after the surrender, Harold had avoided the Bataan Death March. In the Philippines, he was imprisoned at Malaybalay on Mindanao and the Davao Penal Colony. He even survived the sinking of several Hell Ships, finally ending up in Japan as a slave laborer, scooping iron ore into an open-hearth furnace at Nagoya-6B-Nomachi Takaoka. Harold spent over two years as a slave laborer in Japan forced to shovel iron ore into open furnaces in a steel mill.

Of his trip on the Hell Ship, Harold said he had completely blocked it out. The mind is a wondrous thing. Perhaps sometimes it protects us, not so much by what it helps us remember, but what it helps us forget.

Harold always told how he had fought for survival every day for three years. And how he weighed no more than 78 pounds and crawled his way out of the 'Zero Room' back to his squadron, where he was taken care of by his fellow prisoners of war until he was well enough to continue by himself.

He always said, "The day I made it out of the Japanese prison camp was the best day of my life. I came back to the states just smiling every day and I wasn't going to let anything keep me from what I wanted to do."

Harold Bergbower passed away at the age of 99 in November of 2019.

* ★ *

RANDALL EDWARDS

U.S. NAVY
EX-POW

Randall Edwards and his wife came the farthest distance. They flew from Florida to Oregon. Randall served as a first-class radioman aboard the USS Canopus, a submarine tender in the Philippines, a ship that supplies and supports submarines. When the Japanese attacked the Philippines, most of the U.S. Navy ships were ordered to safer waters, but Randall's ship was ordered to stay in the Philippines in order to supply the Navy submarines with torpedoes and food.

"Our ship was attacked by air many times," Randall told the students. "But my luck really turned bad when I was ordered to set up a radio on Bataan. When Bataan fell, I escaped by swimming over to Corregidor. After Corregidor fell, our troops, now POWs, were taken by Hell Ship to Mukden Prison Camp in Japanese held Manchuria.

"We were put in an old Chinese war camp with mud huts and dirt floors, and no windows. We were given a small amount of coal every day to heat our hut during the constantly minus-degree winters. We were forced to work in a machine tool factory. We also built a large factory for Mitsubishi. We worked seven days a week in a factory that made bullets for the Japanese military."

Randall also told how he and other American POWs would secretly try to sabotage their work. "We used to get a lot of knots on our heads from the guards when they thought we were screwing up. If you got through a full day without one, you'd consider you had a good day.

"We were also freezing. In winter, it got as low as 50 below zero. We had little clothing and had to hike three miles to the factory every day. Both of my feet froze during those walks. I still have permanent nerve damage from it."

"What did you eat?" one student asked.

Randall replied, "Cabbage soup for breakfast and cabbage for dinner. It's pretty difficult to work fourteen hours a day with so little to eat. After a year, the Japanese brought in doctors to find out why so many POWs were dying. Their report concluded that we were starving to death. Hell, we could have told them that. After the report, they started feeding us soybean soup."

Another student asked. "Were you tortured?"

"No, I wasn't tortured, but we were hit with closed fists and clubs, and with the butts of their rifles every day. Some were slapped over and over just for fun."

Randall also was asked about what he did to survive all the years as a POW. His reply was, "I thought about my family a lot. However, I think the main thing we did was thinking about menus of what we were going to eat when we got out. We had menus; everything from filet mignon to roast pheasant. You name it.

"When we finally were liberated, we were all lined up and told the war was over, and you could have heard a pin drop. Nobody said a word. A short time later, American bombers dropped cases of food into the camp. I took out a gallon can of peaches and ate it until I vomited."

Randall Edwards passed away at the age of 103 in October of 2020.

★

RALPH GRIFFITH   U.S. ARMY
                                                    EX-POW

Ralph Griffith was a first-class gentleman who always wore a friendly smile. Ralph and his lovely wife Mary flew in from Saint Louis, Missouri.

He was on Corregidor when it fell and was taken to Manchuria, where he was a slave laborer.

"One day a Chinese boy smuggled a small amount of food into the camp and gave it to me," Ralph told the students. "The Japanese found out about this. I was searched and badly beaten before being put in solitary confinement for three weeks. It was during the first brutally cold winter. I was given just one blanket. As for food, I was given a small bowl of rice every other day."

"Did you ever talk about this with your wife and family?" one student asked.

"No," Ralph replied, shaking his head. "I didn't talk about my experiences until I started attending the reunions. I was in my eighties and talked about these things only with the other Ex-POWs. I never told my wife except that I was a POW."

Another student asked, "Why didn't you give up when you were a POW?"

Laughing, Ralph said, "I was too stubborn and determined to give up."

From the back of the room, a student asked, "What was the toughest part of being a POW?"

"To me, the loss of freedom was the worst part of it all," Ralph was quiet for a moment, and then, looking to the boy in the back of the room, he said again, "Yes, the loss of freedom was the toughest part of all."

Ralph Griffith passed away at the age of 96 in March of 2020.

ERVIN JOHNSON   U.S. ARMY AIR CORPS
                                EX-POW

Ervin Johnson and his wife flew in from New Orleans, Louisiana. After surviving the Bataan Death March and a Hell Ship, Ervin was a slave laborer in Manchuria, where he worked in a munition factory. During a panel discussion at the Ex-POWs American Defenders of Bataan and Corregidor National Norfolk Reunion, Ervin explained how he and the other POWs did what they could to sabotage their own work.

"We made sure that none of the parts we made were any good," he said with a grin.

When Ervin spoke to the students, he told them an incredible story. "I wrote a letter home to my parents while I was stationed on Bataan. After the war, I learned that an American submarine found a large bag floating in the ocean. The bag had been on a ship headed for Australia. The ship was bombed and sunk by the Japanese. My letter was in that bag and made it home to my parents over a year later."

Ervin Johnson passed away at the age of 94 in August of 2016.

— ⋆ ★ ⋆ —

JESSE BALTAZAR   U.S.A.F. FAR EAST
                                PHILIPPINE RESISTANCE
                                U.S. AIR FORCE
                                KOREAN WAR

I heard Jesse Baltazar speak at Gervais High School. He had the students entranced. "I was born in the Philippines and was a twenty-one-year-old ROTC student at the American Far Eastern School of Aviation in Manila when the Japanese attacked the Philippines.

"As students, we had no uniforms or weapons. Nevertheless, we participated in the battle on the Bataan Peninsula. Our first casualty was my schoolmate, who stepped on a hand grenade and died in my arms on the way to the hospital.

"On the third night of the March, I escaped. I was helped by a fisherman who rowed me through swamps until I made my way back home. After that, I joined the Philippine resistance movement."

In 2016, Jesse published a memoir, *The Naked Soldier*, in which he talks about his service to America. In it you can read about his service in three wars, four federal agencies, and government travel all over the world.

I also later learned that despite being wounded in action, Jesse had not been awarded the Purple Heart because the Army lost his records. And that his family and other supporters helped reconstruct his records and many campaigned for him to receive the medal. Even Secretary of State John Kerry, who is a Vietnam veteran, helped in the cause.

Jesse finally received the Purple Heart, more than 70 years after he was wounded in action in the Philippines and forced to participate in the infamous Bataan Death March.

I remember Jesse telling a student something remarkable when asked what he remembered most from being a POW. He replied, "I will always be a prisoner to the memory of the worst kinds of brutality and savagery. Yet I also saw courage, nobility, bravery, and the best that human beings can be."

Jesse Baltazar passed away at the age of 95 in April of 2016.

* ★ *

DON LUCERO   NEW MEXICO NATIONAL GUARD
                              EX-POW

I was given Don Lucero's phone number from Bill Overmier. He asked me to call Don and ask him if he would be interested in coming to Oregon. "He hasn't attended any of our reunions lately, Bill said. "I don't think he travels anymore but ask him anyway."

I called Don, and he said, "Sure, I'd love to but under one condition: I don't want to speak to students."

Don and his wife flew to Portland, Oregon, all the way from New York. They were a friendly couple and appeared to have a good time with us. On the last day, Don became very emotional with tears in his eyes. "This experience has been one of the best of my life. Thank you for bringing my wife and me to Oregon."

I was able to later learn from a fellow veteran that Lucero had escaped shortly after arriving at the camp and was recaptured only to escape again. The second time the Japanese guards put Lucero in front of a firing squad.

He wasn't shot but they beat him badly. And then again, he tried to escape and was able because the Japanese soldier who was guarding him felt sorry for him. And when the guard put down his rifle to loosen his shackles, Don picked up the rifle and shot the guard and ran into the jungle

Over the years I lost touch with Don since he last attended one of our events. Although trying to contact I was unable to find out where and how he is doing. Don, I do hope you are well and thank you again for coming to our events. .

* ★ *

JAMES MARTIN

U.S. ARMY AIR CORPS
EX-POW

I was pleasantly surprised to learn that James Martin lived in Oregon. He wasn't much of a talker, and as the other Ex-POWs gathered at the Evergreen Museum in Oregon for a big event, James told me that he did not want to speak to the students. He had come only to mingle with his Ex-POW friends.

All I know about James is that he served with the 19th Bombardment Group stationed at Clark Field. At the Ex-POWs American Defenders of Bataan and Corregidor National Reunion, he said, "We lost all our aircraft to the Japanese bombing but one. We were forced to surrender at Bataan."

James was another veteran that over the years I lost touch with and unfortunately was unable to find any relative or friends who had any information as to his whereabouts. I do hope you are fine, James.

* ★ *

ROBERT HEER

U.S. ARMY AIR CORPS
EX-POW

Robert Heer was another Ex-POW who called me to ask if he could attend with the other Ex-POWs coming to Oregon. His wife and he lived in the state of Washington.

When I spoke with him about his experience he told me, "We were woken up at 2 a.m. by a whistle from our First Sergeant. I jumped out of my bedroll and half-naked grabbed my rifle and helmet, which by the way was an old World War I helmet.

"I was hand-picked for a very important mission and told, 'Remain very quiet and do not fire your weapon during this mission … even if attacked by the enemy.'

"We boarded two Army trucks and left for the docks. There, an officer quickly posted each one of us for guard duty. At sunup, a general begins to yell saying, 'I've got them dead in my sight!'

"We all looked out to where he was looking at through his binoculars. I could make out a small boat bobbing up and down. Soon it was close enough to see it was a U.S. Navy PT boat.

"I'll never forget what happened after it landed at the dock. For there, exiting PT-41 was Gen. Douglas MacArthur followed by his wife and son. We could see they were all really wet and seasick.

"Two days later MacArthur was transported to Australia, and we all got a strong feeling of being left behind. Although Gen. MacArthur said, 'I shall return,' most of us called him, 'Dug-out Doug'."

I also asked Robert what enabled him to survive three and a half years as a POW.

He told me, "Most of the Japanese who were in charge of the POW camps were avid followers of the Samurai or Bushido philosophies. We learned really quick how to read their expressions and their movements and their attitude, so we could judge how to talk with them or not talk to them.

Robert Heer passed away at the age of 94 in May of 2016.

JOHN MIMS

U.S. ARMY
EX-POW

John Mims and his wife flew out from Raleigh, North Carolina. John did not attend the reunions but found out about my offer to bring Ex-POWs to Oregon. He called me and said he was a Bataan Death March survivor, a Hell Ship survivor, and a slave laborer survivor.

John's health was failing, and his doctor discouraged him from traveling anymore. However, he was determined to come to Oregon. In a firm voice, he said to me, "I'll be there."

Although John never spoke to the students, I was able to ask him personally about what had happened to him. He told me, "I got my bottom teeth knocked out by a Japanese sergeant with a soda bottle because he dropped the bottle and I picked it up, but I didn't bow to him.

"I saw a lot of soldiers die from exhaustion, dehydration, and malnutrition. Whatever food we got; you could have fit in your hand. When we got to the camp, I was strung up so that my feet couldn't touch the ground. My neck broke in three places, but the good Lord spared me."

I asked him if he had ever tried to escape.

"Yeah, I did, but they caught me and broke both of my legs with a bulldozer. I survived and was shipped on a Hell Ship on which 3,000 left but only 500 survived. Once again, the good Lord spared me."

As I often do with POW survivors, I asked John how he mentally went through his captivity.

"Two reasons: I spoke Japanese, and the good Lord needed someone to live to tell the world about it."

When John came to Oregon to attend the reunion, we had a wheelchair for him as he could hardly walk without pain. But during the Assembly of Honor, when the Reynolds High School band started playing the 1940s big band hit *In the Mood*, John stood up and asked my wife Malinda to dance. He motioned to the other veterans to get up and dance, too.

John always had a big grin and a smile. He was yet another Ex-POW who was a loving, kind, fun, upbeat, and positive man who lived and loved life to the fullest. John would always end his phone call saying, "I love you, and there ain't nothing you can do about it." He would then laugh loudly, and I could hear his wife laughing, too.

John Mims passed away at the age of 94 in November of 2016.

* ★ *

MARVIN ROSLANSKY U.S. MARINES
EX-POW

Before the war, Marvin Roslansky was stationed in Guam with 147 other Marines. On Dec. 8, 1941, the island was bombed for two days, after which Japanese troops landed on Guam and were met with limited resistance, which led to a quick surrender. Marvin eventually was sent to Mukden in Manchuria, and Japan to work as a slave laborer.

Malinda and I met Marvin at the 2013 American Defenders of Bataan and Corregidor National Reunion in Norfolk, Virginia. Even though he didn't serve in the Philippines, the Ex-POWs welcomed him with open arms.

Marvin was seated with four other POWs at the end of the table for the first panel of a question-and-answer session. When Jan Thompson, the president of the American Defenders of Bataan and Corregidor, introduced all of them and explained the rules to the audience, I noticed a look of horror on Marvin's face. To me, it looked as if he didn't know what he had agreed to do. I whispered to Malinda, asking if she noticed his reaction, and she responded that she did.

When the third veteran started to answer the first question the panel had been given, Marvin had tears running down his face. He looked as if he was in physical and emotional pain. Malinda stood up and said, "I have to go see if he's okay." I got up also and began to follow her.

We both got down on one knee right next to him. Malinda put her arm around his shoulders and started whispering, "It's okay," over and over again. She was also praying.

The event moderator, Jan Thompson, noticed all this, but kept the program going and started the second question with the first Ex-POW at the table. I was impressed with the way she handled this instead of making a big deal about it.

After five minutes, Marvin became composed and said, "I'll try to answer some questions." As Malinda and I stood up to return to our seats, we noticed Marvin's wife sitting in the front row crying. We stopped to console her. "Thank you so much for comforting my husband," she said. "I'm very grateful."

There was only one question Marvin answered, and it was about the living conditions.

"I shared a small structure made with mud and straw with several POWs. It had a place for a window, but there was no glass. There was an opening for a door, but there was no door. We took short shifts sleeping and tried to keep warm with pieces of coal we were allowed to bring into the hut.

We had to keep moving to keep the blood flowing."

Marvin came to Oregon two years in a row but did not want to talk to students. He said to me, "I just don't like to talk about all that horrible stuff that happened to us."

That was fine with me as we wanted him there to honor and thank him for his service to our country. I know Marvin had a great time with all of us. He and his wife were wonderful people.

I was however able to get him to open up a little bit as he told me that as a POW, he was sent to Shikoku, Japan, in the POW camp Zentsuji.

He told me that during that time working on the loading docks, every day was spent unloading freight from railroad cars, hauling it back to a warehouse. Just doing that back and forth 12 hours a day all through the war. And that after the atomic bomb was dropped, he was told that he did not have to work anymore.

Marvin Roslansky passed away at the age of 93 in August of 2016.

* ★ *

In 2013, all of the above sixteen survivors of the horrors following the fall of Bataan and Corregidor came to Oregon to share their stories with high school students.

You have read the stories of fifteen of the survivors. The sixteenth survivor, Phillip Coon, a Native American whose story was best served against the cultural background of the section on Native American Veterans is in *Remembrance Volume I*. If you have not read it yet, please do not miss Phillip's story. It is an amazing narrative.

ARMY AIR CORPS / AIR FORCE

ROGER 'BILL' TERRY   Tuskegee Airman
                           477th Bomber Group
                           Freeman Field Mutiny

Roger 'Bill' Terry was one of more than 100 black officers who refused to comply with 'Jim Crow' policies in the United States Armed Forces during the World War II era. He was also the only member convicted in what became known as the Freeman Field Mutiny.

He needs to be remembered as one of the brave men who were a part of the first steps that led to the nonviolent protests of the civil rights movement in the 1950s and '60s in American History.

In 1945, the Army Air Corps 477th Bombardment Group was assigned to Selfridge Field, outside of Detroit, Michigan. It was there that the first African American officer tried to get into the base's Officers club. The response from the base commander was that as long as he was commander, no bases under his command would allow blacks in the officers clubs.

Despite US Army Regulation 210-10, which strictly forbade segregation of public facilities on military installations, thereby requiring officers' clubs to be open to all, regardless of race, congress appropriated money to build a club for black officers separate from the whites.

The black officers club was never built because soon after, the 477th was transferred to Godman Airfield in Hardin County, Kentucky. After which the 477th was again transferred to Seymour, Indiana's Freeman Field.

At Freeman Field, under the command of Col. Robert Selway, segregation was strictly enforced. Here all black officers were listed as 'trainees', and their white officers were listed as 'instructors'.

It was because of this protocol that Bill and his fellow officers led one of the first non-violent protests in civil rights history by challenging the racist practices of the Army Air Corps. At Bill's base, under the command of Col. Robert Selway, black officers were given their own officers club in an empty room of an old building badly in need of repairs, while the white officers were given a new officers club.

Bill and his fellow officers decided to take action against this policy. On the evening of April 5, 1945, a group of African American officers requested entry into the white only club. They were denied. Then about thirty minutes later the second group, which Bill was a member of, requested entry.

This time, however, there was a white officer, armed with a loaded 45 weapon, standing in the entrance and he dismissively announced, "No niggers allowed!" The black officers brushed by him, with Bill bumping into the white officer as they entered the club.
The next evening saw the arrest of 101 of the base's black officers for entering or attempting to enter the white officers club.

Soon after, the base commander Col. Robert Selway gave new regulations, despite the official US Army regulation in which it was strictly forbidden, to segregate public facilities on military installations.

This new regulation was to be followed by all personnel, officially assigning officers to club by race. In addition, orders specifying strict segregation of not only the officers clubs, but also of the dining halls and housing were issued, and that any violation would result in confinement.

The base commander then ordered every arrested black officer assigned to read an Article of War, threatening death for failure to obey his commands.

All 101 black officers, including Bill, refused to sign the statement. Soon after, word of the arrests got out and Bill and other arrested black officers were transferred back to Godman Field where all were placed under house arrest and guarded by armed guards and dogs.

In contrast, at the time Godman Field held German POWs who had complete freedom of movement, unlike the American black officers. In fact, the German officers often talked about how the American black officers were so badly being mistreated by their own country.

As the news spread, public outcry followed, and all were released and served with an administrative reprimand, with the exception of three men.

Bill was one of those three men. While the other two were fined and released, Bill was court martialed, given a fine, had a loss of rank, and was dishonorably discharged from the Army for 'jostling'.

In 1995, under President William H. Clinton, the reprimands were removed from the permanent files of 15 of the black officers, with the Army agreeing to remove any of the other 86 upon request.

Bill received a full pardon, restoration of rank, and his fine was repaid.

I first met Bill Terry when I picked him up at Portland's airport in November 2001. He lived in Inglewood, California. This was his first-time attending Milwaukie High School's Living History Day. Luckily for us, Bill Holloman had talked him into coming.

At first, he didn't come across as very friendly. As we drove out of the airport, he said, "You're a big guy. Did you ever play any basketball?"

"Yeah, I used to play a lot for fun in my younger days." He immediately said, "I would have run your ass off the court." When I broke out laughing, things lightened up. From that moment on, we had great conversations.

He told me about when he played basketball at UCLA, and that he was also a receiver on the football team for one season. However, the basketball coach forced him to quit football because he didn't want Bill getting hurt.

His best friend and roommate was football, basketball, track, and baseball star Jackie Robinson, the first baseball player of color to play in the major leagues. He also told me that a close friend of theirs was Nat King Cole, who later became the renowned singer and jazz pianist. Bill told me how the three of them would sneak into jazz clubs to party, dance, and meet women in Compton, California, a town known for its jazz scene in the 1930s and '40s.

When Jackie was a senior, Bill was the mutual friend who introduced Jackie to the young UCLA freshman named Rachel Isum, who would later become his wife.
  I asked Bill about the kind of racism he encountered while playing basketball at UCLA. "Well," Bill said, grinning, "you being an Oregonian and all will probably be surprised to hear those kinds of problems happened right here in your home state.

"Our road trips to Eugene to play University of Oregon and Corvallis to play Oregon State University were where we ran into the most racism. We black guys on the team weren't allowed to stay in the hotels or eat in the restaurants.

"Our white players and coaches stood by us all the way. We'd go to the restaurants' back doors and get food to go. All of us, the entire team, and the coaching staff. We'd sleep in the bus after the first game and again in the bus going back to UCLA after the second."

I was really shocked to hear this having grown up in Oregon and always thinking it did not happen much here. I learned that I still had a lot to learn about Oregon's racist past.

When Bill graduated in 1941, he knew he wanted to become a pilot. He was recruited to train at the Tuskegee Airfield, where he earned his pilot's wings and his rank of second lieutenant in 1945.

From there he was sent to Freeman Field Air Base to join the newly formed 477th Bomber Group. They were training to fly B-25s with the goal of sending them to join the war effort in the Pacific. Many of the Tuskegee P-51 Mustang pilots who had flown combat missions in Europe were assigned the 477th Bomber Group.

However, this task force of both young first-time pilots and experienced veterans was never sent to the Pacific because the war ended before they could be deployed.

While the Tuskegee Airmen trained to fight America's enemies abroad, they also had to fight ignorant racism at home. There is so much more to this story so please go to www.tuskegeemuseum.org to read more.

From 2001 to 2009, Bill attended every Living History Day at Milwaukie High School as well as other high schools around the state. It would take several years however before he was willing to talk about the Freeman Field Mutiny.

"I just can't talk about it," Bill said, "because it makes me angry all over again." I told him many times that he should write a book about the experience.

I suggested that doing so might even be therapeutic, but his answer was always no. I did learn that he had been involved with forming the Tuskegee Airmen, Inc., in Los Angeles in 1972, and that he was also involved in helping to form chapters across the United States. Also, that he was heavily involved for years in those chapters and even served as the National President for some time.

My friendship with Bill started to grow in 2005 when his lovely wife Mae came to Portland with him. Mae was the sweetest, kindest lady. She was a class act.

At the time, I had been dating my now wife Malinda, who had suggested I invite the spouses of the out-of-state veterans to come with them to Oregon. I am truly thankful to her for in the end it was a great idea.

As a result, we all became a big close family. Bill's wife Mae was a graduate of Howard University and attended graduate school at USC. Bill and Mae had been married 56 years when he first brought her to Oregon for our events.

During one of their visits, she was able to see something really special happen for her husband. At one of our Milwaukie High School's Living History Days, I told the students, staff, and veterans a short version of the Freeman Field Mutiny and what had happened to Roger 'Bill' Terry.

After finishing speaking, I had Bill come up to the stage, where a couple of students presented him with a coffee mug with our high school's mascot, a mustang, on it. As they handed Bill the mug, I spoke again:

"Years ago, you were denied the opportunity to enter an all-white officers' club to order a drink. We Milwaukie Mustangs want you to know we would be honored to have a drink, a glass of water, a glass of milk, or a cup of coffee with you. We hope this coffee mug will remind you that we Mustangs love you."

After that, he started opening up a little more while telling his story to students in classrooms. It was really wonderful to see how much this was beginning to be a healing experience for him.

In March 2009, Bill agreed to make a presentation to the students at Pendleton High School on their Living History Day in May. The main event took place in their gym. Bill Holloman spoke first, followed by Bill Terry, who gave his best presentation by far. It was the first time I really saw him open up to the audience.

The students were spellbound. They were so quiet, and so intensely following Bill's story. When he became emotional at one point, the students responded with quiet empathy.

When Bill Terry and Bill Holloman both finished, they received a loud, and very long, standing ovation. Soon after, a crowd of one hundred or more students swarmed them to shake their hands and take pictures. Once again, I was in awe by the adoration these young people showed for these heroes. They more than deserved it.

A few weeks after the event, I received a call telling me that my friend Roger "Bill" Terry had passed away in his home. Bill's wife Mae asked me if I would be one of the speakers at his memorial service. I cannot tell you just how honored I was to be able to speak about my friend. She also asked Malinda and me to join her for a private family viewing at the funeral home. Again, I cannot tell you just how tough it was for all of us.

I have many wonderful memories of Bill, but my most special memory is of when Bill and Mae, and Malinda and I, had a dinner date together after the Pendleton High School Living History Day.

At the restaurant, Bill handed me a more than generous donation check to help with our nonprofit organization Remembering American Heroes. Then he took from his pocket, and I will never ever forget this, his Congressional Gold Medal.

The very same Tuskegee Airmen Congressional Gold Medal that was awarded to him by Congress and President Bush in 2007.

He handed it to me and said, "I want you to have this as a token of appreciation from me for all you have done to educate students about the Tuskegee Airmen and especially for me and my story."

Of all the gifts, plaques, and awards I've received over the past twenty years, this is my most prized possession.

Historians of the civil rights movement regard the Freeman Field Mutiny as the catalyst that led President Truman to sign Executive Order 9981, ending racial discrimination in the military.

This wasn't something that could be accomplished overnight. Several years passed before the order took effect. Most of the actual enforcement of the order was accomplished by President Dwight Eisenhower's administration. The last of the all-black units in the U.S. military were abolished in 1954.

After the black military units were disbanded in 1954, military bases in the segregated South became a place where African Americans could escape the South's Jim Crow laws.

Such was the case at Maxwell Air Force Base. In 1955, Maxwell would be the middle of the Civil Rights Movement. It was here on this base that Rosa Parks learned of Executive Order 9981.

Inside the base, everything was completely integrated, including its swimming pool, cafeteria, and its transportation system. However, outside the base, Jim Crow laws were still in effect. This was the spark that led to her refusal to give up her bus seat to a white person.

That in turn resulted in Martin Luther King Jr.'s leadership in the civil rights movement. There are streets, parks, buildings, and schools all over the United States named after Rosa Parks and Martin Luther King Jr. and that is as it should be.

However, something really disturbs me about all this: If the Freeman Field Mutiny was the catalyst setting into motion all these other civil rights accomplishments, what about the one man in the mutiny who paid the highest price for standing up for racial equality, the man subjected to fifty years of distress and anger? Where are all his accolades for his being a part of the first catalyst of the civil rights movement?

Roger 'Bill' Terry, who I will always consider my good friend, passed away at the age of 87 in June of 2009.

* ★ *

ED DRUMMOND Jr.

Tuskegee Airman
World War II
Korea
Vietnam

Ed Drummond was Bill Holloman's best friend. Entertaining and fun, they were headliners at all our earlier Living History Days. Each and every time they wowed the audience. But they were also aware that their stories were about the Tuskegee Airmen more than they were about themselves.

This was especially true of Ed. I always had great difficulty trying to get him to talk about himself. And that, I think, is a magnificent attribute in someone who had the same bigger-than-life ego like all the other Tuskegee Airmen. Unfortunately, it also meant I was not able to learn as much of his personal life as I did with the others.

I did learn that during his time in service, Ed flew the P-47 Thunderbolt, B-25 Mitchell, F-84 Thunder jet, F-86D Sabre, F-80 Shooting Star, and F-106 Delta Dart aircraft, to name just a few.

Completing more than 104 missions, Ed was one of the first two black pilots in the Air Force to fly jets into combat during the Korean War. He also flew missions in Vietnam from 1963 to 1964.

Lieutenant Colonel Ed Drummond Jr. served in the military for 25 years. He was honorably discharged in 1970. I also know he was from Philadelphia and proud of it.

I asked him about his experiences with racism while serving in the military.

"Yes, of course. Especially in the South. I had never experienced anything like that growing up in Philly. I had only read about it. But finding that it was true was shocking. Seeing those 'Whites Only' and 'Coloreds Only' signs was unbelievable. I could never understand the racism I encountered practically every day."

Then, typical of Ed, he added, "But I don't want to talk about that stuff."

I did however later hear him talk one other time. It was when he was doing his gunnery training in Arizona where he was refused a beer when he went into a bar with some of his white squadron buddies.

"I come into the bar wearing my uniform and the bartender says, 'You've had enough.' I hadn't even ordered a drink. But I got the message."

Ed was a very proud, intelligent, and confident man. He had a commanding presence when around people. But he did have what seemed to be a very interesting quirk.

That quirk was that he refused to fly on a plane as a passenger, and because of this he always drove to his destinations.

When I asked him about this, he replied, "I'm not trusting my life to some pilot that I don't even know."

I don't know when he first decided not to fly as a passenger, but I do remember Bill Holloman joking about it at Milwaukie High School's first Living History Day in 1996.

Ed drove to that event, and he continued to come only by driving to Milwaukie's events and any other Oregon high school's Living History Days for the next ten years.

Perhaps Ed's longest road trip took place when he and his wife Alberta drove from Arizona to Washington, D.C., to join the other Tuskegee Airmen in an official ceremony in the Capitol Building to honor them with the Congressional Gold Medal.

That day, March 29, 2007, was a proud moment, not only for the Tuskegee Airmen. but for our entire nation as well.

Ed and Alberta stopped attending the Living History Days in 2008 because of Ed's health concerns and became snowbirds in Arizona every fall to spring. We often kept in touch with them as they were now good friends.

Unfortunately, when his health began to fail in 2012, they had to stay home in Tacoma because of his many doctor appointments. Traveling was no longer possible, so Malinda and I drove up to Tacoma to visit and have lunch together a few times.

They took a final road trip in August 2012, when they drove from Tacoma to Las Vegas to attend one last Tuskegee Airmen National Reunion.

It being a long journey, Ed found sitting and driving for long periods painful, so they took their time, stopping for many breaks along the way.

Despite this, Ed was in a lot of pain and had to spend most of the convention lying in bed in his room once we arrived in Las Vegas.

Malinda and I visited him a couple of times every day during the four-day convention. Many of the Tuskegee Airmen visited Ed in his room, including Roscoe Brown, who shot down a German jet during World War II.

When Ed passed away, his wife Alberta asked if I would be one of the speakers and if Malinda would sing at the memorial service. We of course were honored to do so.

Ed Drummond Jr. passed away at the age of 87 in August of 2014.

ROBERTA LEVEAUX   ROYAL AIR FORCE

Roberta Leveaux was America's last living woman pilot to fly for the British Royal Air Force in World War II. She lived to be 98 years old.

In 1996, at the very beginning of our Living History Day's program, Tuskegee Airman Bill Holloman told me about Roberta and gave me her phone number. "She's a real character," Bill said. "She'll be an inspiration for high school teenage girls."

I called Roberta, and she attended the first Milwaukie High School Living History Day, speaking to two classrooms of students. She was a hit. The students loved her. Both teachers of the classrooms in which she spoke came to me and said that she needed to speak to larger audiences.

During the Assembly of Honor, I asked her to come up on the stage so that I could recognize her. She was dressed in her Royal Air Force uniform and approached the stage with very noticeable confidence. She walked up and put one arm around me, wrapped her right leg around my waist, and jumped up on me.

Laughing, she stated in a voice that carried over the packed gymnasium, "I would have climbed all over your body when I was younger."

Her antics completely broke my train of thought, and I made a mistake in my introduction of her. She grabbed the microphone and said, "That's not correct. It was twenty-two American women pilots, not twenty-five. Get it right." Everyone was laughing, including Roberta, who was cracking herself up.

"Wow," I said, "you are something else. You must have been a real spitfire in your younger days."

"I'm still a spitfire," she declared. "And I flew Spitfires in World War II."

Roberta grew up a country girl in northern Washington on land her father and mother homesteaded. The house had no running water or electricity. On a wall in her Portland home was a painting by her mother of Roberta's childhood home built very close to a creek in the forest.

As a small girl, Roberta was fascinated watching geese fly in a V formation. Her favorite book was a fairy tale of a girl flying on the back of a goose. She would sit on her father's lap as he read the book to her by candlelight over and over again. And at the end of the story, she would say to her father, "I'm going to fly someday."

At age 18, Roberta begged her father to let her attend college in California. This decision wasn't easy for her father. His goal for her was to get married and be a mother and homemaker. "The only thing you can do in college is to study to become a nurse or teacher, and they end up being old maids."

Roberta won the argument. She graduated from the California college and took a job in San Francisco, but she never lost sight of her dream to fly. She had actually had her first plane ride when she was only ten years old. "A barnstormer landed in a field in the small town near us," Roberta said. "I begged my parents to take me there. My mother said no, but my father took me in secret.

"I had a ride in the plane," she said, "and the pilot even gave me a second ride because I asked so many questions about flying. We flew right over our family's house, our barn, and our fields."

Flying was everything Roberta had always imagined it to be when she watched those geese fly in their formations over the farm.

In California, Roberta set that dream into motion. She learned to fly in a crop-dusting biplane. Roberta had begged the farmer who owned the plane to give her flying lessons. He finally agreed to lessons of five dollars an hour.

"I almost starved to death," Roberta said, "because I was spending all my money on flying lessons." But Roberta, who had ridden her horse to school every day until the eighth grade, knew her way around a farm, and the farmer agreed to let her work around the barn to help pay for the lessons.

At the time, despite the amazing accomplishments of women pilots in the 1920's and '30s, in the U.S. the path to receiving a pilot's license had become more and more difficult for women. Schools with flight-training programs were the recommended way to go, but many of those schools did not accept women, and those who did had small quotas for the number of women students they would accept.

Unable to qualify for a pilot's license in the U.S., many women traveled to countries more willing to train and accredit women pilots.

Roberta had been accepted by an American school that offered a flight-training program for ten students per class, only one of whom could be a woman.

"I loved the program," Roberta said. "It was wonderful training." Nevertheless, she decided to follow the path of those women who had been denied the opportunity she had been given. She went to Canada to get her pilot's license.

That was an easy call for Roberta. Her family's farm was close to the Canadian border, and she enjoyed the Canadians she had known there. Also, she was impressed with the English people in Canada. When the English were so heroically defending their country in the Battle of Britain, Roberta knew that she wanted to go to England and join the fight.

She wrote to the British Air Ministry and the Royal Air Force to volunteer her services.

"For a time, I heard nothing from them," Roberta said. "Then one day I received a telegram from Jackie Cochran, the famous woman pilot, who with Eleanor Roosevelt was pushing for women pilots to be allowed to join the effort. I was offered the opportunity, and I took it.

"My train trip to New York took three days. I was so afraid to talk to anybody that I read two magazines over and over. From New York, our group of American volunteers were flown to Montreal to be tested as pilots.

"I was one of 22 American women pilots selected along with one Dutch woman and two Canadians." Roberta beamed with pride as she told me that.

Addressing the new pilots, Jackie Cochran told them how important their role would be: in the war effort. She said he told them, "You have to succeed. I'm pushing hard to get American women flying for the United States."

Roberta continued, "We were shipped to England on a Norwegian freighter," Roberta said. "It was 1942. Crossing the Atlantic was extremely dangerous because of the German U-boats. Most ships traveled in convoys to protect against the U-boat attacks, However, we did not because the freighter was faster than the German submarines. We arrived at a badly damaged Liverpool Harbor, the result of the German bombing raids.

"The day we reported to a British ground school at South Hampton, there were pilots from all over the world there to help the British," Roberta said. "The training was excellent. I admired the British discipline over American discipline. I was a very fast learner. The training was easy, and I proved that I could fly any plane."

Early in their training, a British captain declared that the women would not fly Spitfires. "He told us, 'The Spitfire is too big and fast for you women to fly.' And I stood up and said, 'I'd like to prove you wrong.' Thank God there were other British male officers in the room. They thought it was funny and started laughing. Several of them wanted to see me prove it." Roberta grinned as she remembered this challenge.

"We went out on the tarmac, and I flew that Spitfire with ease. As a result, I was allowed to fly the bigger, faster planes. Some of the other women pilots were not allowed to fly anything fast. I flew the new Spitfires to the airbases and flew the shot-up damaged ones back to the factories. The new planes were never tested with trial runs. When I got in the cockpit, it was the first time any of these planes had been flown."

"What about flying the shot-up ones?" I asked. "That had to be iffy."

"You can say that again," Roberta answered. "Flying those planes was dangerous and scary. Some of them were in really bad shape. I had to crash-land twice, once with the wheels up and once with the wheels down. Many women pilots crashed and were killed flying those planes."

"Did you ever encounter German planes when you were flying?" I asked.

"Yes," she answered. "Twice I saw German planes in the air and once I was even shot at. I was being flown back to the factory in an old Anson taxi plane by a famous pilot, Jim Rolleson, when a German plane attacked us and put some bullet holes in our wing. Jim flew up into the clouds, and we luckily escaped."

Our conversation turned from Roberta's role in the Royal Air Force to her personal life. "I met my future husband, Peter Sandoz, during the war. He was an English soldier in the Cavalry and wearing his dress uniform and spurs the first time I saw him. I was impressed," she said with a big smile.

"We dated for six weeks and then got married. I got pregnant, and that ended my eighteen months flying for the RAF. I intended to keep flying as I was very patriotic and still wanted to continue helping 'The Cause'."

In 1949, Roberta, her husband, and two children moved to the states, where they had one more child. Her pilot's license was not recognized in the U.S. The American women pilots were all offered jobs as airline stewardesses. Roberta shook her head in disgust after telling me that and said, "What a slap in the face. No one took them up on that offer."

For the Milwaukie Living History Day in 2003, I organized a special session in our auditorium with Roberta Leveaux for all the girls and women. Portland's own KOIN Channel 6 news anchor, Julie Emery, interviewed Roberta. It was standing room only with students sitting in the aisles. I was one of two males in the audience as I was not going to miss this one.

It was an amazing experience. Roberta had Julie Emery and the audience eating out of her hand. You could have heard a pin drop as Roberta mesmerized that crowd.

At the end of the presentation, Julie asked, "Is there any last thing you want all these young ladies to know?"

"YES!" Roberta yelled. "Don't ever let a man tell you that you can't do something." The teenage girls cheered loudly and gave her a very long, standing ovation. Many of the girls had tears in their eyes.

After Roberta's husband passed away, she moved into a retirement home. There she formed a veterans' organization. The 36 members were all veterans of World War II. They meet monthly. I was honored to be a guest speaker on two separate occasions.

Malinda and I often visited Roberta. Several times she invited us to join her for the retirement home's Christmas brunch. We were always pleased to attend, especially since Roberta's children and grandchildren lived in other states and would not be there to share Christmas with her.

When Roberta passed away, I received a call from Robert Schuberg. Robert, an Army Air Corps veteran who piloted a B-17 in World War II, had been a speaker in many of our Living History Days. He, too, was living in the same retirement home as Roberta.

"Ken," he said, "there is no funeral or memorial service planned for Roberta, and we can't get any answers from our retirement home."

"Well," I responded, "let's do one for her at your retirement home." Robert agreed, and we worked together to organize a memorial service for Roberta.

The turnout was impressive. It was standing room only. Robert and I both spoke about Roberta, and Malinda sang 'The Lord's Prayer' and 'Wind Beneath My Wings.' We gave everyone a chance to tell their Roberta stories. The stories were full of the joy of having known her.

As for me, my admiration and respect for Roberta Leveaux are as high, if not higher, than all my male veteran heroes.

Roberta Leveaux passed away at the age of 95 in October of 2013.

LARRY BROWN   13th Air Force
                                     B-17 Mechanic South Pacific

Larry Brown attended only one of our events. He was 94 years old at the time and passed away the next year. I was sad that we had only that one time with Larry. He had a fine sense of humor, and he laughed a lot. Also, he was a great storyteller.

Larry had the ability to go from one minute, telling a great story about camaraderie and duty to the next minute, telling another story about the tragedy of war. I remember him always laughing a lot and how much he loved telling stories.

The first time we met, I could see that he would be a great person to come to our events. At that first event where we met, he was not even a speaker. He just came to attend as a veteran to just hear other veterans speak and to give his support.

How I knew he would be great was when I first met him, it was as he was talking to me and telling me a story. There began to gather around us an ever-increasing number of students who were drawn in, wanting to hear him speak.

I had to have him come to Oregon and quickly asked him for his contact information and told him I would really like him to come to our events.

At the event, he told the students about how just before the war, when he was in the Air Corps, he was a mechanic on the ground and a flight engineer in the air. At that time, his group flew in the inauguration of President Roosevelt.

He said it was so intense flying in that group formation over the inauguration because they had to stay close together. So close that their wings were almost touching, and that it was so intense that the pilots looked like they had taken a swim in their flight suits because they were so drenched in sweat.

He also talked about how lucky he was, but how tragic war is because of how many friends he lost. One such story he told was how as he was getting on board his plane, his master sergeant and good friend asked him to stay behind to help with the repair of some aircraft that would be flying in soon. He protested but was ordered to stay.

He heard soon after how the plane full of his buddies, with which he had flown with for a number of years, had crashed and burned, and all aboard were lost. One such story was when Larry pulled me aside that day and said, "I have a General MacArthur story that you'll never read in the history books." He was laughing before he even started telling the story.

"I had the honor of being the mechanic for his personal plane in the South Pacific," Larry began. "It was well known that MacArthur hated flying and traveled by plane when it was his only option. We all thought this arrogant, egotistical man was scared of flying. When he had to fly, he would come out to the airfield the day before to inspect the plane. I had to test everything in front of him. I guess all this was to put his mind at ease."

Larry grinned as he said, "Well, one day I decided to pull a prank on him. I didn't tell anyone what I was about to do." He paused, pulling me into his story.

"What did you do?" I asked.

"Before he came to inspect the plane, I pulled the spark plugs out of one of the engines," he replied. "Of course, when he wanted the engine to start, it wouldn't. I acted baffled when that engine wouldn't start. I kept working on it, trying several times to get it started. MacArthur was pacing back and forth and becoming more and more upset. He started yelling at me to solve the problem."

Larry winked at me as he said, "I was very careful to make sure no one saw me put the spark plugs back in and was able to start the engine. MacArthur, visibly upset, got into his car, and was driven away. After everyone left, I had a great laugh by myself."

Larry roared with laughter after telling me this story. "I never told anyone back then what I had done."

I wish the two of us could have had more time together.

Larry Brown passed away at the age of 95 in August of 2014.

★

ROY DAVENPORT   Army Air Corps
                                 South Pacific

Many times over the years, we have veterans travel with other veterans as we go all over the state putting on events. Roy Davenport and his wife Joyce were two such people, and they were such kind people and loving people who always had big smiles whenever you met them.

Roy always let me know that he flew B-17s in the 13th Air Force. "We were the 'Jungle Air Force'," he said with a grin. "Everybody talks about B-17s flying in the European campaign, but we flew and fought in the

South Pacific as well." Roy told me this every year. He was so proud of the role that he and other B-17 pilots played in the South Pacific.

During World War II, the 13th Air Force took off from tropical jungles on more than 40 remote islands including the Marshall Islands as well as the Mariana and Palau Islands earning them the nickname, "The Jungle Air Force." Roy's units participated in a total of five different operation areas across the Pacific and were involved in 13 different campaigns.

Roy Davenport passed away at the age of 90 in June of 2009.

---

* ★ *

STANLEY P. RICHARDSON Jr.

Army Air Corps
European Theater
Korean War

Stanley Richardson was one of the youngest fighter pilots in World War II, flying P-38s and P-51s, and then in the Korean War, he flew F-86s. He always said, "Of all the prop fighter planes I flew in World War II and the jet fighters I flew in Korea; the P-38 was the best plane of all."

At one point in his military career, Stan was accepted into the space program for training to become an astronaut. However, this opportunity was kept from him by his commanding officer, who refused to release him into the program. After his military service, Stanley had a long career as an airline pilot, logging in well over 30,000 hours, flying until his retirement.

Stanley was a great guy, and we soon became good friends. Stanley was such a great guy that to help Milwaukie High during one of our annual fundraising efforts to keep the Living History Day program going, he donated his own beautiful Thunderbird convertible. And, yes, it was in beautiful condition. It was a big hit because only our students could buy raffle tickets for the car, after selling a lot of tickets the winner was announced in a special assembly.

Stanley was always active in our veteran events and will always be remembered as a longtime supporter and friend to everyone. In 2012, Stanley was inducted into the Oregon Aviation Hall of Fame at the Evergreen Aviation & Space Museum.

Stanley Richardson passed away in his Beaverton, Oregon, home. His service was held in the chapel on the Portland Air National Guard Station, 70 years to the day Stanley flew his P-38, Miss Mona, over the invasion beaches at Normandy.

Stanley Richardson passed away at the age of 91 in May of 2014.

★

ERNIE WAKEHOUSE

Army Air Corps Air Force
Korean War

Ernie Wakehouse had just finished his flight school training with P-51 Mustangs as World War II ended. During the Korean War, he flew P-51s on 100 missions in 90 days. That amounted to 600 hours of flight time.

In one of the missions, as a flight leader, he led a series of attacks on enemy troops, their bunkers, and their large cache of war supplies. Despite the heavy enemy fire and poor visibility, Ernie continued leading the flight's attacks until their ammunition ran out.

One hundred enemy troops were killed in the battle, with their bunkers and their stock of war supplies destroyed. Ernie was awarded the Distinguished Flying Cross for his individual heroism and leadership.

Ernie did not lose his enthusiasm for flying after he retired from his military career. For over 40 years, he owned and flew planes, everything from four-passenger light planes to a Lear jet. He liked traveling across the country to attend meetings and reunions for veteran fighter pilots.

Ernie also enjoyed our Living History Days at Milwaukie High School and attended many of our events in the early years.

Oregon lost yet another of our heroes when Ernie Wakehouse passed away at the age of 93 in April of 2016.

MARINE VETERANS

DAVE SEVERANCE

WWII
Korea
Vietnam

In 2008, I was given the name and phone number of a Marine claiming to be the last living Flag Raiser on Iwo Jima's Mount Suribachi. I of course called and offered to bring him to Oregon. I was so excited that I shared this news with the Oregon Chapter of the First Marine Division Association.

A few weeks later, I received a phone call from a former Marine Colonel introducing himself as Dave Severance, who then proceeded to give me some deflating news. "I was the captain of Company E, the company that raised the first flag on Mount Suribachi. Company F was on our flank as we assaulted Mount Suribachi. I've attended all the First and Second Flag Raisers' funerals, and with other Marines, we've exposed 61 Flag Raiser phonies. This man is obviously an imposter."

I then gave David all the information I had on the man, and he soon mailed me all the information he had gathered on the imposter. I called the man, and upon presenting the information I had exposing him as a phony, he cussed me out and hung up on me. That very interesting turn of events is how I met David. It was the beginning of a wonderful friendship that would last many years.

Throughout the years, David donated generously to the nonprofit, but I could never get him to come up to Portland from his home in Oceanside, California. It finally did happen when in 2012 my wife Malinda and I were in California near Oceanside. I had spoken to him before we left and offered to buy him and his wife lunch if we could meet in Oceanside.

When Malinda and I entered the restaurant that David had recommended, we were directed to a private side room that he had reserved so we could have our conversation without the distraction of the busy lunch crowd.

As we talked over our meal, with our wives enjoying their own conversation, oblivious to us, Dave told me about his extensive collected history on the famous Second Flag Raisers, and how it was used for the book and movie *Flags of Our Fathers*. In addition, he told me how he was one of the Marine Corps advisors for director Clint Eastwood on the set of the movie.

Dave is a truly generous man, for earlier when my wife Malinda and I were shown to the side room, I told the waitress to give me the bill at the end of our meal. However, when she brought the bill to the table, she handed it to Dave without even giving me a glance. I immediately said, "Hey, I'm paying," and then began to tell the waitress to hand the bill to me.

David interrupted me before I could even get the words out of my mouth for in a voice he obviously used when in command he said, "Stand down, Buckles. I'm your senior, and I'm paying for this."

"Yes, sir," I answered back like a lowly private to his superior.

He surprised us by picking up the check, but I also had a surprise for him too. After the bill was paid, and we were about to leave, I looked over to my wife Malinda, who winked at me and nodded her head. "We have a surprise for you, Colonel," I said. My lovely wife then stood up, and in a voice just as beautiful as she, sang two songs for our hosts: *The Marine Corps Hymn* and *Wind Beneath My Wings*.

Dave and his wife loved hearing Malinda sing for them. And, I might add, so did a number of customers in the main dining room, where the chatter of everyone eating and talking quieted so they could listen to the two songs, an honor befitting this heroic man.

Dave Severance not only served in World War II but also as a fighter pilot in both Korea and Vietnam. I would love to write more about this incredible man. Perhaps someday I might.

Dave Severance passed away at the age of 102 in August of 2021.

JOHN CHECKIS   Okinawa

John Checkis was my art teacher when I was a student at Milwaukie High School. I also taught with him at Milwaukie when I became a teacher there in 1982 until he retired in '84. He was a fine artist and a great teacher. Even though I had been his student and we had taught together, I never knew he was a veteran until he joined the other Marines at our first Living History Day.

He never once spoke about any of the horrors of war. Even when I would ask him to speak at our events after finding out he was a vet, he always only spoke about his experiences of being in the Marines, and never about any of the bad things. And of course, sometimes students would inevitably ask, and he always said, "I don't want to talk about it."

When you look at John, you would see a bright and always smiling face full of life. On that wonderful face you also could see a scar that runs from the top right of his head to the top of his right eye. I never personally asked how he got the scar in the war. I guess I just always felt I would get the same answer, "I don't want to talk about it."

Over the years, I have learned that you shouldn't press too hard if a veteran doesn't want to talk about a war experience. When a veteran does say, "I don't want to talk about it," just let them be. If they really do want to talk, with time they will sometimes open up to you because you are a friend, and not because you just want a story. Sure, I could have called his family to perhaps get the story of his scar, but he was my teacher and I respected him.

John Checkis, my art teacher, my fellow colleague, and a man I loved and respected, passed away at the age of 88 in May of 2014.

RICHARD ESPEJO

WWII Guadalcanal
Korea

Marine Richard Espejo would laugh as he told students at our Living History Days, "On my 16th birthday, I was wounded on Guadalcanal. That was my birthday present."

Richard also fought in Korea in the Battle of Chosin Reservoir. He was almost captured when over 100,000 Chinese troops suddenly swept into North Korea from Manchuria and surrounded American forces at Chosin Reservoir.

Encircled and heavily outnumbered, the Marines fought a brutal 17-day battle in freezing conditions and rugged terrain before finally breaking through the Chinese lines to make a fighting withdrawal to the south coast, where U.S. transport ships and evacuation awaited them.

Richard Espejo passed away at the age of 80 in March of 2006.

BENJAMIN CARSON

Midway, Makin
Guadalcanal, Bougainville
Iwo Jima

Ben Carson was a second-generation military man, whose father fought in World War I. While he was working on his family farm, Ben heard about the attack on Pearl Harbor, and knowing he would be called into service, he started looking at which branch of the military he wanted to join. Because his brother was in the Navy, he settled on the Marines.

He talked about his time in boot camp and how bad it was because they were doing training with sticks instead of rifles, or how he had to sleep on the barracks floor because there were not enough beds for everyone. He talked about being a great shot on his farm and because of this he easily became a sharpshooter.

He also told humorous stories about the boredom of guard duty driving him crazy for he wanted to be in the fight. And how he became a member of the 2nd Marine Raider Battalion, later to become the legendary battalion Carlson's Raiders, named for their commander, Lieutenant Colonel Evan Carlson. He talked about how he was chosen by the battalion's recruiter because he, having learned how to do it on his farm, could swim.

Ben, in that famous battalion, would then go on to fight in five major battles of World War II: Midway, Makin, Bougainville, Guadalcanal, and Iwo Jima. He was even part of the very first group of soldiers when the occupation of Japan began. One of those locations would be where his battalion would be given a mission that is renowned in the Marine Corps.

Under cover of darkness on a night in August 1942, his Raiders left two submarines to make their way by small rubber boats to the beaches of Makin Island, an outpost held by Japanese forces. In the mission, over 150 Japanese were killed in the raid.

The Marines lost 19 men killed in action, initially reported as 18, however one first thought to be missing was later identified among the graves where the local islanders had buried them. Of the remaining 11 missing in action, two were found to have drowned and nine were listed as missing.

Those nine missing men were later found to have either been unknowingly left behind in the withdrawal or had returned to the island because their boats were lost trying to cross the extremely deadly heavy seas. They were then captured and transported to another island, where they were tortured and then beheaded.

After the war, Koso Abe, the Japanese general who ordered the executions of those Marines, was tried, found guilty of war crimes, and executed.

Later after returning home, Ben became a member of the U.S. Marine Raider Association, a group that was instrumental in bringing back the bodies of men who were buried by the islanders. After the war, the military stated that they had undergone a retrieval mission to recover the bodies but were unable to locate them and then declared the Marines left on the island as unrecoverable.

Ben's group, with the help of other vets, as well as the relatives of the missing, continually put pressure on the government to keep looking for those left behind.

In 2000, after 58 years, the missing were eventually found, some with service weapons still on them in their graves. What led to the discovery was the search team found an elderly islander who remembered it from when he was a young boy helping to dig the graves of the Marines. It was Ben's group who helped them return home.

Benjamin Carson passed away at the age of 97 in March of 2020.

GORDON MORGAN   Guadalcanal

Gordon Morgan was wounded by machine gun fire during a heroic stand when being led by his Sergeant, the famous Colonel Mitchell Paige. His platoon was given the task of holding a hilltop ridge, at which thousands of Japanese soldiers were going to attack.

Their defense with only thirty-three Marines against the assault of two battalions of the Japanese Army is the stuff of legends. The Platoon Sergeant leading these men was Mitchell Paige, whose remarkable heroism resulted in his being awarded the Medal of Honor.

Gordon's Platoon Sergeant was directing the platoon's machine gun fire when all his men were either killed or wounded, including Gordon. Then, with the enemy ready to break through his position, he started firing two guns single-handed, and when one was lost to enemy fire, he picked up another one to continue his fight.

He even ran to a nearby unit to get another gun, after which he returned to his post through heavy machine gun fire. In the end, he held off the

Japanese until reinforcements finally arrived. Paige was awarded the Medal of Honor for his actions, and Gordon a purple heart, and a story he could tell his grandchildren, and of course our students.

After being honorably discharged from the Marine Corps, Gordon worked for 30 years as a detective sergeant in charge of the Homicide Unit in the Portland Police Bureau. After retiring from the Portland Police Bureau, he then went on to work as a special agent for the Multnomah County District Attorney.

In 1991, he founded and was the first president of the Oregon-Columbia Chapter of the First Marine Division Association. He would also serve as the National President of the First Marine Division Association and the Guadalcanal Campaign Veterans Association.

Gordon Morgan's life was one of service to society and to country, and because of this and his honor, courage, and commitment, he was the ultimate Marine.

Gordon Morgan passed away at the age of 85 in March of 2008.

CLYDE BRUMMELL   South Pacific

Clyde Brummell was born with the bug of aviation, and this led him to be a Marine aviator who flew Corsairs, one of the most formidable fighter-bombers in the battles of the Pacific Theater. Whenever he spoke to students, his favorite stories weren't about himself. Instead, he said how much he admired Charles Lindbergh, one of the most famous pilots of all time.

"He was the famous Lindbergh, so of course no one knew he was even in the Pacific. He came to our unit to inspect our Corsair base. He trained us how to conserve fuel so we could extend our flight range using the same amount of fuel. He showed us that by decreasing RPMs and then increasing manifold pressure, we could get maximum range with the fuel we carried.

"During flight training, we learned doing that would damage the engine, but because it was Lindbergh, we did it anyway. His little fuel saving trick saved the lives of many pilots on long-range missions. At the time he was not a soldier, but just a civilian technical assistant. And of course, they would have been mad as hell if they knew we took him on combat missions. He was told he was not supposed to, but it never stopped him."

Clyde Brummell passed away at the age of 84 in December of 2009.

EDWIN BALL   Guadalcanal Peleliu

Edwin Ball was another speaker whose favorite stories to students were not about his combat experiences. "We were on leave in Melbourne, Australia, after Guadalcanal," he began, "and a couple of buddies and I met three beautiful Aussie women. One of them invited all of us to her family's ranch for a barbecue.

"We'd been there a while when her father asked me, 'How come you n' ya mates aren't drinking the beer I bought for ya? I thought you Marines loved beer.' 'We do,' I told him, 'but we like our beer cold, not warm.' So, the father jumped into his truck, went into town, and bought some ice. We ended up drinking all his beer after it became cold.

"Him being nice to us was typical for all the Australians we met. They were so friendly to us Marines, especially the ladies."

Edwin Ball passed away at the age of 92 in June of 2016.

STAN AIKINS   Iwo Jima

Ray Johnson's best friend was fellow Iwo Jima Marine Stan Aikins. Ray always brought Stan to Milwaukie High School's Living History Days for several years. Being best friends, the two of them would always share a classroom during the presentations with students. Stan also went with us to several of our overnight Living History Days at schools around the state.

Stan was always cracking jokes and telling funny stories and had a great laugh and a big smile. He was a lot of fun to be around. Stan told the students only one story about his Iwo Jima experience, laughing all the way through it as if he were doing a standup comedy routine.

"I was a machine gunner on Iwo Jima. We were pinned down by Japanese machine gun fire. Over a field phone, an officer issued a command to advance. I told him it would be suicide if we moved forward into the brutal fire we faced.

"Then the son of a bitch officer yells back at me, 'I don't give a damn! I said move forward right now!' So, I grabbed my machine gun and stood up to move forward. I was immediately hit by the Japanese machine gun fire.

"I never did find that son-of-a-bitch who gave that stupid order, "Stan said, laughing. And the students laughed with him.

Stan Aikins passed away at the age of 81 in December of 2006.

ROBERT BUSH   Okinawa
                                    Medal of Honor

I am always searching for veterans to come attend our events and speak to our students. Many times, you will read about or hear about someone who you should try to contact. In 2001, I was given one such name, Robert Bush, and soon called to invite him to our Night of Honor tribute to veterans at the Rose Garden Arena.

I asked if he would give a short speech during the event, and then, if possible, speak the next day to students at our school. Robert, who lived in the state of Washington, agreed, but unfortunately because he was having health issues, he could not stay to speak to students the next day.

Robert received his Medal of Honor while he was attached to a Marine Corps rifle company as a hospital corpsman in the Battle of Okinawa. He was also the youngest member, at age 18, of the U.S. Navy in World War II to receive a decoration of valor.

"I dropped out of school at age sixteen," he told the audience that night, "and joined the Navy, and as a Corpsman was attached to the Marines. I was badly wounded in an action. That resulted in my receiving both the Purple Heart and the Medal of Honor. When I came home from the war, I enrolled back in high school. I was eighteen years old."

That night he was not feeling very well, so many felt his speech's length was due to this. However, I can tell you that I felt that even if he were not feeling well, he would have said the same thing. He was a very soft-spoken man, who when you talked to him, you just felt at ease.

You also got a feeling that he was more concerned about others than himself, which makes sense when you hear about how he received his Medal of Honor.

Just before landing on the island of Okinawa, his entire 1st division in which he was a medical corpsman, was told that they were expendable. That their mission was to take a hill by the early morning.

Soon, all hell broke loose, and his platoon leader was hit and lay dying in a trench ahead of him. At that moment he went against his training of the medical corpsman being a vital part of the platoon and that the needs of the many outweigh the needs of the few, and he ran across to the fallen man's position.

He then opened a can of plasma and started giving it to the man via an IV. When he looked up after finishing, he spotted the head of the enemy a few yards away. He picked up the platoon leader's rifle and shot fifteen rounds into the enemy position. As he was doing this, his platoon leader woke up and walked back to his platoon then was taken to an aid station. Soon after, from the Japanese position above him, three grenades were thrown and went off close by and shrapnel took out his right eye.

Even though seriously injured, he then started walking around the hill to return to his platoon, trying to avoid any enemy positions. Along the way and with only one eye, he came upon some Japanese soldiers manning a machine gun. He snuck up behind them, pulled out a pistol then shot one round into each one of them, after which he walked back to a battalion aid station. He knew because of his injuries that he could start thinking about his return home.

It is unfortunate that Robert, not feeling well, was unable to properly speak to our students about his experiences. I think we would have really enjoyed hearing in his own words of the story I just shared of his 'conspicuous gallantry' on that day in 1945.

Robert Bush passed away at the age of 79 in November of 2005.

— ★ —

ARMY VETERANS

PAUL SCHWERTMANN   41st Sunset Division
                                    New Guinea, Philippines

Paul Schwertmann attended all fifteen Milwaukie Living History Day events in addition to traveling to other high schools throughout Oregon. He was a first-class and a sweet and very kind gentleman.

When I visited him at his home in February of 2013, he was eager to show me his office. On one wall he had pinned every name tag and program from each of the Milwaukie High School Living History Days he had attended.

With tears in his eyes, he told me. "I'm so proud of those Milwaukie students. Those Living History Days were some of the best days of my life."

Paul had written a book about his life entitled From My Earliest Memory: Peek into My Past. In it, he wrote about his life and how there were many bumps in the road, but in the end through his faith how God straightened them all out. I thoroughly enjoyed reading it.

I never heard him speak to the students, but on my visit to his home, he told me two stories about his World War II experiences.

"During the battle for New Guinea, we had secured a landing beach without any fire from the Japanese. We spent all day unloading big crates of all kinds of ammunition that we stacked on the pier and the beach. The stacked crates were as big as a couple of large warehouses.

"What we didn't know was that the Japanese waited until everything was unloaded and stacked. Then that night they blew it all up with artillery shelling. When the shelling started, most of us ran down the beach, getting as far away as possible. We just sat on the beach and watched the most incredible fireworks show we'd ever seen.

"After the New Guinea battle, we were sent to a small island to rest and regroup before joining the invasion to take back the Philippines. As soon as we got there a lot of us stripped and went swimming at the beach.

"All of a sudden, we see a jeep racing toward us. An officer jumps out and tells us to leave because the Army is filming about two hundred yards down the beach. We asked if we could watch, and he said, 'Yes, but stay up on the hill and keep quiet.'

"What we witnessed was something else," Paul said, breaking into laughter. "There was MacArthur practicing for his landing on the beach in the Philippines in a few days.

He was in charge of everything and yelling and barking orders left and right to the cameramen, the props, and even the extras. He must have practiced that landing a dozen times. Man, he had an ego."

Paul Schwertmann passed away at the age of 89 in March of 2013.

* ★ *

TOM LATTANZI   41st Sunset Division
                             New Guinea

Tom was a proud 1938 graduate of Milwaukie High School and attended all of our Living History Days at Milwaukie. "All my children and grandchildren attended Milwaukie High, and we are all proud of these Milwaukie Students for honoring us veterans," he said.

He was another first-class gentleman who always had a beautiful smile. I'm so grateful to his widow Betty and her daughter Christi who I interviewed for his story in March of 2021 at Milwaukie Floral.

Betty wanted me to know that "Tom was very close friends in high school with several guys who were Japanese Americans. There were many Japanese American farms in Milwaukie then and he was always very upset about them being interned."

Christi loaned me a DVD recording of Tom being filmed and interviewed in 2009 by the family.

"I was born in an Army hospital in Manila, Philippines in 1920 and was named after the ship the USS Thomas which was docked in Manilla. My father was an American soldier in the 31st Infantry stationed there, and my mother was Russian from Siberia. They met when my father was stationed in Siberia for a short time.

Betty told me, "When Tom was just a baby, his father talked his wife into getting a babysitter and going out to dinner for the first time. Right after being seated, she told her husband, 'I feel something is terribly wrong, take me home now.' As they pulled up to their home, baby Tom was being handed through an open window to a man outside next to a car that was running. They stopped a kidnapping, and the pair was arrested."

Christi also told me that her father was involved in sports in high school. "He was the State High Hurdles Champion and held the record at Milwaukie for over 40 years," Christi stated with pride.

In 1937, Tom and his best friend attended a yard meeting one evening at an Oregon National Guard base, Camp Withycombe, and all of them lied about their ages so they could join that night.

After graduating from high school, he was off to Ft. Lewis for boot camp in the 186th Infantry of the 41st Sunset Division.

Tom said in the video, "I was also first trombonist in the Army band. We all were great musicians as joining the military was the best way for musicians to make some money as the depression was tough on them. It was a great, soft job, playing revelry, retreat, parades, and other events. Every morning we would play 'Oregon My Oregon' and the Oregon boys would all cheer.

"Then I was sent to officer's training school at Fort Benning in Georgia. In 1940, the 411th was activated and I was commissioned."

When asked if he felt they would be going to war he said, "We knew it was coming as most of Europe had fallen, we were three years late."

"Right after the attack on Pearl Harbor, I was ordered back to Oregon to be shipped to the Philippines. I had six days to report to Oregon, I took trains and hitchhiked and made it just in time." Tom said laughing.

"We were shipped out on a Dutch luxury liner but were diverted on route to Australia after General MacArthur was ordered to Australia and there, we trained for jungle fighting."

In Australia, Tom helped to design and build raised platforms for trenches and fox holes because of the heavy rains they were expecting.

Biak Island in Papua New Guinea is where Tom was awarded his first Purple Heart - "We landed on the beach and advanced into the jungle taking a left turn and another left turn until reaching the beach again, thus surrounding the Japanese troops.

"However, up in the hills, the Japanese started firing anti-aircraft guns at us all on the beach. The bombs would explode above us and rain down shrapnel. As I was talking over the phone to our regimental commander inside our headquarters tent, I got hit bad in the leg.

"My parents received a telegram saying I had been shot but they did not know if I was still living. I was taken to a hospital on Lae, the same island in Papua New Guinea that Amelia Earhart took off from.

"My leg took two months to heal, and my doctor told me I was going home. But I asked to be reunited with my company still in New Guinea and I knew our plans were taking back the Philippines. I wanted to be a part of liberating the Philippines because I was born there," Tom said with pride.

Second Purple Heart.

In the video, Tom was asked to talk about how he got his second Purple Heart. Tom paused, and tears formed in his eyes, and he looked down. The video goes black and then restarts but now Tom is smiling. I have no idea how long it was before he could resume the interview.

"We were on patrol in the jungle and got in a firefight. A bullet ricocheted off a rock and went into my face right next to my nose and went down my esophagus into my stomach. I threw up blood and the bullet.

"My men, twenty of them, took turns carrying me over the twenty miles out of the jungle. When word got back to the beach, many others raced to find and help save me." Tom paused and got emotional again.

It is obvious to me that Tom was a very much loved and respected leader.

"I was sent to the same hospital with the same doctor. This time I was sent home and stationed in Texas until after the war ended. But I'll always remember being put in the back of a two-and-a-half-ton truck and taken to quite an outdoor celebration when it was announced the Japanese had surrendered."

When asked how he had earned his Bronze Star, Tom said, "I guess they thought I did a good job or maybe because I got two Purple Hearts."

Then Tom became very serious, "I wasn't a hero, I know what a real hero was."

Tom was also asked about the nickname the Japanese gave him and his men.

"It was actually Tokyo Rose who called us 'Bloody Butchers' and we never knew why. We listened to her on our radios."

I then asked, "So Betty, how did you and Tom meet?"

"I was working in the downtown Meier & Frank Store and Tom would come in to visit a co-worker a couple times a week for coffee. We were introduced, started dating, fell in love, and were married in 1948."

"How did he deal with the memories, or did he have any nightmares?"

"He never talked about it, and only opened up to me a little when our kids were grown and out of the house. It wasn't until becoming heavily involved with 41st Sunset Division Oregon Chapter and attending National reunions that he started to open up.

"We were invited to the 50th Anniversary of the battle of New Guinea 41st Sunset Division in Australia and excited to go. But Tom could not get a passport because the Army misspelled my father's last name and my mother's full name and refused to change it. They told him to change his last name.

"It took two years to get a passport because we found papers in a family bible with a birth certificate of Tom's grandfather born in America. We finally got to travel to Australia and had a marvelous time with the Aussies. They were such wonderful people."

Tom owned a grocery store with two gas pumps on Johnson Creek Road in Milwaukie.

When asked what he would tell high school students at Milwaukie High School's annual event to honor veterans, he said, "I would look into joining the service to learn a trade or a skill, get the money for college. There are a lot of opportunities."

"I retired after 27 years as a Lt. Colonel. I had 17 years with the 186th, and 10 years with the 104th Division Armored Reserve. My dad always wanted me to become a Captain and I didn't let him down," then Tom smiled.

Tom Lattanzi passed away at the age of 89 in March of 2010.

DR. PHILLIP LEVEQUE   European Theater

Dr. Phillip Leveque was quite an outgoing character. He always wore his Army uniform at every Living History Day event. At the end of each Assembly of Honor in the Milwaukie High School gym, he would stand up and yell, 'Konnichiwa' and 'Guten Tag.'

Then he would yell, "If it weren't for us veterans, you would all be speaking German or Japanese." Next, he would salute the students and yell, "Veterans, join me in saluting these students." All the veterans would then follow his lead.

I learned a lesson on the first Living History Day when several veterans stepped up on the stage, grabbed the mike, and started talking. This was not good because the students needed to leave the gym immediately to get on their buses.

The following year, we included in the mailed or emailed itinerary this notice: "No one will be allowed to speak at the end of the assembly." Also, a reminder was given near the end of the event. But nothing stopped Dr. Leveque, who was a 'don't take no for an answer' kind of guy.

"I walked from Luxembourg to Dresden most of the way under fire. I spent more time on the point than anybody else in my battalion. I don't have any idea how I got out of it alive" he shared with me.

Dr. Leveque even wrote a memoir called *General Patton's Dogface Soldier of WWII from a Foxhole* to help him with the nightmares he was having after the war. Later he began speaking at events and helping others.

Dr. Leveque was a proud World War II Army veteran. "I was one of General Patton's 'Dogface Soldiers,' he would say. "I helped liberate the Dachau Concentration Camp." He told me with pride.

He was also very proud of his role as a pioneer in the use of medical marijuana for veterans with PTSD. He helped legalize the use of marijuana as a medicine with Oregon's 1998 Medical Marijuana Act.

I remember many veterans joking around him, calling him the 'Pot Doc,' but that never fazed him one bit. He was proud of his efforts and never backed down.

Dr. Phillip Leveque passed away at the age of 92 in May of 2015.

DESMOND DOSS Jr.

Desmond Doss Jr. is the son of World War II Medal of Honor Desmond Doss Sr., whose incredible life story was shown in the movie Hacksaw Ridge. For three years in a row, Desmond Jr. has traveled to Oregon to join us in our high school speaking engagements. Ever since the movie came out, his life has changed dramatically. He has been flown all over the country speaking mostly to business audiences about his father.

We were lucky to get him because he enjoys speaking to high school students the most. After his first trip here, he pulled me aside and said, "Ken, this week has been an enjoyable experience for me. As long as you do this, I would be honored to be a part of your program."

Malinda and I went into the classroom where he was speaking at Gervais High School. In all my years of hearing public speakers, teachers, professors, coaches, veterans, others, Desmond Dross Jr. is the best. He mesmerized everyone in that classroom, especially the students. He had them in the palm of his hand.

Desmond is extremely loyal to his father's wishes. "My father," he said, "did not consider himself a hero. He considered himself as just an average man who loved God, his family, and life. He felt he was just doing his job. He was not Superman.

"In the movie, my father supposedly saved over 70 wounded soldiers by lowering them down the side of a cliff all in one night. Do you students really believe one man could do that? The truth is, this did happen but over the course of many days." The students gave him a standing ovation and crowded around to shake his hand.

On a personal note, Desmond fit right in with the Native American veterans with their sense of humor and constant jokes. Two years ago, I made a huge mistake while introducing Lieutenant General Russell Davis to the student body at Gervais High School. I meant to say, "How many stars does a lieutenant general have?" Instead, I said, "How many stars does a three-star general have?" Of course, the veterans broke out laughing, some of them hysterically. And the students followed their lead.

I joined in the laughter, but all I could think of was how much ribbing I was going to take from all the veterans, especially the Blackfeet veterans who would never leave this mistake alone. As it turned out, I didn't have to wait for the Blackfeet to kid me. As soon as the assembly was over, Desmond sidled up to me and said, "Ken, I need to call 911. What's the phone number?" And with that, we both exited laughing.

Desmond Doss Jr. is still living and still traveling around the country talking about his famous father. This last year, in 2020, he traveled to the very spot where his father so heroically saved the lives of so many.

---

* ⭐ *

W. DAVID KOLB   Third Army
101st Infantry 26th Division

In January 2014, I received a packet in the mail from David Kolb. He had attended all of our events from the beginning. Included in the packet were a handwritten note and a typed copy of his memoirs.

Dear Ken,

Here is a copy of my World War II memoirs. I thought it might be helpful for the book you are writing. At eighty-nine, I'm probably one of the youngest veterans with World War II experience. I can still walk three to five miles a week, though.

Best Wishes,

W. David Kolb

In 2019, as I was writing the book, I swear I heard a little voice say, "Ken, don't forget about me." I grabbed David's memoirs from my bookshelf and called his phone number. His wife answered. She told me that David had passed away in March of 2018. She gave her blessings to include her husband's experiences in this book.

David was a corporal in the 2nd Platoon, Company D 101st Infantry, 26th Division, Third Army. What is amazing to me is that David wrote his memoirs in 1946. He is the only veteran I ever met who did this so soon after the war.

> We arrived on the beaches of Normandy on September 7, 1944. We spent a couple of months working with the Red Ball Express. We supplied many of the trucks and drivers, loading supplies and gasoline that was delivered to General George A. Patton because his 3rd Army had outrun its supplies.
>
> After resupplying Patton's troops our company was ordered to the front. It took three days of driving to catch up with Patton's frontline forces. Once there we were ordered to accompany our captain to a meeting with all Division officers with ranks of captain and higher.
>
> It seemed that each officer was to be accompanied by a noncom. I think I was chosen because I didn't need a shave.
>
> We assembled, and General Patton, the Third Army Commander, walked in. It turned out the reason for this assembly was to give old 'Blood and Guts' a chance to give us a pep talk, and that he did. He looked and talked like a real soldier, and by the time he finished, I was ready to march to Berlin.

Many times, in his memoirs, David wrote about how beautiful the countryside was but how sad it was to come to village after village that had been destroyed. He also described something that those of us who have never served would not realize what daily life was like during the times between combat. Walking daily in deep mud and water sometimes knee deep. Digging foxholes in mud and water. Trying to sleep while cold and wet with rain. Trying to keep warm with wet blankets.

One night I had to crawl in the same hole with a buddy. The hole was small, and we had to sit up with me kind of lying across my buddy's lap. We were cold, wet, and miserable, but I did manage to sleep for a couple of hours.

We couldn't build fires because we were so close to the line. The mud was our worst enemy. We were caked with it from head to toe. Sometimes we could not leave the foxhole to urinate or defecate. We had to do our business in a K-ration box.

David wrote in detail his thoughts of his first time under fire in a battle in the vicinity of the old Hindenburg Line.

I was ordered to lead our platoon over a bare hill. We were to keep well dispersed and maintain contact with the other rifle troops and our artillery.

We hadn't gotten more than three hundred yards when German machine guns opened on us. Immediately we hit the ground. I was scared, yes, but not as bad as I had been afraid, I would be. I think what a soldier fears most about his first battle is not being killed but becoming so frightened that he won't be any good to himself or his buddies.

I remember that after this attack I felt quite proud of myself because I had not lost my head. No one ever knows for certain whether or not he is going to be one of those who lose control. Quite often it is the fellow who is least suspected to go off his nut that does so.

Oddly enough, I found that I was angry. I wanted to get one of those gunners with my rifle. I found myself cursing and praying in the same breath. After five minutes, the guns stopped firing. To this day, I don't know why.

As we attacked Metz and pushed the Germans out of France, the weather started getting colder. Most nights we tried sleeping in the rain and wind. Then came the snow. I would lie there and shiver for about fifteen minutes then get up and walk around to get warm. The only protection was purely in my imagination.

Once again, we were slowly crossing over a hill when the Germans opened up, this time with artillery fire. We hit the ground in a rain of shells. They would land on the right, then on the left, or right in front of us. What a helpless feeling it was to just lie there and take it.

It was then that I realized what an insignificant and unimportant bit of this universe I was. What did it matter to the world whether or not the next shell landed on my head and blew me to hell? But I lay there pressing myself into the ground and praying that it wouldn't.

David didn't escape injury in that firestorm. He was hit with shrapnel in his right leg. The next day he was evacuated to a 103rd field hospital in Nancy and then to another field hospital before being moved once again, this time to a hospital in Paris.

From there he was sent to the 110th Station Hospital outside Southampton, England. His final stop was the 91st General Hospital in Oxford.

In January 1945, David was sent back to join his outfit in Luxemburg. He was with the 3rd Army when they crossed the Rhine River into Germany in March.

This was all on foot with some pretty tough fighting. I remember passing several G.I. bodies as well as dead Germans. I remember a wounded German who kept calling out for wasser. He sounded pretty pathetic, so I stooped down and gave him a drink from my canteen.

I remember entering a small village that our artillery had heavily bombed. Strewn all around a rail yard were many damaged boxcars. One car was full of food and booze. Several riflemen drank too much and were bullying some civilians. I could see the civilians were terrified. That was probably as close as I ever came to deliberately shooting an American soldier. So, I left the area in disgust.

David became very sick and was sent to an aid station, where he was diagnosed with hepatitis. He was flown to the same hospital in Paris and eventually back to England again. The war with Germany ended while he was hospitalized.

Those of us in the hospital were told that when released, we'd probably get a thirty-day leave to go home to the States, but after that most of us would be shipped out to the Pacific to prepare for the invasion of Japan. You can imagine how happy and relieved all we wounded were when we heard the news that Japan had surrendered.

W. David Kolb passed away at the age of 93 in March of 2018.

NAVY VETERANS

TUDOR DAVIS   USS Halibut

Tudor Davis Revisited as Tudor opens up to me!

We've decided that this new, incredible information from Tudor has to be remembered and included in this Volume II.

My computer crashed in 2010 and the backup was on an antique floppy disk. I lost the contact information of many veterans. Thanks to Doc Collins, I reconnected with Tudor Davis in 2019.

In November of 2019, Tudor agreed to be one of five WWII veterans to speak to a crowd of 275, mostly veterans from WWII to Iraq and Afghanistan during a banquet to honor veterans.

Tudor was a submarine combat veteran on the USS halibut from 1943 - 1945, whose short section was in Volume I. Tudor followed Jack Owens, Army Air Corps, B-17, Top Turret Gunner, with thirty three missions. At the end of his presentation, Jack joked and told everyone that, "When that anti-aircraft flak started exploding all around and hitting our plane, we all felt we were in a flying coffin."

Jack laughed after saying that and the audience then laughed, and he handed the microphone to Tudor.

Tudor started laughing and said, "We all felt we were serving in an iron coffin under the sea." Everyone laughed at that.

His presentation was the shortest and just told everyone some facts about the USS Halibut and that was it. He didn't open up. But I figured that was going to be the case anyway because he was a submarine veteran who experienced depth charges and he was not going to suddenly tell a group of strangers about his experiences even though they were veterans. I was happy he was there, and so was everyone else because a lot of veterans asked if they could take a selfie with him.

In September of 2020, my Board Chair Paul Henderson was contacted by the Save The PT Boat, Inc. PT - 658 Heritage. They own and operate the beautifully restored PT - 658 that is kept down at the Naval Reserve on Swan Island in Portland, Oregon. They wanted us to ask a couple of WWII Navy veterans if we could bring them and take a ride on the PT-Boat.

I called Tudor, and he responded with, "I've never been on a PT boat before, this will be exciting," said Tudor Davis. His son, Fred, also a Navy veteran, brought him.

PT-658 was manned with an all-volunteer crew, all veterans, mostly Vietnam veterans. It was a sunny Saturday on a beautiful fall day. The ride up the Willamette River was awesome. They asked Tudor if he would like to drive. He was like a little kid in a candy store. Everyone was moved and taking pictures of him.

After reading Volume I, Tudor called me to talk about his section. In the last months of 2020, I had several more conversations over the phone with him. Every time, he shared more information and even mailed me more information on the Halibut.

During one phone conversation, he told me about the sub's mascot, a dog named 'Skeeter'. It's a great and unbelievable story included in this section.

I called Doc Collins and told him the dog story and he responded, "This is historic. This is a miracle. You got him to open up to you!"

Doc Collins was a submarine veteran and Navy corpsman attached to the 1st Marine Division at the Chosin Reservoir during the Korean War.

I asked him why he joined the Navy.

"We were a very poor family. There was no work available in town," Davis said. "I had a job in the small steel mill, but there was no future, and the Navy looked like the place to be.

"So, I joined the Navy in October of 1941, and was put on a waiting list until December 7, 1941, when I was called in and sworn in as an Apprentice Seaman on December 31, in the Old Seamen's Institute in Philadelphia.

"Right after Boot Camp and Seamanship training, I was assigned to the USS Tuscaloosa and participated in the Murmansk Patrols and the Invasion of North Africa and Casablanca.

"I requested submarine duty, was transferred to Naval School for Submarine Training and then spent the rest of WWII on the USS Halibut's 5th through 10th war patrols."

The following is from a letter to me by Tudor Davis in November 2020:

We had just sunk an AK (supply ship) and had to go deep and rig for depth charges. We were in a Reload Torpedo Tube operation and at 250' depth when our pet dog 'Skeeter' started barking like mad at the Port After section of the forward Torpedo room.

Sonar could not pick up any sounds, we could not get him to stop barking so we called the conn and told them about Skeeter's barking. The Control & Conning tower started in maneuvering action. We in the Forward Torpedo Room had a torpedo on the skid moving it into position to reload when the 'Shit hit the Fan'.

All hell broke loose. A mass of depth charges exploded over the forward battery forward torpedo room. The depth charges were exploding so close, it was determined there could have been over 40 detonations. The starboard skid was being moved to reload in free position and it was jumping above the runners by one or two inches, and the five of us who were moving the torpedo, felt safer when we got it in position and locked in place. We left it there!

We had other things to check and open and close while being Depth Charged. The Depth Gauge in the Forward Torpedo Room read 480 and we still had 15 degrees down angle. We never knew what depth we reached as the gauge was frozen stuck at 485. It was estimated by engineers that we reached 600.

Thank God the torpedo in the skid was strapped down during movement. Once locked in the loading position, safe, right where we left it! Four hours later, our sub was rigged for hand operations as many systems in the automotive operation (high pressure air, electrical, hydraulic) were in need of repair. We surfaced and the enemy was not in sight.

What caused Skeeter to react like this? We had recently learned that the Japanese had dropped a new vehicle (Jiki Kon Tiki) to find and send enemy positions by crisscrossing a target and then the patrol craft dropped everything they had. Had he not been with us, God only knows! To this day, we who were on this 10th patrol know that God and Skeeter saved our lives.

Messages were sent quickly asking for assistance and possibly an escort. We dove in manual operation to get hidden. It took us 15 minutes to get to a depth of 60 out of Radar Contact. More analysis was made to determine instant repair we could perform back on the surface and head for safe harbor. Electrical systems were corrected that could be, air systems, etc.

Then we surfaced again and worked on Engine Room problems and all other problems to insure we could surface to get out of the zone we were in and headed for Saipan. This was Nov 14th, 1944, and we had taken Saipan back by then. We were informed that the USS Pintado (SS 387) was rendezvousing with us and would escort us to Saipan. After Saipan we were sent to Pearl Harbor where we were put in dry dock.

While in dry-dock the damage to the hull was revealed. The hull and outer hull (fuel tanks etc.) were pushed in approximately 3 to 4 inches 6 to 15 feet high. From the bow to the frame 58 which is the FWD Bulkhead of the Control Room. It looked somewhat like mother's washboard instead of a smooth hull.

We were eventually sent to Mare Island Naval Shipyard and then on to Portsmouth Naval Shipyard in New Hampshire where we were decommissioned.

In December of 2020, I decided to ask him a tough question. This would be a risk as I did not know how he would respond to my question.

"Mr. Davis, I would like to ask you the same question I asked four of the Ex-POWs at the Defenders of Bataan and Corregidor's National Reunion in 2013. As a coach, we always pushed our athletes hard to hopefully make them mentally tougher and to never quit, etc.

"When you were going through the depth charges and the Halibut had submerged to extremely dangerous depths, how did you deal with this emotionally? What did you draw back on? Was it your father, a coach, a Pastor, etc. What got you through this?"

Tudor just laughed and said, "Well, my father, Tudor Davis, Sr., Army, Purple Heart, was a tough WWI veteran. He was a Doughboy, who served in the trenches and was gassed (Mustard Gas). He suffered badly with a lot of physical pain until dying from ulcers at 53 years of age.

"My father was also a coal miner, and my mother Louise Ann Davis, was a homemaker. Our family of five lived in Pottsville, Pennsylvania. Most of the fathers in our neighborhood were WWI veterans and they built a makeshift boxing ring in the street. Every boy had to start fighting at six years of age. Boxing was huge in those days. We had to fight all the time and there was no getting out of it.

"Once, when I was in fourth grade, it was a very cold day, rain mixed with snow, and I put my books under my coat to walk home. A boy told me I looked pregnant. I punched him right in the mouth and knocked him down. The principal saw this, grabbed both of us, and brought in the school and whipped us both good.

"My father asked me why I was late coming home from school, so I told him. He was so upset, he went down to the school and roughed up the principal and yelled 'I'm preparing my son for the next war, don't mess with him.' Dad was also the Constable of the 6th Ward.

"As young boys in the community, we were so afraid of letting our fathers down. I started working out at ten years of age, you call it lifting weights today. I boxed all through elementary school and through high school. After joining the Civilian Conservation Corps (CCC) in October 1940, I went from 113 pounds to 165 pounds of solid muscle. I left the CCCs in March 1941. I still lift weights today, obviously lighter weights.

"We submarine sailors know we are in that iron coffin together, with only each other, and we depend on each other very much. Another factor was the constant training aboard the sub. We were so focused on doing our job. And that dependency led to forever friendships."

I then said, "I'm so grateful to you for sharing more of your experiences. It means a lot, and the dog mascot Skeeter story is amazing."

Then Tudor says to me, "I also have a more detailed version of the Australian Digger Hat part. The Digger Hat became part of our WWII Submarine Veterans when we became an organization in 1951. It was voted on by the group of founders who were stationed and made war patrols out of Australia.

"Many submarine sailors met and dated Aussie Ladies. After the war, they married their girlfriends (Aussie Ladies). Because of the deep respect our sailors had for the Aussie Soldiers, we wore the Digger as part of our Dress Uniform for all honorable meetings, parades, and remembrance services we attended, etc. We used the color Blue to match our vest."

Tudor Davis served on nine different submarines during his twenty year career and served on his last submarine, the USS George Washington (SSBN 598), when he retired from the Navy as a chief torpedoman in January 1961.

After completing Polaris Training School in April of 1958 and in 1959, Tudor had the good fortune to work with LMSC Engineers on ships and in the shops at Cape Canaveral. When he retired from the Navy, Tudor was hired by Lockheed Missile and Space Co. and worked on SSBNs as a Field Engineer, performing phase testing on the Polaris Missile system for six years and completed his career with LMSC as a supervisor of the Missile Parts Operations, retiring in January 1987.

Tudor Davis is still living at 97 years of age, and still working out every day.

Thanks to William Galvanti, author of *Sea Dogs*, Published in American Heritage in Oct 1994.

> Skeeter the mascot of the USS Halibut was a swashbuckler too. The crew acquired him in Lefty's bar in San Francisco while the sub was undergoing overhaul in '44. During his tour on the Halibut, Skeeter appeared at the captain's mast twice, perhaps a canine record. He was first charged with disturbing the peace in the forward battery compartment and with being surly and belligerent. Cmdr. I. J. Galantin, the Halibut's C.O., dismissed the case with a warning. Skeeter's second trip to mast came when he mistook a chief petty officer's leg for a fire hydrant. But the dog eventually received an honorable discharge and was mustered out of the Navy in Portsmouth, New Hampshire in July 1945.

WILLIAM 'BILL' TUNSTALL

DOROTHY 'DOTTIE' MAE TUNSTALL

USS Hornet
Doolittle Raid
Navy Waves

Bill and Dottie were the first veterans to publicly thank the Milwaukie High students soon after our first Living History Day in 1996. They asked if they could have the opportunity to speak to the entire school at our annual Holiday Assembly held right before Christmas break. Their thank-you was so emotional and heartfelt.

They told the students, "You have no idea what you students have done for us veterans, and we are so proud of you." I saw many teenagers crying as Bill and Dottie presented the student body president a U.S. flag that was flown over the U.S. Capitol building.

"I am extremely proud," Dottie told the students, "That I was the very first woman in Oregon to join the WAVES during World War II." That brought a standing ovation from the girls. "Also," she added, "Bill and I were the first couple in Oregon to be married in our uniforms."

The WAVES was the first women's branch of the United States Naval Reserve. It was into this group of highly dedicated women that Dottie entered. The WAVES (Women Accepted for Volunteer Emergency Service) accepted women into the Naval Reserve as commissioned officers or at the enlisted level. This group of women was vital in helping the war effort because they replaced positions in shore establishments when those men were called for active sea duty.

After the assembly, the three of us chatted some more. I wondered how they managed since they obviously were apart for long periods of time. Dottie smiled. "Bill and I created our own secret code to communicate with each other when he was in the South Pacific." It wasn't until March of 2021 that I finally learned about their secret code.

Bill first served on the Heavy Cruiser, USS Chester (11 Battle Stars) and after it was bombed during an attack on Taroa, Samoa in January of '42. He asked to be transferred to the USS Hornet (4 Battle Stars), and when it was damaged during the Battle of the Santa Cruz Islands in October of '42, he asked to be transferred to the USS Kitkun Bay (6 Battle Stars), which was damaged by a Kamikaze attack on October 25, 1944. He asked to be transferred again, but this time he was promoted to an Ensign sent stateside as an instructor.

The Hornet was the aircraft carrier from which sixteen B-52B medium bombers, under the command of Lieutenant Colonel James Doolittle, launched the first bombing raid on the Japanese mainland. It was April 18, 1942, four months after the Japanese attack on Pearl Harbor. The Doolittle Raid was a tremendous lift for American morale.

"I was in sickbay for two days but came up on the flight deck to witness when those B-52's took off," Bill said. "Being on that flight deck when all of those B-25s started their engines was such a powerful, emotional moment. The enormous pride and jubilation we felt was incredible."

Bill followed that up with, "I'll also never forget seeing a sailor lose his arm when the final B-52 rolled back out of position, and he lost his arm from its propeller. And one of the pilots approached me before taking off and tried to give me his wallet, 'Please get this to my wife if I don't make it.' I refused, telling him, 'No, you are going to make it.' I learned later that he never made it back home. I've always regretted not taking his wallet and sending it to his wife."

The Secret Code

I needed to learn more about their secret code. I learned from their daughter, Sally, that an impressive display including both of their uniforms and love letters were at the B-17 Alliance Foundation in Salem, Oregon. Their mission is to restore their B-17 and to educate generations. (www.B17Alliance.com)

Terry Scott, Executive Director, and singer in the trio 'Two Sisters and a Mister' (Patriotic and WWII era songs, and they have sung at many of our events for years) told Malinda and I the story.

"This is a story of love and romance that lasted over seventy years. First, Dottie, her sister, Nancy, and their cousin, Betty all joined the Waves together, and were stationed at Sand Point Naval Air Base on Lake Washington in Seattle, Washington.

"She rose to the rank of Petty Officer. She loved to tell me how their Drill Instructor, a male, hated the fact that women were now being allowed to join. When teaching the women how to march, he would slur his words on purpose, and we couldn't understand him. This would cause constant confusion with women bumping into each other. The DI would let all know that this was proof women should not be in the Navy. Well, that just made us women more determined to learn anyway, and we did.

"Bill was stationed at Sand Point also where planes practiced aircraft carrier take-offs and landings. The women and men were kept segregated, but during lunchtime they would pass each other, walking on opposite sides of the street. Bill noticed Dottie and yelled "Hey Babe" and Dottie would yell the same back to him. This went on many times, and they started seeing each other and soon fell deeply in love and eventually married on August 24, 1943."

Terry got tears in her eyes, stopped talking, "I'm sorry this part always gets to me. Bill was so romantic and always showered Dottie with Roses. Before shipping out, Bill got two giant maps of the Pacific from National Geographic. Using grid coordinates, he created many squares and wrote different salutations on both maps.

For example, My Dearest Darling would be in the Marshall Islands. My Darling Dearest would be somewhere else. Dottie would always know where Bill was located when he wrote the letter. She always felt very comforted as it was confirmation, he was alive.

"The Navy censers never broke their code. Once, she didn't receive a single letter in six months. His family assumed he was killed in action but finally received a letter letting them all know he was safe."

Bill Tunstall passed away at the age of 93 in June of 2013.

Dottie Tunstall passed away at the age of 97 in March of 2018.

WARREN SCHAFER   Navy South Pacific

Dr. Warren Schafer attended many Milwaukie High School Living History Days. All of his children attended Milwaukie High, and he was also a popular dentist in the Milwaukie area.

In 1968, when his son, Donald Schafer, was killed in Vietnam, Dr. Schafer buried Donald in the Willamette National Cemetery. What he saw in the cemetery disgusted him. Thousands of graves did not even have permanent markers.

In addition, there were acres and acres of mud where there should have been beautiful grass surrounding the dead. Dr. Schafer decided to do something about the horrible conditions into which this national cemetery had been allowed to fall into disrepair.

He knew the dead deserved better, so he started to look for a better way to respect those buried there. He then started a campaign and spearheaded it to beautify the cemetery and give the National Cemetery greater stature.

Five decades later, Willamette National Cemetery is considered to be one of the most beautiful of all the national cemeteries, second only to Arlington National Cemetery in Washington, D.C.

I often go there to put flowers on my parents' graves, and every time I go, I look around and thank Dr. Schafer for what he did to make my mother and father's final resting place so beautiful, for them and for all of us.

Malinda and I attended his memorial service, and the family had displayed many pictures of Dr. Shafer from his childhood to his elder years. I knew, of course, that he had been a Milwaukie dentist for years, but when I saw pictures of him as a dentist, I said out loud, "Oh my gosh, Dr. Schafer was my dentist when I was a kid."

Dr. Warren Schafer passed away at the age of 99 in February of 2019. He was laid to rest in Willamette National Cemetery beside his son Donald.

* ★ *

GENE CLIFT   USS Little

Two Navy destroyers were named after George Little, a Navy officer who was in the Revolutionary War. Both ships fought in the Pacific Theater of World War II, and Japanese forces sank both.

The first USS Little, a Wickes-class destroyer, was first commissioned in 1918, decommissioned in 1922, and then reclassified for recommissioned service in 1940. It went down in a fight with three Japanese destroyers on September 5, 1942, in the Battle of Guadalcanal.

The second USS Little, a Fletcher-class destroyer, was commissioned in August of 1944. Nine months later, while on radar picket duty during the invasion of Okinawa, four Japanese kamikaze planes hit and sank her. She broke up and went down. Thirty-one of the USS Little's 320 crew perished. Among the survivors was Gene Clift.

Gene and his lovely wife Naomi attended several of our Living History Days at Milwaukie High School. They always had a table display about the USS Little.

Gene's story always fascinated the students. "I was one of twelve sailors in the boiler room when one of the kamikaze planes crashed into the room," Gene would begin. "It all happened in slow motion. I saw the giant red meatball on the side of the plane. I climbed up the stairs and out of the boiler room. The next thing I remember is floating in the water. The explosion blew me over fifty feet off the ship. Of the twelve sailors in the boiler room, only me and one other guy survived, and I have no idea why. And I didn't have a scratch on me, but I lost my hearing.

"We were in the water for about four hours until rescue, but it seemed like an eternity. We taught some of the sailors how to swim, and we sang the song 'Mairzy Doats' over and over again for a couple of hours. Don't ask me why. Also, a sailor had smuggled a small dog aboard the Little, and she survived the sinking, too. Her name was Dee Dee, and we took turns holding her in the water. After we were rescued, that sailor took the dog home."

Gene and I both lived in Canby, Oregon, so I ran into him often and visited him in his home many times. He was a great guy, and we enjoyed each other's company.

In 2006, Gene was diagnosed with cancer. The doctors said he had three to six months to live. When Gene told me this, he declared, "I'm going out in style." In his house, he had a cigar room. Gene enjoyed a good cigar and a single malt scotch every afternoon. After the diagnosis, he bought very expensive scotch, and from a good friend living in Spain, he got a box of Cuban Cohiba cigars, the famous brand specially rolled for Fidel Castro.

This extravagance however lasted three years as Gene proved the doctors wrong. "Hell, Ken," he said, "I can't afford this anymore. I'm going back to the cheap stuff." His 'cheap stuff' was still high quality, though.

During one of my visits, while enjoying a cigar and scotch with Gene, I told him about Eugene Morgan, the USS Indianapolis survivor. "I'd love to meet him," Gene told me. So, I called Eugene to see if he too was interested.

The next week Eugene drove down from Seattle and met Gene at his home. They settled in the cigar room, and as they talked, they became emotional. They hugged each other as if they were long-lost friends.

I think because the two of them having the connection of being survivors of their ships' sinking, they were able to seem like old friends. I have seen time and time again how veterans who have endured the horrors of war open up only with other veterans who have gone through the same experiences. I sat mesmerized for the next two hours as they shared story after story of their experiences. It was as if I were not in the same room.

When their conversation started to die down, Gene realized that he had not offered us a drink or a cigar. After pouring three glasses of scotch, Gene raised his, and said, "To the men of the Little and the Indianapolis still at sea." We raised ours and then drank in remembrance.

Before his cancer diagnosis, Gene and his wife Naomi were heavily involved with the USS Little's national reunions, with the two of them attending many of them over the years. In 2007, the next national reunion was to be held in Portland, Oregon, and Naomi, helping with many of the details and planning, was a big part of it being such a great success.

After having introduced the two, Gene invited Eugene to come to Portland and be an honored guest. They even had a plan to sail with the Little's survivors on the Navy frigate the USS Vandergrift up the Columbia and Willamette Rivers to be part of the annual Rose Festival Fleet's arrival. Eugene struggled with this invitation. The thought of being on a ship sailing up the rivers would be an emotional challenge for him, so he told Gene he would think about it.

Several days after the invitation, Eugene called me. "Ken," he said, "I'm going to do it. I think it will be good for me." And it was, for he had a wonderful time on the ship with the Little survivors. Everyone, especially the ship's crew, treated Eugene like a rock star.

During the trip, one of the sailors had decided to reenlist in the Navy, and the ship's commander asked Eugene to do the honors for the young man. It was a very emotional, powerful, and moving ceremony led by Eugene. Everybody cried or had tears in their eyes. The ceremony was on the ship's helipad. It was damn impressive! The sailors and the officers were so honored to have this happen on their ship.

This whole experience meant the world to Eugene. "Thank you," he said to Gene, "for pressuring me into joining the cruise. I had a marvelous time."

Gene's battle with cancer continued. At age 92, the cancer had metastasized, and he went into hospice care. Naomi called me and told me about the news over the telephone. She was very emotional and kept saying over and over again how sad she was feeling.

We kept talking and had a long conversation just talking about Gene the entire time. I felt sorry for her because I kept asking her questions because I wanted to make sure that I had Gene's story right so I could write about him and give him the honor I knew he deserved.

"My best memories," she said, "are attending the USS Little's reunions. I remember at one of the first reunions in the '80s where we witnessed two sailors reunite. They were best friends who served on the Little. Neither knew if the other had survived because different ships rescued the sailors, and they lost track of each other.

"When they saw each other for the first time since the sinking of the Little, they hugged and cried. They wouldn't let go of each other and held hands. They were inseparable for the entire reunion." Naomi cried as she told me this.

On November 8, 2016, some of Gene's veteran buddies brought him to our annual veteran's dinner event at the FOB Taproom in Canby. When they brought Gene in, he was in a wheelchair, bundled in heavy winter clothes and a blanket, and obviously very ill. Before the start, everyone was engaged in conversations, while Gene sat silent, slouched with head down, barely acknowledging those around him.

I opened the evening as I usually did by introducing the vets in attendance and saying a few things about their backgrounds. When I came to Gene, I shared the story of Gene's persuading USS Indianapolis survivor Eugene Morgan back on a Navy ship for the cruise up the Columbia and Willamette rivers.

Hearing this everyone in the room rose to give him a standing ovation. When they did that, Gene threw off his blanket and sat up straight, touched by this show of admiration by his fellow veterans.

Gene Clift continued his battle with cancer for two more years and passed away three days short of his 94th birthday in May of 2018.

———— ★ ————

PT BOAT VETERANS

From 1996 to 2004, a group of fifteen PT boat Veterans attended our Living History Days events. During that time, they were heavily involved in restoring an original PT boat to its 'as-built' condition.

The story behind the boat, PT-658, was that it had been purchased after the war by a person in California, who converted it into a pleasure boat. No longer being used the boat fell into disrepair.

Then in 1994, the California owner's family donated the boat to this group of PT boat veterans in Oregon. The PT Veterans then had the boat carefully transferred to a barge and then moved to Portland's Swan Island behind the Navy Operations Support Center where they then began their restoration work.

These men often came to our events many times over the years, and they would talk to our students about their PT experiences. They also often invited me to come see the PT boat they were restoring. I regret not going down to Swan Island to see them at work on their restoration of the boat.

So they could help raise and manage funds, the vets formed the nonprofit organization, Save The PT Boat, Inc. For the next ten years, from generous donations to many hours of many unpaid volunteers, in 2004 their dream came true. That October, after a few trial runs, their boat cleared the dock and they proudly sailed on the Willamette River.

Their legacy lives on with the PT-658 at the Heritage Museum and Education Center on Swan Island in Portland Oregon.

PT BOAT VETERANS WHO ATTENDED LIVING HISTORY DAYS

John Akin	Don Brandt
Brian Tedder	Jim Brunette
Roth Bruckner	Don Carter
Frank Lesage	Richard Lowe
Al McCready	Ken Nissen
Gordon Smith	Harry Wiedmaier

Don Foidel   *Class of 1939 PT squadron crewman w/ John F. Kennedy

PART II   THE KOREAN WAR

We didn't do much talking,
We didn't raise a fuss.
But Korea really happened
So please - remember us.

We all just did our duty
But we didn't win or lose.
A victory was denied us
But we didn't get to choose.

We all roasted in the summer
In winter, we damn near froze.
Walking back from near the Yalu
With our blackened frozen toes.

Like the surf the Chinese kept coming
With their bugles in the night.
We fired into their masses
Praying for the morning light.

All of us just had to be there
And so many of us died.
But now we're all but half forgotten
No one remembers how we tried.

We grow fewer with the years now
And we still don't raise a fuss.
But Korea really happened
So please - remember us.

~ Lt Cdr Roberto J. Prinselaar, USCG (Ret)
New Jersey Korean War Veterans Memorial

SOUTH KOREA: THE MOST GRATEFUL COUNTRY ON EARTH

"Freedom is not free." The majority of South Koreans understand this more than most people and are the most grateful people to American veterans I have ever met.

I have many experiences that have deeply impacted me and have been extremely healing and now I honestly believe my father's death was not just another casualty of the Korean War. It was not in vain.

The first experience was with a South Korean Tour Group on the beaches of Waikiki, Honolulu, Hawaii.

During a two-week period where I worked for the University of Hawaii's Head football coach, June Jones, as the FB camp director for high school players and with my children in 2001, an amazing experience happened to me. One I shall never forget!

One late afternoon, I was walking on Waikiki Beach with my son, Anthony, and my daughter, Breanne, heading back to our hotel. I was wearing my swimming suit and a t-shirt with 'United States Marines Corps' on the front.

As we got to the street, there was a charter bus parked right next to the beach with a group unloading right in front of us. The guide was holding a South Korean Flag high in the air, and all of the South Korean tourists gathered around him. The majority of them were senior citizens.

I stopped my children and said, "Let's wait to let these people pass as a group. As they started to walk by us, the guide approached me and said, "Some of the ladies have asked if you are a US Marine"?

I responded, "No, but my father was, and he fought in the Korean War." Immediately, nearly everyone came up and surrounded me, speaking in Korean, and bowing.

The guide said, "They are all saying thank you for your father." Several elderly women cried as they thanked me. One older man pulled out of his backpack a bottle of the popular Korean alcohol 'Soju'. They gave several toasts to my father, and they offered me samples of different Korean food.

I have never been treated with such respect and honor. Their gratitude towards me for my father (an American Korean War Veteran) is something I will never forget.

Revisit Korea Trip

Another amazing experience was the Revisit Korea Trip that the Government of South Korea had been sponsoring for years. They have been thanking and honoring American Korean War veterans with an all-expenses-paid four-day trip to Seoul.

Because most Korean War veterans have passed away or are unable to travel, South Korea opened this trip up to the children of the veterans.

I learned from many veterans from The Chosin Few and the Korean War Veterans Association (KWVA) who had gone on the trip in the past that it was not to be missed. They all raved about the gratitude of the South Korean people. I felt I needed to go for my father and I'm so thankful I did.

Everything about the trip was a five-star, first-class experience, from the lodging to the meals to the impressive heartfelt receptions everywhere we went.

The trip included visits to The Seoul National Cemetery for a moving remembrance ceremony, the DMZ, attending a Korean professional baseball game, in front of thousands of South Koreans being honored and entertained at a large indoor arena, and on the last night, a banquet honoring us with more outstanding entertainment and gifts.

I must have been told, "Thank you for your father," and bowed to several hundred times during the trip. It was all so emotionally moving and healing for me. I shall never forget this experience.

To the people of South Korea, Thank you so much.

LT. GENERAL EDWARD L. ROWNY

Army WWII
Korea Vietnam

I was blessed to meet this impressive man while on my first trip to Korea. He was 98 years old, and his son helped bring him on the Revisit Korea Trip.

At that time, he was just finishing writing his book *Smokey Joe and the General.* I chatted with him for a few minutes and learned he was on General MacArthur's staff during WWII and the Korean War.

He told me, "I helped plan the Inchon landing and the famous bridge drop at the Chosin Reservoir."

"Wow! What was it like working for General MacArthur?"

He laughed and then told me, "Well, this short story will tell you everything you need to know about General MacArthur.

"I flew from Korea to the General's headquarters in Tokyo, Japan for a meeting with him. There were two elevators in the lobby. One was guarded by a Marine because that elevator went straight to the General's office. The second elevator was for all the other floors, and everyone was required to take the second elevator and then request permission to take the first elevator to the General's office, one floor up."

The Lt. General laughed again. "I was in a hurry and approached a Marine who was guarding MacArthur's elevator. The Marine guard quickly stepped forward blocking the elevator and barked, 'This elevator is reserved for God only.'"

The Lt. General laughed and looked at me and said, "Does that answer your question?"

Lieutenant General Edward L. Rowny passed away at the age of 100 in December of 2017.

* ★ *

SAE EDEN PRESBYTERIAN CHURCH, SEOUL, SOUTH KOREA

Malinda and I had the opportunity to travel back to South Korea in June of 2019, for five nights and six days, compliments of Sae Eden Presbyterian Church in Seoul. It was the church's 13th annual event in which the congregation tithed every service to raise the funds for this Honor Trip, to honor Korean War veterans in person.

The church has over 40,000 members. The budget was $400,000, and they graciously paid for everything, including airfare, baggage fees, transportation, and lodging (Jamsil Lotte World Hotel, over $500 a night, with all meals, many at five-star restaurants). We spent four and a half days there filled with many impressive events organized to honor the veterans.

This trip all started when we were invited by Hannah Kim, a Korean American, who had spent two years traveling across America to every state as well as to every member country of the United Nations to personally thank Korean War veterans. Hannah traveled to Oregon in 2018 to attend our annual events. Hannah was so impressed that she told Elder Kim of Sae Eden Church about us.

Elder Kim was the person in charge of organizing the entire event. When I first met him, he greeted us in a ROK (Republic of Korea) Naval dress uniform. He was a retired Admiral, and I was so impressed and in awe of him, I always call him Admiral Kim.

After learning what we had been doing in Oregon for over the last twenty years, Sae Eden asked us to come on the trip. This trip and experience were however only for Korean War veterans and the families of MIAs and KIAs, and many times we told Hannah that it would not be appropriate for us to go as we would be taking the place of a veteran who should attend.

Well, Admiral Kim would not accept no for an answer, and in the end, we graciously accepted the invitation.

It was also a blessing because our good friend Bill Chisholm, a Chosin Few who had refused to go back to Korea as he was worried that his memories of his time there during the war would worsen, agreed to go if we 'promised' to hold his hand. Bill had told us several times that he was very nervous about going.

When we arrived in Korea and disembarked, we were all greeted by dozens of high school students, college students, and adults. Even the press and media were there to cover it. It was unbelievable.

Then we found out that a high school student was going to be personally assigned to each veteran and guest. It was then that for some reason Bill was swarmed by several of the high school girls who acted like he was their long lost relative. The look on Bill's face was priceless. He turned to me and Malinda and smiled and said, "I'll be OK now."

Sunday started with a church service in the hotel with a sermon from a pastor from Sae Eden. This was then followed by a cruise and an incredible buffet lunch on the Han River.

It was something else to see the Korean War veterans' shock at how modern and huge Seoul was as many of their personal memories were that it was completely destroyed during the war. They told me that there was only one bridge connecting the two sides of Seoul. Today however there are thirty-one.

That evening we attended the Welcome Dinner, Worship Service, and Commemorative Ceremony in the promise Hall of Sae Eden Church. As we unloaded the charter buses, we were greeted by hundreds of Korean children dressed in traditional clothing waving ROK and US flags all singing a 'Thank You' song. We were led through this gauntlet of children that was probably 50 yards long into the church, and then to the Welcome Dinner filled with hundreds of South Korean War veterans and then escorted to our assigned tables.

As we ate a fantastic dinner of Korean food, we were entertained with traditional Korean songs. After dinner, we were led into the Worship Hall that holds over 7000 people, again all singing the 'Thank You' song. We were led down the middle aisle to the front. It was a moving and impressive ceremony, filled with a lot of tears.

The next day, Monday, June 17, we were taken to a Wreath Laying Ceremony at The Korean National Cemetery. Again, very moving, and emotional. It was then on to visit the headquarters of the ROK Marine Corps and Review Honor Guard with traditional Korean drumming on large drums, The ROK Marine Corps Band performed, and an elite rifle silent drill team gave an incredible performance.

After lunch, we were taken to the 2nd Fleet Command base to visit the Cheonan Memorial where lies a patrol ship sunk by a North Korean submarine on March 6, 2010.

At the site, we learned how The Republic of Korea Navy brought up the entire severely damaged ship, which is now on display at the memorial site. The Cheonan Memorial was opened in 2017 commemorating the 46 sailors who were lost in the sinking of the ROK's Cheonan warship.

From an article posted on December 28, 2016, by Korea Bizwire:

> An exhaustive investigation revealed that on the night of March 26, 2010, the ship was hit by a North Korean torpedo, although North Korea has consistently denied the claim.
>
> The memorial was built at the Second Fleet Command's naval base in Pyeongtaek, adjacent to the recovered hull of the Cheonan. Construction began in June 2015, with a 4.47 billion won ($3.7 million) budget, and covers a total area of 1,340 square meters.
>
> The exhibit is comprised mainly of a detailed history of the event, including rescue efforts and the recovery operation for the vessel, a place to commemorate the fallen, and pictures and the military ID tags of the 46 soldiers.

This was another very emotional visit as all were moved to tears. Several of the American Navy veterans wept openly. The following day, we visited the 8th US Army Command Base, and we were given an impressive early dinner at Pan Moon Jeom Business Center in Seoul hosted by the Federation of Korean Industries.

The next day, we toured the Korean War Memorial & Museum Complex in Seoul. It was beyond impressive. We were led to the long (open to the outside), approximately 75 yards long. On both sides of the hall, from the floor to the ceiling, were bronze plaques covering the walls.

They were separated with each representing a US state, Washington DC, and territories. On each state's plaque were the engraved names of every American serviceman or servicewoman killed in action while in Korea. It was overwhelming.

Several of the Korean War veterans were so overcome with emotion they could not walk through it. All of the South Korean volunteers offered to find the names of their buddies on the wall.

For lunch, they split us into two groups. All of the Marine veterans and their family members were invited to a luncheon hosted by Brigadier General Park Jung Soo ROK Marine Corps Ret. and two retired former Commandants of ROK Marine Corps at the Dragon Hotel in the US Army Garrison Yongsan Base in Seoul. It was awesome!

On our last day before departing South Korea, we were taken to the ROK Army Special Warfare Command which is off limits to the general public. Stationed at this base were American Special Forces and it is also the home to the 'Black Berets' who were modeled after US Army's Special Forces Green Berets.

To get on the base, it was about a two-hour drive south out in the country and up in the hills. The entire time we were ordered not to take any pictures. When we got out of the transports, we were met by ROK Special Forces all dressed in all black, even covering their faces with special black goggles. They were very impressive and very intimidating.

They then proceeded to put on several displays of their unique abilities such as two of them running full speed down the side of a four-story building and stopping about two feet from the ground. Another two jumped off the top of the building holding the rope in a free fall and then came to an abrupt stop just a few feet from the ground.

Next, four of them repelled down into a second-story window from the top of the same building, throwing hand grenades in and just seconds after the explosion flying through the window, machine guns ablaze and then silence with the ROK Special Forces men leaning out the window yelling all clear. It was an adrenaline rush and awesome!

That evening was the farewell dinner at Lotte Hotel World in Jamsil. Another impressive event, at which there were many thank you speeches and songs. At this event, we were all given a coffee table book full of pictures of our daily activities, and each one was individualized for each and every one of us.

The volunteer photographers and others worked every night, with only a couple of hours sleep, to put these books together and finally publish them only just before they were handed out to us at the farewell dinner. We were also given many other wonderful gifts. We could never say thank you enough.

But the most impressive moment was when all of the adults and high school students, including Pastor Kang Suk So, Rear Admiral Chong Dae Kim Ret., and General Lee Chul Hyee Ret., all got down on their knees and gave us the traditional Korean Bow. Wow. I will never forget that moment.

Thursday, June 20, we were taken to the new Seoul Incheon International Airport for departure home. I've never seen a more impressive Airport. Upon entering, we were greeted by a life-size robot asking us if we needed any help. Again, all of our fees were paid for by Sae Eden Church.

I have included this in this book because I have never in my life experienced such sincere, heartfelt love and gratitude from anyone such as the Congregation of the Sae Eden Church. It is something I'll never forget, and I want Americans to know how grateful the South Korean people are to our Korean War veterans.

The man in charge of organizing this entire event was Elder Kim of Sae Eden Church, also a retired Admiral of the ROK Navy. I've never been more impressed with a man as I am of him and I've known many great professionals, and college coaches.

The organization, the logistics, and the attention to every little detail were awesome. I told him, "I have to call you Admiral Kim from now on because I know it's a difficult title to earn, and you deserve to be called Admiral Kim for the rest of your life."

SAE EDEN PRESBYTERIAN CHURCH - 70th ANNIVERSARY OF THE KOREAN WAR COMMEMORATION

Sae Eden Presbyterian Church was planning on having this event in San Diego, California on the deck of the aircraft carrier the USS Midway, unfortunately, due to the Corona Virus in 2020, it was canceled. They were so determined to honor and thank Korean War veterans that they instead decided to hold a live Zoom presentation from the Church with the goal of reaching as many of the veterans as possible. This was the first online event in the world to honor veterans.

Again, Admiral Kim led the charge, and this time with the help of Susan Kee, a Korean American living in the states, to help coordinate with anyone who could help with veterans living in their state. I was responsible for some Oregon veterans and almost every one of them needed their adult children to help out with the computer end of it.

It was a beautiful program with heartfelt speeches of gratitude, some traditional Korean songs, and a very moving tribute to several MIAs and KIAs. Many family members were recognized on screen, several of which the remains were never found and are presumed to be in North Korea.

I have spoken to many of the veterans since this program, and every one of them was extremely grateful and moved to tears during the program. It was very healing for many.

Thank you and God Bless everyone at Sae Eden Presbyterian Church.

JOHN LIM   OREGON STATE SENATOR

I've heard former Oregon State Senator Lim speak at several veteran related events, especially the Korean War events, on Veterans Day, Memorial Day, and South Korea's Memorial Day.

Every single time, he thanked American Korean War veterans with an emotional, heartfelt thank you. His sincere gratitude has always brought tears to the eyes of the veterans as well as me.

I was eager to talk to John, and when I started interviewing him, he stopped me and said, "I'll email you my story that I already have written, use whatever you need."

John Lim grew up in the small town Yeoju, South Korea with his parents, four brothers, and a sister, where they worked together as farmers and operated the only sawmill in the town. "I learned early the value of cooperation and hard work.

"I was in the eighth grade when the North Koreans invaded South Korea on June 25, 1950. My father, Eun Kyu Lim, was forced to serve as a firefighter under the North Korean military occupation for three months. Right after the North Korean soldiers were pushed back to the North, he was executed by the South Korean police because he worked for the Communists.

"Times became very difficult for my mother, me, and my brothers and sisters. Without our uncle giving us food, we wouldn't have made it."

During his teenage years, he suffered from tuberculosis for more than five years. The townspeople thought he suffered from mental illness "During these years of suffering from tuberculosis, I memorized 7,500 English words and also volunteered at the Yeoju hometown orphanage. I was able to finish high school but was not awarded a diploma because of non-payment of tuition.

"I went to Pochun near the Demilitarized Zone (DMZ) to work as a houseboy for U.S. soldiers for one year in order to pay back the tuition and then receive my diploma.

"I then entered Seoul Theological College and was able to finish college working part-time as a U.S. military missile base student chaplain."

In 1966, John Lim and his wife, Grace, came to the U.S. where hope and opportunity afforded him a life with prosperity and purpose. John's life in America is a shining example of achieving the American dream. He earned a master's degree in divinity and later was awarded a Doctorate in Humane Letters from the same seminary.

He was heavily involved in many causes and organizations. He founded American Royal Jelly Health Products, which is an international health and beauty supply company. He has served as the local President of Korean Society, President of the National Korean American Federation, and President of Asian American Voters Coalition.

In 1990, he ran for the nomination of the Republican candidate for the gubernatorial race in Oregon. In 1992, he ran for State Senator for District 11 (East Multnomah County) and garnered 60% of the vote. He became the first Korean American as a first-generation Korean immigrant to serve in any State Senate in the United States.

During his first tenure, he worked on reforming the public welfare system, tort reform, international trade, plus many other issues.

John Lim is a good family man, a successful businessman, and a sacrificial volunteer. "I believe that we cannot accomplish all dreams we pursue, but without any dreams, nothing is accomplished."

John and Grace Lim have three children and five grandchildren. Currently, John Lim is serving as Chairman of the World Korean Political Association.

John is just one of the millions of South Koreans and Korean Americans who are extremely grateful to American Korean War veterans.

John Lim is still doing well at 86 years of age.

WOMEN VETERANS - KOREAN WAR

MARILYN SHOEMAKE   Army Nurse Corps

Marilyn was a first lieutenant nurse with a MASH unit during the Korean War. She attended many of our Living History Days but would never go into a classroom to speak to students.

At a Korean War veteran luncheon in the early 2000s, I asked her if she would reconsider, and I tried to tell her that there were so few women veterans speaking to the students and it would mean a lot to the high school girls. When I asked her, she suddenly became noticeably quiet and didn't respond for a long time, for she just was looking straight ahead.

Then she got tears in her eyes and looked at me and said, "I'm sorry, Ken, I just can't talk about it. The memories are just too painful. But I have a book I want you to read so you can understand how devoted we nurses were. Please come see me at home, and I'll give you a copy of the book."

The next week, I visited her at her retirement home, and she handed me the book *We Band of Angels: The Untold Story of the American Women Trapped on Bataan* by Elizabeth Norman. Marilyn opened up the cover to show me that she autographed it and that it was a gift for me. She wrote, "Milwaukie High School and Ken Buckles, Thank you for the Remembrance - Living History Day," Marilyn Shoemake, Nurse, MASH unit, Korea.

I read the book in three days - could not put it down. I've read hundreds of books from most American Wars from the Revolutionary War to today, and this book is one of my favorites. Those nurses are so inspirational. I am in awe of these women, the nurses who served at Bataan & Corregidor.

After reading this book, I truly believe that the nurses who served in all of our wars and conflicts deserve our utmost respect and admiration. I was so moved by this book that for over 15 years now, at every LHD assembly, I have recommended reading this book to all high school students as it is a must-read book!

Even though Marilyn was unable to personally tell her story, she gave me and possibly hundreds of students, a tremendous gift. The legacy of our amazing military nurses lives on.

Marilyn was born August 24, 1924, the same birthdate as me, except I was born in '54.

Marilyn Shoemake passed away at the age of 85 in August of 2010.

Freddie attended every single Living History Day around Oregon until health issues impacted her life in 2012. She always wore her uniform and looked very sharp. Freddie was extremely proud of her service and being a veteran. She loved talking to the high school girls, telling them at every school, "Joining the Navy was the best decision I ever made, and I would do it all over again if I could."

She was always in a great mood, positive, upbeat, and had a great sense of humor. Her presence at every event brought joy to everyone and the students loved her. She always had the biggest and most beautiful smile.

After every event, Freddie would approach me and give me a hug, and thank me for such a wonderful time. She said to me every time, "Look at what you've done, Ken. All of these veterans from all over who never knew each other and now we're all close friends like a big family. I hope you are proud of yourself because we are proud of you."

Thanks, Freddie, I sure miss you.

Freddie McBride passed away at the age of 86 in December of 2014.

Also Attended MHS LHD's
Jean Kirnak, Army Nurse Corps, Korea, MASH unit

CHOSIN FEW

Introduction

I first met this amazing group of veterans in 1995 at one of their chapter's monthly luncheons when I was trying to find out about my father's Korean War experience. There must have been around 50 of them in attendance.

The chapter president gave me an opportunity to talk to the group and as soon as I finished, four of the men stated they knew my father. Lew Rumpakis said, "Your father and I were in the Leatherneck's Drum & Bugle Corps together." Gene Shirley said, "I was in the Marine Corps Reserve with him." Frank Kaiser and John Baird said, "We worked at Pacific NW Bell with your father. None of us ever knew we were Marines or Korean War veterans as we never talked about it."

It was only after Tom Green founded the Oregon Chapter in 1987 and put an ad in The Oregonian newspaper that they started talking about their experiences at the Chosin Reservoir, but only with just each other.

In November of 1997, I invited all of the Chosin Few veterans to our 2nd Milwaukie High School Living History Day, at which they were divided into many classroom groups to speak to students. During the Assembly of Honor, I recognized them as a group, and it was the first time publicly that they had ever been recognized.

Most people knew nothing about the Battle at the Chosin Reservoir, and afterward even some veterans of WWII and the Vietnam War asked them, "Why do you call yourself the Chosin Few?" and "Why is it misspelled?" In fact, I too knew nothing until learning from them during the classroom sessions.

The Battle of The Chosin Reservoir was one of the most brutal battles in the history of U.S. military history. The X Corps, composed of the U.S. Army's 3rd and 7th Infantry Divisions, the 1st Marine Division, British Royal Marine Commandos, and ROK units had pushed the North Korean Army back into its own territory, and it was believed the war would be over by Christmas.

American and UN commanders were unaware that 12 divisions of the Chinese Army, 120,000 men, were gathering along the border. Then on November 27, 1950, the Chinese forces came across the border and completely surrounded the 30,000 UN forces.

The battle lasted 17 days until breaking out on December 13, 1950. According to the U.S. Department of Veterans Affairs, the 17-day battle took place in temperatures that dropped to -50°F (-45°C), with a wind chill factor of -100°F (-73°C).

The US X Corps and the Republic of Korea I Corps reported over 10,000 casualties during the fighting around Chosin, with the brutal cold adding over 7,000 as non-battle casualties. On the Chinese side, historians believe the Chinese suffered over 19,000 combat casualties and almost 30,000 non-combat casualties from cold weather.

The stories of these brave men are something everyone should hear. Not only the ones that follow, but all the other amazing books and videos that everyone should read.

In December of 1997, The Chosin Few Oregon Chapter invited me to their annual Christmas Banquet and presented me with a beautiful plaque thanking me for recognizing them at MHS.

This was the beginning of a beautiful friendship that is still going strong today. Of all of the many veteran organizations I've come to know, The Chosin Few Oregon Chapter veterans and wives have the strongest bond with each other. And that is saying a lot because all veteran organizations have very strong bonds with each other.

We football coaches like to say that a football team is a family and has strong bonds to each other, but I can say with experience that a football teams' bond is nothing compared to a veteran organization's bond, especially combat veterans.

A huge percent of the credit of the strong bond and close relationships of the Chosin Few Oregon Chapter goes to their wives. The wives had a requirement at every event: everyone had to be greeted with a hug. The wives even had their own monthly luncheon meetings when the men met for their monthly lunches.

But the wives were also involved with all of the rest of the gatherings such as the annual Christmas Banquet, the annual Spring Banquet, the annual Memorial Day Service at Willamette National Cemetery at their impressive Korean War Memorial (they raised the money and built this memorial), the annual weekend retreat to the Oregon coastal town Florence, and an annual summer BBQ picnic.

Most also attended the Chosin Few's National Reunions. They were one large, extremely close family. Every gathering was full of love, laughter, and good times. I became friends with all and good friends with many. They were all so very friendly, loving, and such great people.

The Jacket

During our MHS 2007 LHD Assembly of Honor, Bill Chisholm, and Audrey Rumpakis (wife of Lew Rumpakis) got out of their chairs in the front row and walked up on the stage carrying a large package. I was in the middle of recognizing all the veterans and this was not planned. Bill grabbed the microphone from me and introduced himself and Audrey.

"For the past three years, the Chosin Few has been collecting military patches and pins from all the veterans who attend this annual Milwaukie High School event every year. Audrey has handsewn these patches onto this jacket."

When Bill opened the box and took the jacket out, I was simply without words -which is unbelievable to everyone who knows me, for the jacket was beyond impressive. The jacket was full, both front and back, including both arms with the patches and pins from the veterans.

Bill stated, "This jacket is a token of us veterans' appreciation to Ken Buckles for all that you have done for us. Thank you."

I was speechless as I put it on, but the first thing I said was "I hope it fits" as I was XXXL at the time. I yelled, "It fits!" Everyone laughed. I was deeply moved and thanked everyone.

When they sat back down, I looked at the patches on the jacket and then looked at Audrey and asked, "You sewed all of these on the jacket?" She smiled and said "Yes." I then asked the crowd to please give her a round of applause and they gave her a standing ovation.

The jacket is one of my many prized gifts from veterans and I only wear it at veteran related events. I recently learned that the Chosin chapter's historian, Clyde Henderson, donated about half of the patches from his personal collection.

It is the topic of many conversations and questions whenever I wear it. And every year since Audrey has sewn more patches onto the jacket. There is not any space left, but I was, however, able to fit one more special patch.

When I spoke at Holocaust Survivor Alter Wiener's memorial service in the winter of 2018, I put my jacket on in front of all, and said: "I consider Alter Wiener an American hero and I'm going to have a patch made in his honor and put it on this jacket."

A few weeks after the funeral, I received an email from Gracie Goddard, who attended the service, asking me if I had a patch for Alter Wiener. Soon after that, we met her, and she presented to us her homemade Star of David patch. It includes the words 'Love Over Hate' and it also has barbed wire in the shape of a heart surrounding Alter Wiener's name.

OREGON CHAPTER CHOSIN FEW WHO ATTENDED LHD

TOM GREEN   Marines
                            Wife-Patricia

Tom was the founder of the Oregon Chapter of Chosin Few. He placed an ad in the newspaper The Oregonian back in 1985. Many responded and came to Tom's house for their first meeting.

He never shared his experiences with me or students. He did present me with a framed print of the famous *The Eternal Band of Brothers* by Col. Charles H. Waterhouse, a Chosin Few veteran. It portrays the breakout at the Chosin Reservoir, and I had all of the Oregon Chapter veterans sign it. I felt it was very important to have something about him included in this book because, without his effort, I never would have met so many wonderful veterans and their wives from this Oregon Chapter.

Even though I tried several times to get him to speak at our events Tom always declined. Even his son, Jerry, told me, "My dad never shared anything about the Korean War with us." Luckily, Col. Mike Howard, Marines, Iraq, shared Tom Green's greatest memory of the Chosin Reservoir Battle with me.

Mike told me that Tom said to him, "I will never ever forget all of us in the 1st Marine Division singing the Marine Hymn over and over as we marched into Hagaru." Mike told me this as his voice cracked with emotion.

Tom Green passed away at the age of 73 in April of 2002.

BOB JACOBSON

Marines
Wife-Janet

Bob was close friends with Tom Green and was one of the original founding members of the Oregon Chapter.

I'll never forget the many Memorial Day weekend potlucks the chapter would have at the Jacobson's home. First, all would meet at the chapter's Oregon Korean War Memorial at Willamette National Cemetery for their annual memorial service.

The beautiful Memorial has every Oregonian killed in action during the Korean War engraved on its bronze wall. The Oregon Chapter helped raise the funds needed to have it built. Bob's legacy with the memorial is a beautifully sculpted bronze of Bob from a picture of him as a Marine taken during the war.

Bob's daughters, Susie and Linda only had one story about their father and learned it from their mother, Janet.

"He never slept with his arms under the sheets and blankets for the rest of his life. During the war, he slept holding his rifle on the outside of his sleeping bag."

Bob Jacobson passed away at the age of 73 in September of 2001.

BILL CHISHOLM

Army
Wife- 'Amazing' Grace

Of all the great veterans of The Chosin Few, Bill Chisholm, Pete Cummings, Chesley Yahtin Sr., and Art Wilson were the only members of the chapter who served in the Army, and the rest were all Marines who always let everybody know that fact with pride. But of them all, the one member I became the closest to was Bill Chisholm.

Bill was a founding member, and he was responsible for the Chosin's annual donations to our Living History Days. Every year, he would encourage the chapter members to vote to donate generously to support our mission. Bill attended all of our events, traveling around the state of Oregon. He was never much for talking to students but would join the classroom sessions with his buddies.

He tried many times to talk about his experiences but would become overcome with emotion and would leave the room. He just could not talk about it. I have been asking for years because I wanted to get his story for this book, but Bill has just kept refusing.

I know that he served in the 31st Infantry Regiment nicknamed 'The Polar Bears'. Bill's unit was along the eastern side of the Chosin Reservoir as part of the 31st Regimental Combat Team (RCT-31). They were badly outnumbered and surrounded by Chinese troops.

The fighting was hand to hand and brutal. Then, with the enemy advancing upon their position, the covering aircraft were forced to drop napalm right in front of Bill, causing casualties among both Chinese and US troops.

Bill was wounded and earned his 1st of two Purple Hearts at 16 years of age. Bill's unit of nearly 3300 men had only 385 survive unwounded. Bill and the other survivors managed to make it across the frozen reservoir to fight with the Marines in their withdrawal. Not even a vehicle or a piece of heavy equipment was able to make it back to the American lines.

In July of 2017, I called Bill to tell him about the book *Devotion: An Epic Story of Heroism, Friendship, and Sacrifice* by Adam Makos that I had just finished reading. I told him the book went into detail of several Marines' personal experiences during the battle at the Chosin Reservoir and how the Marine Corsairs had saved them all from complete annihilation from the tens of thousands of Chinese Soldiers who had them surrounded when they dropped napalm bombs on them.

Bill then tells me, "Our jets didn't just Napalm the Chinese, they hit us bad also."

I immediately responded, "I'm sorry Bill, I know better than to bring this stuff up with you." There was a pause and I heard Bill getting emotional, and he then said, "I still hear the screams."

I apologized again and realized that this was the first time since meeting Bill in 1995, that he ever told me anything about his experiences. It did not stop there though for then Bill began telling me about something incredible that happened to him at a birthday party for a friend.

"I'm talking to an elderly man who tells me he was in the Air Force and served during WWII and the Korean War. I asked, 'Did you ever fly into North Korea?' He said, 'Yes, I flew a C-119 and parachuted the Bailey bridges to help the retreat from the Chosin Reservoir.'"

Bill says to him, "Can I give you a hug? Those bridges saved our lives as we were trapped. I was one of the soldiers down on the ground at the reservoir."

Even though he never spoke at any events, I was able to get some experiences out of him eventually. One interesting story was one that he always enjoyed telling called his 'Tootsie Roll Story.'

During the battle of The Chosin Reservoir, a group of Marines radioed in that they were running out of 60 mm mortar shell ammunition, so they called in for them using the code name 'Tootsie Rolls'. They later found out that the radio operator who received the call was missing the code sheets to tell him what a 'Tootsie Roll' was code for. The request was sent up the line and soon pallets of actual Tootsie Roll candies airdropped to the men.

At first, the Marines were angry, but soon they learned that they could hold the Tootsie Rolls close to their bodies to thaw them enough to eat. Because of the freezing temperatures, everything else was frozen and the Tootsie Rolls were all they had to eat for over a week. The men of the Chosin Few believed this mistake was Heaven sent because the Tootsie Rolls saved them as they provided much-needed energy.

I heard from Chosin member Don Mason, as well as from Al Lane's grandchildren, that soldiers also used warmed Tootsie Rolls in bullet holes as well as gas tanks and radiators, because when they refroze, they would seal the holes up nicely.

In March of 2018, Bill and I met at Rose VL Deli in Portland. This Vietnamese American family-owned restaurant is consistently highly rated, winning many awards for having the best Vietnamese soups in the Pacific Northwest.

We have become friends with the owners, Major William Hanh Vuong and his lovely wife Christina. As we were eating, the Major was visiting with Bill at our table. I said to both of them, "How do I ever get you two to share your experiences with me so I can include them in my book?" They both just laughed, but I said, "I'm serious."

Bill turns to William and says, "Major, if you agree to talk, I'll agree to talk. The Major sticks his right hand out and they both shake hands and promise each other. The Major's unbelievable story will be in *Remembrance Volume III*.

Bill then turns to me and said, "I need you to interview me as soon as possible before I change my mind." Then he laughed. Well, I did exactly that for we got together at my house the very next day.

I began by asking, "Where and when were you born and where did you grow up?"

"I was born on May 31, 1934, in Stockton, California. But my lying birthday was 1932. That's the date I gave the Army when I joined because I was only 16 years old."

"Why did you join the Army at 16 years of age?"

Bill answered with a tone of anger, "Because my stepmother and I didn't see eye to eye, so I got my aunt and uncle to help get me into the Army at 16."

Bill was shipped to Korea in September of 1950 on the ship the USS General H. B. Freeman. He laughed and said, "When we were shipped out, I remember asking, 'Where the hell is Korea?' Hell, we didn't even have American maps of North Korea, we had to rely on old Japanese maps."

I knew asking about his experiences in Korea would be tough for him, so I first asked, "Did you get seasick? He laughed and said, "Of course."

I then asked him, "What do you want your grandchildren and great-grandchildren, and future generations, 100 years from now to know about your experiences during the Korean War?"

Bill started getting emotional with tears in his eyes, "I just wish we could all get along, no more war."

He then asked me if I had any tissue and as I went to get him some, I thought to myself, I hope he can do this, but if he can't it's OK.

Again, I decided to start with easy questions about the food, the drinking water, going to the bathroom, and sleeping, in the hope that it might ease him into telling me more about Chosin.

"We had to eat snow every day as we had no water. Those Tootsie Rolls kept us alive, rations were frozen stiff. I had a mummy sleeping bag and half a pup tent and was always cold."

Bill paused and looked away and then looked at me and said in a very serious tone, "I don't know what people will think of this, but when you're freezing, you do things that're hard to understand later. We would strip the clothes off of dead Chinese soldiers to use. You have to remember, we were issued summer clothes, not winter clothes.

"We were sent to the eastern side of the reservoir to relieve a company of Marines who were ordered to reinforce the Marine lines on the west side. We just took over their very shallow foxholes. It was already so damn cold, minus thirty, and the ground was frozen solid.

"That first night, the Chinese hit us hard and didn't stop for the next three days. I got hit that night in the left leg just above the knee, and the medic just dug the shrapnel out and patched me up and I stayed on the line. I was lucky, the shrapnel was only about the size of a 22-caliber bullet.

"By the way, I just remembered the medic was a black man. I asked him if there were other black soldiers at Chosin. He said, "Oh yes, there are seven that I know of." Bill then told me that he knew of one who was an ordained minister, and on their first Sunday, he gave a sermon to everyone, and how greatly appreciated it was for them.

"I was just a rifleman at first, then issued a BAR (Browning Automatic Rifle), and when I made corporal, I was issued a 57mm Recoilless Rifle. We set it up on a hill. One of the older soldiers says, 'There's a bunker hidden over on that ridge,' and then he fires a shot at the bunker with a tracer. We loaded the 57 and fired a phosphorous round and it blows up the bunker. Suddenly, we hear these popping sounds and see the ice on the ground popping all over.

"Someone yells, 'What the hell is that?' and I scream, 'It's incoming! Get the hell out of here!'"

Bill got emotional again and paused. I knew he had two Purple Hearts, so I asked, "Were you wounded a second time at Chosin?"

"No, that was June 6, 1951, at the Hwacheon Dam. We put down these 15' long by 4' wide panels painted bright yellow and red on the ridge so our jets would not bomb us but instead fire at the Chinese who were attacking our ridge."

Bill raised his voice and with a tone of anger stated, "Our own jets hit us with Napalm. I saw the bomb coming down towards us, and I dove into a bunker, which saved my life, but was still burned on my backside."

Bill got tears in his eyes again and stopped talking. I thought I should change the subject a little. "Did you end up in a hospital in Japan with lots of nurses?"

He laughed and said, "No, it was a MASH unit, and I have no idea where the hell it was. But before we got there, I woke up strapped down to a stretcher in a lot of pain. My eyes were all bandaged up and I was blind for over two weeks. All I heard was a very loud whoop, whoop, whoop sound. I was on a helicopter being taken to the MASH Unit.

"I remember these women called 'Grey Ladies' who would come around every day and write a letter for us wounded. I wrote many to my mother."

Bill then told me his mother Mary Jane Colver's address. I said, "Wow, you still remember her address and you tell me your memory is going." We both laughed.

Bill then paused and got tears in his eyes again and said, "This next story is cool, and I still can't explain it. I was asleep and then felt this hand on my forehead and then I heard this voice saying, 'How are you, my son?'

"I immediately asked, 'Who am I talking to?' The voice answers, 'This is Cardinal Spellman from New York. Keep the faith, everything will be ok.' A few minutes later, I hear some nurses talking about Cardinal Spellman. One of the nurses says, 'What a wonderful man he is.' That meant a lot, having a Cardinal visiting us wounded so close to the front."

I asked him, "Were you sent home after your second Purple Heart."

Bill laughed and said, "Are you kidding, I was put right back on the front line.

"I did get my first R&R though in Japan. We were ordered to strip, take showers, and then we were issued brand new fatigues. My top had a USMC on the left chest. I thought it was cool, so I kept it.

"After getting dressed, we got in the chow line, and they served us huge steaks with a huge baked potato. Our stomachs were shrunk small, so I asked them to cut everything in half. But when I saw the milk, I started chugging glasses and got so full, I could hardly eat any of my dinner," Bill said laughing again.

"I was finally sent stateside in the fall of '51 and finished up training recruits." Bill then told me that he would always laugh when the recruits would salute him, and he would always tell them, "What the hell are you doing, I'm not an officer."

Bill came home eventually and got married and had three girls. When they were five, three, and one, his wife and mother of the girls left them, and Bill raised them all.

Bill told me that he still suffers from nightmares.

Over the years, there were opportunities for Bill to travel back to Korea, but he always declined. However, in June of 2019, Bill finally agreed to travel to South Korea, and this was his first time back since 1951. He previously refused all invitations but agreed this time to go only if my wife Malinda and I escorted him.

The entire trip was sponsored by The Sae Eden Presbyterian Church in South Korea with every expense being covered by them as their way of showing their gratitude towards American Korean War veterans.

I think the reason why he finally decided to go was because I had been telling him that it would be a healing experience for him, and also because the South Koreans are so grateful to the veterans.

Bill told me, "I believe you. I experienced it first-hand when years ago, many of us from the Chosin rode on a float during a Veteran's Day parade. We had a large banner with 'Chosin Few Oregon Chapter' on it. As we were moving, I noticed an elderly Asian woman on the sidewalk Bowing to us and she was crying.

"I had the float stop, I got off, walked up to her, and asked if she was okay. She looked at me and said, 'I was a refugee from North Korea, and you brought us out to safety. Thank you so much.'

"She kept bowing and thanking me over and over. I gave her a hug and got back on the float."

My good friend Bill Chisholm is still living at the age of 87.

LEWIS RUMPAKIS   Marines
                                   Wife-Audrey

My wife and I became very close to Lew and Audrey. Malinda unofficially adopted Audrey as her second mom and her daughters, Teri and Cheryl, as stepsisters. They are such wonderful people.

Years ago, when Lew was the President of the Chosin Few Oregon Chapter, he welcomed everyone at the beginning of their annual Christmas banquet, and I will never forget his opening speech.

After welcoming everyone Lew said, "I was remembering our first hot meal we were served when we finally reached safety in December 1950."

Lew paused then mumbled, "I'm sorry," and started to cry. After about thirty seconds he continued but paused several times to regain composure.

"They put us in this very long tent, probably 100 yards long with over 1000 cots. We all picked out our cots at one end of the tent and we were settling into sleep when I noticed probably over 90% of the tent was empty."

"Then it hit me, they had no idea that such a large number of Marines didn't make it out."

Lew broke down and started crying profusely, and Audrey came to his side, hugged him, and helped him to their table while all applauded him.

One of my pleasant surprises from getting to know Lew and Audrey was that they were good friends with my parents when Lew was in the Color Guard of the Leatherneck Drum and Bugle Corps in the late '50s with my father.

With the help of her daughters, Audrey threw a surprise 80th birthday for Lew and set up a table with pictures. She pointed out a picture of two soldiers in French uniforms. "Lew and your father performed in the Portland Opera performance of *Carmen*, playing two French soldiers, and they sang a song together."

I told Audrey, "I am shocked, I never knew this. I didn't know my dad could sing." Audrey responded with a tone in her voice of expertise, "Oh, your father had a beautiful singing voice."

I never interviewed Lew, but I did learn that he started writing a book on his experiences, but he passed away before finishing it. Audrey gave me a copy and permission to use whatever I needed to include in this section on the Chosin Few. I copied the parts of his writings that I felt needed to be remembered.

> We sailed into a typhoon and what a truly gut-wrenching experience that was. I was on port watch in the wheelhouse. The bow of the ship would disappear into a large wave before raising out of the water. When the bow was going into the war, the fantail was out of the water, shaking the ship. The props made a noise like someone hitting the sides of the ship with a huge sledgehammer. We were ordered to our compartments, and everyone got seasick, heaving in their helmets, on the floor, in the passageways, on ladders, and in the heads. What a mess. When the storm was over, we were issued mops, brooms, and buckets...bad duty.

Lew had a wonderfully sounding laugh and beautiful smile, and I believed he would have laughed many times telling this story.

> Once in Japan, we were allowed to go into town, and we all went to this bar where there was music and dancing. All the Japanese girls wore brightly colored strapless formal dresses. As they danced the dresses dropped down low enough to expose their Cheaters (Falsies). I think this is where the first frisbees were invented because you could pull them out and sail them across the dance floor. It wasn't too long until the air was filled with them. What fun!...

> The cold - ...Everything was frozen even hot coffee would freeze within a minute. On Thanksgiving Day, we were served a hot meal with all the trimmings, but by the time I could find a

place to sit, the food was almost frozen. But it tasted wonderful, almost like home.

It was so cold we did not take off our gloves as your fingers would stick to your gear. There was a warmup tent that each man could warm up for ten minutes and then relieve the next man so he could warm up. Digging foxholes was impossible as we had to dig through about 18 inches of ice and dealing with the constant wind blowing and the snow coming down. Vehicles were never shut down for fear they wouldn't restart.

We didn't think about how the Chinese were dealing with the cold until we saw their dead. They wore rubber sandals with two pairs of light socks and their feet were black from being frozen. Their winter uniforms were handmade yellow khaki cloth, and some wore fur made of cat's fur. Some wore white sheets to blend in with the snow. I'm sure they lost more men to exposure than we did due to improper clothing.

We learned not to use oil to lubricate our weapons to keep them dry. We used the lead of a pencil to lubricate because the graphite in the lead would not freeze.

Walking on the ice-covered road was extremely difficult as you slipped and slided (sic) all the time. Our feet became numb and we would stomp our feet on every step to keep the blood circulating and keep them from freezing. Because the water in our canteens was frozen, we ate snow, and the ice crystals sliced the inside of our mouths.

First Combat experience - Around 1:00AM we were awakened by red, green, yellow, and white flares are going off in the sky and the ridiculous sounds of bugles, whistles, and pots and pans being banged upon. All kinds of noise and yelling. It scared the hell out of us. Our left flank was attacked first, then the whole damn place was under attack except our front. The noise was unbelievable. Then we started getting fired upon, spewing ice all over us. I was so scared, I started reciting the 26th Psalms from the bible. I believe God saved us that night.

Later, we were ordered to go up a hill to retrieve the wounded and the dead. They had all been attacked in their sleeping bags and not too many were left alive. As we were getting the dog tags, the Chinese started firing on us. Our sergeant yelled 'Grab a sleeping bag and get the hell out of here.'

It was very difficult leaving our buddies, but we were able to bring back the few wounded. One of these was a friend of mine, Dan Gogerty and over the years whenever we would get together, we would embrace and shed a few tears with each other.

We headed to the town of Hagaru where our division had been cut off. It had been a slow pace of fighting all the way. We came upon an Army convoy of ambulances that had been hit. Everyone was dead, the Chinese had even killed the wounded inside the ambulances and then set them on fire. It was after midnight, very dark and with the burning vehicles giving off a reddish glow and only the sound of our boots crunching on the ice. It was like a terrible dream.

The Chinese blew up a bridge and a Treadway bridge was parachuted down to our engineers. Sounds good but it had never been done before. The first span had normal parachutes attached to it and they shredded on the way down, the spans were rendered useless. The second attempt the span went into a marshy area and could not be recovered. Anyway, finally there were two parachuted down with cargo chutes, landed in good shape and were put in place by the best engineers in the world.

We continued on to safety where the Army was waiting for us. It was on this walk that I fell asleep walking and walked into the guy in front of me knocking us both down. We both laughed as I realized this probably kept me from walking off the road and over a 1000-foot cliff.

Anyway, we kept moving down the road and stopped. Coffee! I could smell coffee; I mean real coffee. We saw this big open cast iron pot steaming over a cook stove. We couldn't believe our eyes as it was the biggest pot I had ever seen and full of coffee.

We got out our cups and dipped them in to fill them when this dumb-ass Army Staff Sgt came out of his tent yelling obscenities at us and told us to get the F- -K out of here.

One of the guys raised his rifle and was going to shoot the asshole. I grabbed the rifle and pushed it away before he could shoot, thank heavens. Just then an officer came out of the tent and looked at the Sgt with disbelief and ordered him to get back in the F- -king tent. The officer told us to get a cup and tell the others. If we forgot to say thank you, Sir, please forgive us and THANK YOU!...

Reaching Safety - ...While in Manson, they gave us liberty to go into town. The Marine Corps was looking out for us because they put MPs at the Black Cat, a house of ill repute. As I approached one of the MP's, I was shocked to see he was one of my high school chums from Portland, Vic Saraceno. I said, "What the hell are you doing here, and he asked the same question back to me."

Shipping out - ...The ship was so crowded that men slept everywhere, outside on the decks, passageways, lifeboats, paint lockers, it didn't make any difference. The second day we lined up for showers. It had been 33 days since we had showered, lots of dead skin. We looked and smelled nasty. The Navy guys plugged their noses whenever they walked by one of us. It was bad...

This was as far as Lew got. I asked Audrey to share with me her memories of Lew having any issues with the memories of the war.

"He had nightmares, but when I tried to talk to him, he would just say, 'Just had a bad night.' He was so protective of me and our children. I do remember when the kids were little, Lew could not handle loud voices, and there was no screaming, and he would lose his temper really bad. I had to keep the children quiet. I told them to never wake him up if he's sleeping because he'll start fighting. But he kept so much from us, so protective."

Lew's daughter Cheryl then added, "My high school history teacher gave me an assignment to ask Dad about the Korean War. That evening I asked if I could interview him, and he lost his temper and yelled at me to never ask about Korea again, so I never did."

"I miss him every day," Audrey then responded with tears in her eyes. She is still going strong at 86 years of age and sewing more patches on the Jacket as I write this.

Lewis Rumpakis passed away at the age of 87 in May of 2017.

★

DR. VERN SUMMERS
Navy
Wife - Patti

Dr. Summers served with the Navy, but was attached to the Marines during the Korean War. Dr. Summers was a very kind, caring gentleman. He attended many Milwaukie High Living History Days. I know he would go into the classrooms with other Chosin Few veterans, but not speak. I'm grateful that his son Eric and his widow Pat were able to give me information on him.

"My father never talked about his Korean War experiences to me. All I know was that he had neuropathy nerve damage as a result of the cold at the Chosin Reservoir. He wore gloves in the house often. He absolutely hated the cold. The only experience I ever heard was having to amputate the frozen limbs of men. The limbs were black and frozen and like a block of ice.

"My father would make house calls to many local Asian Americans for their health issues and would never charge them. I know this because he was well-loved and respected by them. We were always treated to free dinners at any Asian restaurant in Portland.

"Halfway through his general family practice, he decided to go back to school to become a psychiatrist. He was way ahead of his time when it came to dealing with the emotional well-being of veterans dealing with the effects of combat. In fact, he was on the ground floor of founding the VA's PTSD program, which is still in place today.

"Most everything I learned about dad was during his funeral. Many men came up to me and said with tears in their eyes, 'I would not be here today if it wasn't for your father in Korea.'"

In a telephone conversation with Dr. Summers' wife Pat, she told me, "He never talked about it, and it never dawned on me to ask him questions. I was 14 years younger than him. I still remember his mother telling me that they received a telegram stating that Vern was killed in action. Obviously, they were devastated, until three days later when they were notified it was a mistake.

"I do know that he was very upset because he felt the government just swept the mental conditions under the carpet.

"I remember, after talking to Dr. Dean Brooks of the Oregon State Hospital in Salem, Vern came home and said, 'How do you feel about moving to Salem? I want to go back to school and go into psychiatry.

"I loved him so much, I would have followed him anywhere. We sold our house and moved to Salem for the next four years. At the time, our children were in grade, middle, and high school. He worked the ward of the State Hospital with the patients with severe mental issues.

"A big surprise was he was asked to be the physician on the set of the movie *One Flew Over the Cuckoo's Nest*. This movie was filmed at the Oregon State Hospital and won the Academy Award for Best Picture. We got to know all the actors and crew.

After finishing filming, the crew asked me what Vern liked for a gift idea. I said he loves the ocean and the beach. They gave him a beautiful large brass artwork of flying seagulls. It's still hanging in my living room.

"I know that Vern enjoyed his friendships with the Chosin Few immensely. He never complained about anything, except when I turned on the air conditioning," she said laughing.

"He started having his own health issues and had to go on kidney dialysis, and our German shepherd dog would go with him, rest his head on Vern, and Vern would lay his cold hands on our dog."

Pat became emotional telling me this. "I get goosebumps just thinking about it. One day he fell and broke his hip and leg. In the hospital, he told all of us family members that he was not going to dialysis anymore.

"He passed away the next day."

After a long silence, Pat said to me, "I write to him every day in my journal."

Dr. Vern Summers passed away at the age of 84 in November of 2006.

OTTO OLSON

Marines
Wife- Marcelene (Marcie)

Otto was a soft-spoken, unassuming gentleman. He was always calm and very friendly, very easy to speak to. If he had PTSD, he hid it very well. I did hear that his nickname was 'Mr. First Platoon' because he served longer than anyone in his platoon during the war.

The only thing he did tell me was that one of his lifetime dreams was to travel the Alcan Highway in a camper, and he was able to fulfill that dream with his wife Marcie. He also said that he loved traveling around the United States and to England to attend the Chosin Few gatherings.

I became rather impressed when Otto told me how he built his own house on what he called 'five country acres' in La Center, Washington.

Otto Olson passed away at the age of 77 in January of 2006.

* ★ *

PETE CUMMINGS   Army
                                        Wife-Verna

Pete attended all of our events right up until his passing and would always speak to students about his experiences. Later after Pete passed, I learned that the Chosin chapter members all had written personal messages for the last two living veterans to read. However, when their numbers reached only around ten, they voted to open and read those messages to all at the next Spring Banquet.

Pete's message was the following:

> My parents divorced when I was a toddler and my mother placed me and my baby sister in an orphanage. She got both of us back after remarrying. After being knocked around a lot by two different stepfathers, I ran away, rode freight cars for a while, and got in some minor scrapes with the law.
>
> When the Korean War started, I lied about my age and joined the Army. On my third patrol northeast of the Changlin Reservoir, my unit was ambushed by the Chinese. Our jeep patrol was almost annihilated, most were killed, and a few were captured. I caught a bullet in the scalp but escaped with another man. We stayed

together for two days and joined North Korean civilians until we got to safety at the Koto-ri perimeter.

I don't remember much except I was shipped to the 4th Field Hospital where I was treated for my head wound and the shrinks pronounced me sane and fit for duty.

I was rewarded by an assignment to be a machine gunner and was seriously wounded on June 1, 1951, almost losing my arm.

(Pete would spend the next three years healing at Madigan Army Hospital, Ft. Lewis, and then Portland's VA hospital.)

Pete lost most of his left hand, but he would play a medley of beautiful music on the piano at every Chosin banquet. His wife Verna told me his PTSD was so bad he could not hold down a job, and he only found comfort and peace growing and hybridizing flowers in his garden that had over 1000 roses.

Pete Cummings passed away at the age of 78 in June of 2007.

★

BILL CALL   Marines
                                      WWII Iwo Jima
                                      Wife- Dolores

Bill was very proud of his Iwo Jima experience, but would never talk about it or his Inchon landing and Chosin Reservoir experience. I tried many times over the years, but the last time I asked him was in 2018 and he responded with, "Ken, I have found that not talking about it or thinking about it at all has really worked for me and I'm going to keep it that way."

He was always very supportive and generously donated to the non-profit over the years. He owned a large warehouse that he turned into a personal museum called 'Bill's Place.' It was amazing, dozens of restored beautiful classic cars and trucks, (mostly Plymouths), hundreds of displays of memorabilia, pictures, and giant patriotic murals painted on the walls. There was also a beautifully painted wall with the famous "Raising the Flag on Iwo Jima" and *The Eternal Band of Brothers*.

Bill Call is still living at the age of 95.

★

GLEN CROSBY   Marines
                               Wife-Gloria

Glen was a retired high school teacher and coach from Ontario in eastern Oregon, and I was told several times he was an outstanding public speaker. He would hang maps of Korea and use a long pointer when speaking to the students. After his classroom sessions, the students knew more about the Battle at the Chosin Reservoir than most veterans.

When I was starting to write the book, I contacted his daughter, Deb, who had in her possession a handwritten rough draft of his story. She scanned it and emailed it to me. It is an extremely detailed and thorough account of the Inchon Landing and the battle at the Chosin Reservoir.

Everything from names, dates, times, locations, every weapon, artillery, ammo types and sizes, all military vehicles, etc. was included. A military buff would really enjoy his rough draft. I'm including parts of his story that I believe most readers of this book will enjoy the most.

> After graduating from high school in '48, my best friend Glen and I drove to Boise, Idaho to register for the draft and join the military. The recruiting offices were all in one building but the

first office we walked into was the Marine Corps. Two hours later we walked out with 'Pie in the Sky Dreams', dreams of wearing dress blues and knowing we signed up with the best.

I told my mother and she angrily said, 'No you haven't, I won't sign the papers' I replied, 'No you won't mom, I'm 18 years old and I don't need your signature.'

Another classmate ends up joining too, and all three of us report for boot camp. That's when 'All hell broke loose' and I remember thinking, 'What the hell did I get myself into?'

But they instilled in me high values and standards, and pride that we are the best, not arrogant but proud. All the while the DIs were hazing, shouting, degrading us verbally, and making us all miserable. Were we intimidated? Yes, all 100% of us.

I broke my wrist the second week and after it healed, I had to join another outfit and start boot camp all over again. My best friend had moved on and I would not see him again for over five years. I drew the toughest three DIs on the base, all WWII veterans. Sgt. W. Clark was a Bataan Death March survivor and Ex-POW. They were all very mean.

After graduating from Boot Camp, many of us got to visit with our DIs in the barracks. They told us they were just trying to make us good Marines and we concluded, they were humans after all.

On Sunday, June 25, 1950, I arrive home for thirty days of my first R&R in two years. A friend asks, 'When are you going to Korea?'

Why would I go to Korea and where is it anyway? He told me that the Communist North Korean Army had invaded South Korea that morning. That was my introduction to a war I was about to enter, but I tried to enjoy my leave.

That lasted for ten days until I received a telegram saying, 'Leave cancelled, report to Camp Pendleton immediately.' When I reported to our company headquarters, I asked the Sgt. Major when we are shipping out. He said, 'You are the 50th guy who has asked me that, I don't know, now get out of here and leave me alone.'

We shipped out to Kobe, Japan, and six days after arriving were shipped out to the Unknown. We all assumed it was Korea, but were not told anything. Finally, the word got out that we were headed to the port city of Inchon on the west coast of South Korea. We were to capture the city of one million people and march an additional 30 miles east to liberate Seoul, the capital.

As we got to about maybe two miles from the shoreline, I leaned on the rails on the fan tail end of the ship and suddenly realized I might not make it back home. A few moments of great anxiety and fear swept over me. I gathered my senses and said my first prayer in my young life. Dear Lord, please don't let me die in this God forsaken country.

The Navy was short on anti-aircraft gun crews, so I was assigned to a five-man 44mm AAA Battery. With binoculars we watched the dive-bombing assault and the constant barrage from Navy ships on the city. When we moved in closer, and the guns fell silent and when the smoke cleared the destruction was shocking. Then a second shelling started, I felt shockwaves from each blast was as the sound was tearing my ears apart.

We had it easy that day as there were no hostile plane activity. The next day, we witnessed the assault on the city, all of the land craft loaded with Marines hitting the beaches while the aerial bombing from our planes to the Naval bombardment on the city continued. It was a grand sight. All 'D' Day objectives were achieved on the first day by darkness. It took one day and an afternoon to secure the city.

On D-Day + 2, my outfit was unloaded on the beach and trucked to the eastern side of Inchon. I was shocked at the destruction, and it reminded me of WWII pictures of the aftermath of the bombings of London, Berlin, Hamburg, and Tokyo but I was a part of this as a spectator while on duty aboard ship.

The next day, Russian T-34 tanks with 200 North Korean soldiers approached the city to launch a counterattack, but the Marine's firepower was too much as all were destroyed and killed in ten minutes with only one Marine being wounded.

Glen's duty for the next couple of months was perimeter guard for trucking, food, and fuel supplies for the final advance on Seoul.

On the third night, my Sergeant ordered us, 'Whatever you do, do not leave your post for any reason.' Later that very dark night, no lights, looking down the road about 200 yards away came a stream of bright red lights headed straight for me. Instantly I recognize them as tracers and me and my partner dropped to the ground. I rolled over on my back and saw 9 or 10 tracers maybe six inches or a few feet over my head.

As I laid there, I hear the pop, pop, pop sound of an automatic weapon and did not learn until in North Korea, that the Chinese tracers were green, the North Korean tracers were blue, and American's were red. Could this be friendly fire? I will never know. We soon recovered our wits and stood up. Were we scared? Yes, but we did not lose our composure.

I'll never forget all of the civilians returning to their destroyed homes with nothing left but the clothes they were wearing. They left the city the day before our invasion because our aircraft had dropped warning leaflets. We helped them as much as we could under the circumstances.

On September 24th Marines and Army had made it to the streets of downtown Seoul but fighting was fierce, building by building, casualties were high, but huge losses were inflicted on the North Koreans.

During the last days of the campaign, I decided to look for the grave of a dear friend of mine who had been reported KIA in the outskirts of Seoul and was buried in the First Marine Division's Cemetery. Walking down the many rows of white crosses with dog tags placed on them, I found Glen Dyer, USMC.

I was immediately overwhelmed with emotion and despair. As I stood there looking at his cross thinking of not only what a good Marine he was, but also what a devout person to his faith and country he was. I remember him every Sunday morning leaving our barracks on base, Camp Pendleton, going to church with his bible under his arm while I was lying in bed relaxing.

It was a sunny hot, dusty afternoon and Marines were burying over one hundred South Korean soldiers. The smell of death spread over the cemetery so strong that I thought I was going to throw up. I left wondering why Sgt. Dyer and not me. This question has haunted me to this day.

Chosin Reservoir

We were shipped out and around the peninsula to Wanson on the east coast of North Korea. An assault landing was scheduled for October 10th but the harbor was filled with over 2000 mines. It took ten days for minesweepers to clear the waters.

Once we got on land, our Sergeant ordered us to gather driftwood on the beach to start fires and cook our own meals. I started to walk north up the beach to look at the North Korean defenses and trenches that were built, but turned around and walked south instead. Two Marines passed me walking north.

About two minutes later, I heard a tremendous explosion and a big shock wave hit me. The explosion was catastrophic as both Marines were blown to pieces. They could not identify either of them as their bodies were blown apart into pieces. It was determined that they were killed by a booby trap bomb.

Thanksgiving Day was our first, and would end up being our last, hot meal until Christmas as we began what would be known as the 'Frozen Chosin Campaign.'

The temperatures dropped below freezing and most units had not even been issued cold wear clothing. My outfit was stationed in Hungnam, where we were on work detail for unloading ships, and loading trucks to resupply our men from sunup to after sundown.

For the rest of the campaign, we worked in misery in what we felt were rotten conditions. We complained about our conditions until we learned that our Marines at the Chosin were sleeping out in the cold. At least we had tents we could sleep in.

Glen has put a lot of time into researching this battle as his writings include very detailed numbers, dates and locations for the Marines, Army, and the Chinese. He must have been a very thorough teacher at the high school level, and his rough draft manuscript could be used for a college class or serious military buffs.

The Army's High Command in Japan was convinced the Chinese were just a rag tag bunch of coolies. The First Marine Division's intelligence response was 'General, there's a shit load of Chinese up in these surrounding hills.' It was unknown how correct that statement was at the time as history is recorded that ten divisions of the Chinese Army, 120,000 men, were rapidly surrounding our troops.

As the temperatures continued to drop, we became miserable but then a very cold wind called the Siberian Express made our lives even more miserable. It was brutal. We started hearing the bad news that the Chinese were advancing everywhere, and we began to believe it was a matter of time before they reached us. The Marines were not retreating but fighting a frontal assault all the way to the coast.

We now were rigging parachutes which seemed like endless tons of small arms, ammo, hand grenades and food that was parachuted into our men. Even though we weren't on the front lines, we started to believe that our part in this war was saving lives. We were told that our air drops had saved the lives of over 1000 Marines.

But on several of our drops were containers of millions of Tootsie Rolls which we thought were requested. We got called every vulgar name in the dictionary until they learned that the Tootsie rolls provided much needed sustenance and energy as all food supplies were frozen and saved them.

As I reflect back on those days, some days I remember as if it was yesterday, other days are hazy. But everything in this document is true to the best of my ability as I researched everything in the official Manual of US Marines operations in Korea.

My last memory was of my last day there, Marines were putting in explosives to blow a bridge about thirty minutes out of Hungnam and we were waiting by our 10-wheeler truck. Someone said, 'The Chinks are about three to four miles down the road' and just then the artillery assaults started just north of us.

I said, 'Guys, I think we better give our souls to God because I believe our butts belong to the Chinese.' No one said a word but rushed back to safety. The next day we all shipped out to Pusan, South Korea. Thank God for the US Navy!

When I later asked Glen what he thought about his experience in Korea, He said, "People were dying around me every day and I just kept asking myself, 'Why not me?' I have no idea and I have counted my lucky stars every day since."

Glen Crosby is still living at 91 years of age.

---- ★ ----

WAYNE SPARKS   Marines
                               WWII Navy South Pacific
                               Wife- Romana

Wayne's joining the Chosin Few was an interesting one for while playing golf one day with some friends he discovered a bench that was next to the tees with a plaque saying it had been donated by the 'Chosin Few'. So, he did some investigating, found the group, and joined.

My favorite memory was of how Wayne and his good friend and fellow Chosin Few member Pete Cummings would agree to travel to high schools around the state under one condition, "We will drive ourselves, and only speak in the first classroom session, but after that we are going fishing for the rest of the time, take it or leave it." I always took it.

Wayne Sparks along with Bill Chisholm were responsible for convincing the other veterans of the Chosin Few Oregon Chapter to donate generously to all of our events since 1997.

"In WWII, I served aboard the USS Rixey, a troop transport with full hospital facilities. One trip we picked up Marines from Guam to take to Okinawa. One of the Marines was Albert Lane and we've been friends ever since.

"I remember that our first trip was to San Diego to pick up around over 200 women sailors and women Marines (WAVES- Women Accepted for Volunteer Emergency Service) and transported them to Hawaii. Our ship was loaded with replenished supplies, then we sailed to The Marshall's and Guam before going to Okinawa.

"At Okinawa, we were hit by a terrible typhoon. We tried to get out to open sea but couldn't, so we rode out the storm in the bay. From

Okinawa, we sailed to China to drop off some Marines we had picked up in Guam. While there we picked up some men who had been prisoners of war and held by the Japanese. They were a horrible sight. All skin and bones.

"Later I had enough points to be eligible for discharge and I was sent to Bremerton, Washington for discharge. After being honorably discharged, I decided to join the Marines Reserve.

"Why," I asked. He laughed and said "The only reason I joined was to make a little extra money. I never thought I would end up in Korea fighting another war.

"We were at Udamni, North Korea, headed to Hagaru-ri in late November when the Chinese attacked. The column moved so slowly, we had no sleep or rest for three days. I was so tired I climbed up on a 6X6 truck behind the cab and got in my mummy sleeping bag. I kept my M1 rifle in my bag with me.

"The next morning, I woke up with five to six inches of snow covering me. Well, snow had gotten into the barrel of my rifle, and it was completely frozen."

"How did you get your rifle thawed?" I asked.

"Well, it was a scary situation for a while. There were some Chinese troops in a small grove of trees, and they started shooting at us. I tried to cock the rifle, but the shell was frozen in the chamber. I placed the stock on the ground and kicked open the bolt.

In doing so the cartridge separated from the shell and was still frozen inside the weapon. I tried to find a ramrod so I could get the projectile out. I had to place my rifle against my body to warm it up. I finally found a ramrod and got the projectile out."

Wayne made it back to America to live a long life, and in the last days of life, he had only one request from his daughter Tracy. He wanted her to promise to give him a full military honors funeral, gun salute included.

Tracy kept that promise for after her father passed, she had everything her father requested for his funeral. However, on the night before her father's scheduled funeral, she received a call telling her that everything was set for the next day, but there would be no military gun salute because no one was available.

Tracy told me that she responded by telling them, "That's unacceptable, cancel tomorrow's funeral and I demand a new date that includes the gun salute, or I'll cancel it again."

I've attended many, many Military Funeral Honors and always wondered why most had included the gun salute and some did not. Tracy and I both believe this has happened to others also and we feel that it shouldn't happen to any veteran!

Tracy, daughter of Marine Wayne Sparks, fulfilled her father's wishes by giving him a full Military Honors Funeral that took place over three months later.

Wayne Sparks passed away at the age of 92 in January of 2021.

CLYDE HENDERSON   Marines
                              Wife- Polly

Clyde was the historian of the Chosin Few Chapter and had an impressive collection of memorabilia. He told me that he liked to travel and that he and his wife had traveled visiting England and China as well as Korea.

He loved square dancing and photography which was one reason why he was a great historian for the Chosin Few. He attended every event we ever had from 1997 until passing in 2018, but he could never speak about it.

He told me with tears in his eyes, "Ken, it's just too emotional for me. I know I would break down and start crying if I tried to talk about it." The only thing he ever told me was "I was in on the Inchon landing, too."

Clyde also loved sports, especially baseball. He was a walking encyclopedia when it came to baseball. He loved talking about it, and his knowledge of its history in Portland, Oregon was incredible.

I had to ask him, "Were you a good baseball player, and what position did you play?"

"I was a hell of a shortstop; I was quick and fast, but I was average at the plate. I had a tryout with the Portland Beavers AAA baseball team, and if I had been a better hitter, I would have made the team."

Clyde Henderson passed away at the age of 90 in November of 2018.

BOB WESTLUND   Marines
                                Wife- Hazel

Bob was another great guy, a retired Portland Police Officer, on the motorcycle patrol. He attended every single Chosin Few event, but I could never get him to attend just one of mine.

Al Lane of the Chosin veterans told me, "Bob had it rough and was lucky to make it out of there. He never talks about it."

The only thing I ever got out of him was, "It was my second time in the service. After World War II, I was called back for the Korean War. We went all the way to Yudami-ni in North Korea, then made our way out. It took two weeks to do it. We didn't have winter clothing at that time and the ground was frozen so we couldn't dig a foxhole. We dug big graves to bury the ones who couldn't make it out."

At Bob's funeral, I learned that he had not told even his wife about his experiences and that the only person who knew was his daughter Cindy. Cindy told me that she had no explanation why her father shared with her explicit details of his experience at Chosin.

This started off and on from when she was a little girl through her teenage years. I tried several times to get Cindy to share her father's story, but it was just too difficult for her.

I'm sorry, Cindy, I believe I pressured you too much, please forgive me.

Bob Westlund passed away at the age of 91 in June of 2018.

RICHARD CALDWELL   Marines
                                 WWII Wake Island
                                 Ex-POW
                                 Wife- JoAnn

I met Richard when we organized a Living History Day at Redmond High School in Central Oregon. He attended our Welcoming Dinner at the local Veterans of Foreign Wars the night before. I approached him because I noticed he was wearing a Maroon-colored vest with patches and pins on it that I knew represented the American Ex-Prisoners of War service organization.

Richard was extremely outgoing and friendly, and the first time I met him he said, "Hey Ken, pull up a chair and talk. I'm so glad I finally get to meet you. I've been following you for years and I would love to drive over the mountain for one of them (Bend to Portland via Mt. Hood is a three-hour drive), but at my age and health issues, I just can't do it."

As we sat down together, I started by asking him, "When were you a POW?"

"I was captured at Wake Island and spent the rest of WWII as a guest of the Japanese," he laughed.

I responded, "Wow, you are the second Wake Island Marine I've ever met. The first was Elmer Drake from Portland."

He said, "I knew Elmer well, he was a fine man."

Richard then asked me if I was a veteran to which I said, "No, but my dad was a Marine in North Korea from 1950 to '51.

Richard responded, "What a coincidence, I was called back and was at the Chosin Reservoir."

I was shocked, "Oh my gosh, Wake Island, POW, and the Chosin Reservoir too. You are lucky to be alive."

I was, in the end, able to talk him into coming over the mountain for our next Milwaukie High School LHD and he made it happen. He enjoyed the experience immensely. Sadly, Richard passed away the next year.

Richard Caldwell passed away at the age of 85 in December of 2005.

GENE SHIRLEY
Marines
Wife- Bertha

When I asked Gene about including him in the book at the 2019 Spring Banquet, Gene said "I'll think about it, but I probably won't. Four days later at the monthly Chosin luncheon, he changed his mind. I called him and he said, "I've got some humorous stories that I'll share."

"We were supposed to land at Wonson for a planned invasion, but the harbor was mined, so we had to wait a couple days until it was cleared. When we finally landed, the South Koreans had already secured the area. The Marine's top brass were pissed.

"We found out Bob Hope was doing a USO show in the area, but they would not let us go. We had to set a defensive line in case of a counterattack.

"Another story, we were assigned to unload barrels of gasoline, and we stacked them three high in rows. There were many rows at this gas depot. North Korean peasants were used as laborers. They were very poor and used the money to buy food. They were nicknamed 'Coolies' as that was a name used back then for Oriental workers.

"It was so cold that the laborers started building campfires between rows of barrels of gas to stay warm. Even after telling them, 'You're going to blow the whole place up!', they still kept building fires," Gene laughed.

"Then we were assigned to keep the North Korean laborers and the Japanese crane operators apart as they hated each other. The North Koreans would beat the hell out of the Japanese every chance they could. So, while unloading a British merchant ship, the Japanese would try to drop the cargo nets of food and rice on the North Koreans. It was something else," he said laughing again.

"We worked outside in shifts and were allowed to warm up on the ship. The British gave us three big slabs of bacon that were supposed to go to the Army. We decided to sneak it out of the ship and wrapped it around our necks and covered it up with our coats.

"When we got back to our tent and started frying the bacon, well, the smell must have got outside, for a captain came in. We gave him a piece of bacon and never heard anything more.

"When we came out of the reservoir, we ended up at the seaport town of Hungnam. It was a large town. After a month of no shaving, haircuts, or bathing, we wanted to clean up. My buddy and I walked into town and found a local barbershop.

"My buddy went first and when he was done went next door to a bar. I'm all alone with this North Korean Barber, and he's sharpening his razor to shave me. I started to worry, so I cranked a round in my weapon and held it over my shoulder. Afterward, I realized that was dumb because if he wanted to kill me, he could have done it before I could get a shot off."

Gene ended our conversation with, "Ok that's it, and you get all that for free."

Gene Shirley passed at the age of 90 in January of 2021.

RAY GOODY   Marines
                                   Wife Marcella

Ray Goody was the first veteran of the Chosin Few I became friends with at the chapter's summer potluck at the Rumpakis' Rockaway Beach cabin on the Oregon Coast in 1998. There were two tables, and everyone was sitting at one of the tables, so I sat at the second table by myself. Ray got up and moved to sit next to me. That small gesture meant a lot to me.

That October I was invited by the chapter to their annual fall weekend retreat in Florence, Oregon on the coast. After the evening banquet, Ray pulled me aside to thank me for his previous Living History Day experience. He stated how healing it was for him and so many of his buddies. He also told me that it was the first time most had spoken about the Chosin in public.

He then put his hand on my shoulder and said, "I have something I've been wanting to tell you. It's terribly sad that your father took his life before this chapter had been formed because I believe joining a group like the Chosin would have saved his life. This group saved my life and saved the lives of many of us here.

"Did you know that some of us have a support group we call 'The Coffee Klatch Group'. We meet sometimes a couple of times a week, always during the middle of the night. Whenever any of us has nightmares or flashbacks and needs someone to talk to, we will meet at a restaurant for coffee just to be there for each other.

"So, Ken, please forgive your father. We understand what he went through." I was stunned, but very grateful to Ray for sharing this with me.

I later learned that fellow Chosin member Dr. Vern Summers started this support group with Bill Chisholm.

Sadly, Ray passed away in 2002 from cancer, and I was never able to get his personal stories. But he did write his own book, *Korea- Shadows in The Night,* but only made copies for his family and members of the Chosin Few. Ray gave me a copy before his passing.

I never read it until May of 2019 and was blown away at the detail of his experiences in the Korean War and the Chosin Reservoir. He kept a detailed day by day diary and I'm including parts of Ray's experience.

Ray was the leader of a wire team of seven Marines attached to the Fire Support Coordination Center. Their jobs were to lay and repair wire for communication. They had a jeep with a 30-caliber machine gun. It was very dangerous work as they were always in harm's way.

We received orders, we will land at Inchon, about 20 miles from Seoul, the Capital of South Korea. Due to the terrible tidal conditions, the North Koreans will not expect us to land there. Our section will be in the second wave. It's the early evening prior to the landing, and the sky is alive with 16" shells from the Battleship Missouri. We hear that Seoul is a city on fire. I'm on deck with my wire team watching the destruction of Inchon with flames thirty to fifty feet high.

Our landing craft is now ready, and we climb down the Jacobs ladders into the landing crafts. Before I climb down, I try to light a cigarette but can't because I'm shaking so bad. I say to TJ (Marine in our team), "Hey man, I'm a bundle of nerves. What about you"? TJ replies, "I can't stop shaking." A Navy Chaplain starts praying for us.

When the landing craft becomes full, we shove off from the ship and begin to circle, waiting for the wave to form an attack formation. With my nerves tingling throughout my body, I strike a match and try to light my cigarette. A sailor grabs my shaking hand and lights it for me and says, "Damn, I don't know if I'd have the guts."

He looks me straight in the eyes and says, "Hell, you're just a kid, how old are you?" I tell him, "I'm 18." The sailor with tears running down his face says, "God All Mighty, you're all just kids, God Bless you all."

My thoughts wander to my wife of five weeks. We got married on August 8th, 1950, and it's now September 15th, 1950, and I'm going into battle at Inchon, South Korea. God! What a selfish bastard I am, putting her through this. I should have waited, but I needed to know she would be there waiting for me. She would be my strength, my life, my reason to survive the ordeals ahead of me. This young girl, Mickey, my wife, I love you.

We hit the beach and run for cover. A marine is wounded in front of me. I yell out, Corpsman, Corpsman, need help here, come on…. Wounded Marine here. I look into his staring eyes, he's gone. I slump on the ground and throw up. With tears in my eyes, I'm screaming, "Where is everyone?" TJ slides next to me, grabs my head, and holds it next to his chest, saying "It's OK. It's OK." Another Marine a few yards away is dead, too. My first taste of battle, God it's tough!

We come into Seoul and it's a city destroyed, hardly a building left standing. Our section is given cold weather issue. "Damn it, TJ, those crazy bastards at Division Headquarters have given us four parkas for seven men." We learn that President Truman has called this a Police Action, but we'll call it a war."

The Reservoir.

The darkness of night and the evening stillness is shattered by the freezing cold blasts of North Korean winds bounding off the steep mountains. The cold bites into my flesh.

TJ whispers to me, "Ray, do you think they are out there?" I stare into the valley below, "Let's put up a flare." My skin is crawling, I just know they are out there. Two flares light up and slowly parachute down to earth. The Chinese are black in the valley and start firing up at our bunker. The valley is alive with crawling bodies. Bugles are heard, those damn bugles. The cries, "Marines you die, Marines you die."

They are attacking from all directions, the bugles, and the horrible terrifying screams of attacking Chinese Soldiers. With both section 30 caliber machine guns firing constantly, the black figures fall on the valley floor. Flares refined one after the other keeping the sky illuminated for minutes at a time. Clip upon clip of M-1 shells are expended. The Chinese dead and wounded cover the valley floor.

We have been under attack for several hours, and I believe we are outnumbered 20 to one. We learn ten Chinese Divisions have come across the border from Manchuria. For God's sake, we are surrounded, the entire 10,000 Marines from Koto-ri to Yudam-ni are surrounded. Over 120,000 Chinese are in this battle with the objective of destroying the 1st Marine Division.

"Damn it to hell TJ, those son-of-a-bitches Chinese have us all surrounded. We are in the battle of our lives!" I yell out, "Good Luck and give them hell." Hour after hour they attack and line after line is cut down by our overwhelming firepower. The Chinese are setting up mortar and our bunker site is in great danger. The mortars pounded the side of our bunker hill. We name our position 'Bunker Hill' and the valley, 'The Valley of Hell.'

Later the next day, the Chinese retreat back into the mountains to regroup. They have left hundreds and hundreds of dead in the valley.

My section is so tired and weary from the battle. I rally my team, "TJ and I are really proud to be associated with this section. You guys are damn good." I pass around a canteen filled with Canadian Club Whiskey, given to us by sailors from the troopship. I get up to walk over to the other Marines next to us and I suddenly fall to the ground.

"What's wrong, Ray?" Asks TJ. "Hell, I don't know, my leg is all wet, and feels warm as all hell." TJ, "For Christ Sakes Ray, you've been hit." After cutting his pant leg up the side, TJ says, "You took one in the side of your leg but punched through. I'll put sulfa powder and a bandage on it. You'll be alright, hell it's not going to bleed much in this frozen hell hole."

Burial at Koto-Ri

Our section seven joins the Convoy and immediately the Chinese attack from all sides. The lines of Chinese seem endless, and the battle goes on hour after hour. The Marines' firepower is overwhelming the Chinese forces and they are paying a terrible price. This attack is huge as they keep coming, screaming, blowing their damn bugles.

God! My nerves are about to explode but I keep my finger on the trigger, delivering hot steaming bullets of fire into a wall of quilted, uniformed enemy soldiers. The Chinese are suffering terrible losses, hundreds killed and wounded with each attack.

We are also feeling our losses of our dead and wounded. After two hours of continuous battling, the smells of war are everywhere. The snow in the valley is stained with the blood of men, Chinese, American, and British. The battlefield is covered with the courageous men who have died for their cause.

The Chinese called off the attack and withdrew into the mountains. The Marines have named this 'Hell Fire Valley'. We must bury our dead! My wire section team has been under attack for twelve straight hours, physically, mentally we are beat. And now we must bury our dead! We must not let our fallen brothers lie on the battlefield. They shall be honored as the heroes they are. They will always be in our hearts as brothers for all time. They have given the supreme sacrifice; they have given their lives.

Bulldozers have bladed the icy ground for burial. We place our brothers side by side in the graves of ice. Many break into tears as prayers are said and the bulldozers cover the sacred grounds of Koto-ri. Now these men of valor, Marines, Army, British Commandos will forever be bonded together in true brotherhood.

I gather the section team together. I am a very young eighteen year old, but I speak from the heart, "Hub, Pasq, TJ, Hannis, Kerrick, I love you guys, you're a great team. I'm so proud of each one of you. I'm so proud to be a part of this team. I know we can make it out of here, but we must stay together and fight as one." Tears are streaming down my face and tears are flowing down their cheeks as well.

We all have a toast to the Canadian Club in our canteens. TJ says, "Here's to us, the All Corporal Wire Section Team, and damn it men, we are good!"

Day after day, night after night, the battles rage on with the terrible, terrible cold. We can only move about one to two miles. The battles are furious in this valley as the Chinese know Funchilin Pass is ahead as they are trying to inflict as much pain as possible on us before we enter the narrow pass.

Marines name it 'The Valley of the Shadow of Death'.

Thousands and thousands of civilian refugees are traveling ahead of us. We are ravaged from the terrible, ever present, freezing cold. The numbness consumes our entire bodies, and the misery goes on and on, and on, hour after hour. A Staff Sergeant approaches the section and yells, "Men, you've been through hell, I know, but you are going to go through it one more time, then again one more time, and then again till we are out of this hell frozen over. You will battle these damn Chinese again and again. You will win each battle. Now get on your feet damn it. You are not going to die on this hill."

As suddenly as they left, the Chinese troops return. Bugles are blaring as they rush us from both sides yelling "Marines you die. We destroy Marines."

Hand to hand combat is taking place throughout the convoy. As the Chinese charge our wire section, I spray with bursts of carbine fire, many fall to the ground but many continue to charge. We now are all fighting hand to hand with our bayonets. As TJ bayonets one, I slash at another who falls at my feet. Hannis and Kerrick draw their 45s and finish off two more of the attacking enemy troops.

The horrible fighting continues, and the snow is covered with deep red colors of war. As the last of the fighting stops, I drop to my knees, cover my face with my hands and cry, my tears flow onto the bloody snows of Funchilin Pass.

Later I try to give our section words of encouragement, "You men, we've been through the battles from hell. Our nerves have come to a breaking point. We must fight as one or die alone. Let us remember the words of the Staff Sergeant, 'We are not going to die on this hill.'"

Parachutes are landing on the grounds a short distance from us. We grab a container and open it and find boxes of Tootsie Rolls. I unwrap one and take a bite, damn good. "Hell, guys, something to eat that's not frozen." The civilian refugees receive the same nourishment from the candy. For the majority, it is their first taste of American sweets.

God! Be with me, as I struggle, stumble, one foot after the other, can't feel my feet, so very cold, face of red and blue, icicles on my mouth, eyes of snow, lips that won't move, and ever longing pains for sleep.

Suddenly a voice came through. I know who this is. It's the "We are not going to die on this hill," Sarge. He is singing and yelling at us to join in.

"From the Halls of Montezuma to the shores of Tripoli..." Marine after Marine joins in and our steps quicken, as the spirit of the Corps shows through. We look at each other and know we are going to get out of this mess.

My eyes swell with pride as I have fought the fight. I took them on and beat them in their own park. Colonel Chesty Puller

(Marine Legend) told us, we are not retreating, hell no, we are attacking in another direction.

With wind chill factors of 50 to 60 degrees below zero, I think to myself, how can any man stand this terrible God forsaking cold? It is inhuman and beyond description.

I see a spotlight over the tree line and it's the beach. God! What a sight. Jeeps, trucks loaded with wounded, and the dead tied onto fenders, on top of hoods and lying with the wounded. Marines stumbling along, half frozen to death, putting one foot in front of the other, dragging their weapons and God... singing the Marine Corps Hymn.

I watch in awe. One hundred twenty thousand Chinese were no match for this Marine outfit. Many of us drop to our knees crying, sobbing for the dead, the wounded, and the ones we had to mass bury at Koto-ri.

Personally, not having been in combat, it is hard to imagine just what the men went through, but Ray's words in his book made me further understand the sacrifices these brave and courageous men made during those days.

He was such a great guy, and I still miss him a lot.

Ray Goody passed away at the age of 70 in April of 2002.

PAT MILLER   Marines
                             Wife - Liz
                             Chosin Few Chapter's Chaplin

Pat was the Chapter's Chaplin for years and every prayer he gave before any chapter related meals, he would always include in his prayer those men who never made it out of the Chosin Reservoir.

Pat Miller passed away at the age of 89 in June of 2018.

DON MASON   Marines
                             Wife- Sheri

Don has been my inspiration in dealing with helping to raise grandchildren. He and his wife Sheri have been raising his granddaughter and grandson since they were little.

When I asked how he did it at his age he said, "I have no choice; it's not my grandchildren's fault and they deserve a decent childhood. My wife and I would love to travel and relax, but we won't until they are raised. We have no regrets, and we feel blessed to have them in our lives."

Don was born and raised in Whittier, California, and graduated from Whittier High School in 1948. I asked, "Did you join the Marines after high school?"

"No, I enrolled at a Jr. College and joined the Marine Corps reserves. After the North Koreans invaded South Korea in the summer of 1950, all reservists were assigned to the 1st Marine Division to fill in the holes. I was assigned to Artillery and 105 Howitzers. The majority were WWII Marines, and many were in the Raider Battalion.

"So, how was your trip on the ship sailing to Japan? Did you get sea-sick?"

"No, I had been fishing before out on the ocean, but a lot of the guys got sick. I became good friends with a WWII Marine who was a barber and cut anyone's hair for donations. He was also a great gambler. He would play poker all night, and I was his money holder."

I asked, "Weren't you nervous keeping his money?"

"Not really because nobody knew I had his money. Every once in a while, he would wake me up to ask for more of his money when he was losing, and he would usually win it back by morning."

"Were you in on the Inchon landing?"

"Yes, we left Kobe, Japan on LSTs. I'd never been on one before. All of the crates of ammunition were stacked on the bottom floor, then it was covered with plywood. The next level was all of the 105s, but all of the guns' wheels had to be changed because they were too big to fit.

"On top of the guns was another floor of plywood. Also, loaded in the LST were many DUKWs which we used for the beach landing. It was a good thing we were not hit because we were a floating bomb."

"Is there any memory of the Inchon landing you feel should be remembered?"

"Sadly, several of the first Ducks coming out of the LSTs flipped over and sank, killing all."

Don immediately changed the subject. "Ken, did you know that Inchon was an island and is now the site of the Incheon International Airport? They filled in the bay, and you would never know there was a major battle there.

"A memory which was different for us artillery Marines was setting our guns up on the beaches of Wanson. We got to direct fire on an unidentified ship entering the harbor, something we had never done before."

Don got silent for a moment and then said, "A lot of Marines were sleeping up on top of a hill where the railroads were. In the middle of the night, they were attacked and killed in their sleeping bags. That morning the sight of Marines carrying the bodies of dead Marines away was terrible.

"Later that morning, many enemy soldiers were marched down to the beach and lined up. I heard machine gun fire, turned around and saw the enemy soldiers were all shot and dead."

"Have you ever shared any of your experiences with your wife or children?"

"No, only with other Chosin Few veterans."

"So, what do you want your future great, great-grandchildren to know about the battle at the Chosin?"

"We lost a lot of guys up there, and anyone who hasn't experienced that severe cold will never understand.

"I do have kind of a funny story though. After we reached safety, we were given daily rations of beer, and I was assigned to guard it. I slept on top of the cases of beer." Don laughed telling me that.

"Did anyone try to steal any?"

"They didn't dare," laughing again.

Don Mason is still living at the age of 92.

JOHN BAIRD   Marines
                                    WWII
                                    Army- Battle of the Bulge
                                    Wife- Dorine

John attended the majority of our events, but would never speak to students. When I learned that he served in the Army in WWII during the Battle of the Bulge, I asked him if he would like to talk to students about that experience. His quick angry response taught me to not bring the subject up again.

"No, never, I can't even think about it without getting angry. We fought the SS troops and I saw first-hand their atrocities. I still hate them."

But that is not my only memory of John. I'll always remember him as a real first-class gentleman.

John Baird passed away at the age of 87 in October of 2013.

* ★ *

RICHARD JACKSON   Marines
                                    Wife-June

Dick should have been a stand-up comedian as his wit was very quick and funny. He never attended any of our events as he told me over twenty years ago, "I just don't go there."

For many years, Dick was a full-time caregiver for his wife, and he brought her to every Chosin Few event. For years, everyone advised him to put her in assisted living care. Dick would not even consider it. He told me, "I made a commitment to her when I married her, and I promised her I would never put her in a home." Even during hospice care, Dick was still helping out. June passed away in the winter of 2019.

At the Chosin Few's annual Spring Banquet, I told the seven veterans and the many adult children, "Believe it or not, I'm close to finishing Volume I and will continue writing Volume II. Would any of you be interested in sharing any of your experiences with me so I could include you in the section on the Chosin Few Oregon Chapter? My goal is a hundred years from now, you will be remembered."

To my surprise, Dick said, "Yes, give me a call."

The next day I called him, and he started before I could ask a question.

"I joined the Marines Reserves as a Senior in 1947 at Central Catholic High School with five other senior friends. I wanted to make extra money. I started working for four hours a day after school at the Post Office at 16 years of age, and after graduating I worked full time as a Post Office clerk. But my life changed drastically on August 25, 1950.

"Every Marine Corps Reserve Unit nationwide was called up and ordered to report to Camp Pendleton immediately. We were all formed on the parade grounds when some officer yelled, 'Anybody needing more training, take one step forward?' Nobody moved. I was smarter than that.

"On September 1st, we were shipped to Korea and landed at Inchon five days after the original landings. There were still snipers around. I was attached to the 11th Marines, then on November 10, the Marine Corps Birthday, I was transferred to a Firing Battery- Artillery.

"At Chosin, I was transferred to the 7th Marines and came out on foot with them. We were in firefights all the way from Hagari to Kotori. We were out in the elements for three weeks, in an average of minus thirty-five degrees.

I have permanent nerve damage to my arms, hands, feet, and legs. It took thirteen years of fighting the VA to get disability benefits."

"I'm so sorry, I've heard the same from all of the other Chosin Few veterans of having to fight for disability benefits also," I said.

"Let me continue on. As we got close to Kotori, there was a huge firefight going on with all the houses on fire. There were twelve Marines lying on the side of the road still holding on to their rifles looking like they were going to shoot. I yelled at them and realized they were all dead and frozen.

"Later, we walked up to a huge pile covered with snow with a hand sticking out. As I got closer, I noticed under the snow were the dead frozen bodies of British Marines and the US Army. They were eventually buried in a mass grave.

"We approached where a bridge had been blown up, and we waited for two days till parachuted bridges were put in place. My platoon was ordered to go back up the road to rescue trapped Marines. We got up there and into another firefight. Well, the info was either false or too late as the eight Marines were dead.

"We started to head back to safety when a tank came around the corner, stopped, and its big gun turned around and aimed at us. I thought, 'Oh Hell, we are dead now.' The tank started towards us and out pops one of the soldiers who yells out, 'Hey Marines, if you want a ride back, climb on board.'"

"Wow, what a relief! How have you dealt with the memories?" I asked.

"I still have the same nightmares, seeing frozen dead Marines stacked like cordwood."

"Have you shared any of this with your wife and children?"

"No, just other members of the Chosin."

Dick is one of the original Chosin Few Oregon Chapter members who first responded to Tom Greens' notice in The Oregonian newspaper.

"Do you have any funny stories?" I asked.

"Oh yes, it's funny, scary, and a lucky story. There was this Black American Sergeant standing next to me. He must have been top-notch as a black sergeant was extremely rare in those days. A mortar hit a rock right next to us and did not explode. The sergeant turned to me and said, 'That will make a black man turn white.'" Dick laughed.

Dick Jackson passed away at the age of 91 in May of 2021.

— ★ —

ELBERT 'DOC' COLLINS   Navy
WWII- Submarine
Wife- Gerrie

Doc was a Navy Corpsman who served primarily on submarines. He even served on five submarines between 1952 and 1964: USS Hancock, USS Diachenko, USS Catfish, USS Thomas Jefferson, and USS Proteus. When the Korean War broke out, he was deployed with the 1st Provisional Marine Brigade, 1st Marine Division Fox Company as a Line Corpsman.

At a monthly luncheon, I told Doc about a Korean War medic who had no training. "They were so desperate for Medics that many riflemen were told they were now Medics." Doc laughed and said, "Hell, there was no training to be a Corpsman either. (Medics are attached to the Army and Corpsmen are attached to the Marines.)

"We were told, 'Just stop the bleeding and give them a shot of morphine.' And, 'If someone is shooting and wounding marines and you run over there to help the wounded while the enemy is still shooting, you will get shot too.'

"My Sargent, a WWII veteran, ordered me to stay in my foxhole, and he would give the order when to leave foxholes to aid a wounded Marine. Well, when I saw the first Marine get shot, I left the foxhole and ran to help him, but I got shot myself. My Sargent runs over to me and starts cussing me out for disobeying his orders. He doesn't even ask me if I'm OK."

I then asked Doc, "How did you go from submarine service to being on the ground in Korea as a Corpsman?"

He laughed. "That's a hell of a story. I was stationed in the states and during August 1950 was helping process Marines who had all been called up to report to Camp Pendleton ASAP and were being sent to Korea. I was stamping each Marine's paperwork, and when I handed it back to him, I was having fun being a smartass. I was saying have a nice trip or enjoy your vacation.

"The very next morning, I came back to work, and my seabag is packed with a letter attached. I was ordered to report immediately to Camp Pendleton, in fact, there was a cab waiting for me. I flew to Southern California, reported to Camp Pendleton, and then was flown to Japan, and attached to 1st Marine Division, all within 48 hours."

At one of the Chosin Few monthly lunches, I asked him, "Did you all get seasick on the ship traveling to Korea?"

Doc laughs, "Hell yes, but this was on the way to Inchon. It was so rough, we were all sick. Down below where we slept, there was puke all on the floors, guys slept with their helmets and puked in them. The smell was horrible."

I responded, "I thought you were on a submarine, didn't you get your sea legs?"

"Hell no, I never got my sea legs, and a submarine was worse because when on the surface it would roll from side to side. There was always puke on the floors and the smell inside the sub was disgusting.

"This is funny now, but not back then. I went to the urinal trough to piss and next to me was a sailor throwing up and out flies his dentures and into the trough. His dentures flow down the trough, so he hurries over and grabs them, rinses them off, and then puts them back into his mouth. Then I and everyone else threw up."

Doc Collins passed away at the age of 90 in April of 2021.

★

FRANK KYSER   Marines
                               WWII-Merrill's Marauders,
                               Saipan
                               Wife- Myla

Frank became my next good Chosin friend as he went out of his way at every gathering to pull me aside to chat. Probably because he worked for Pacific Northwest Bell with my father for thirty years.

"Neither of us ever knew we were Marines and served in the Korean War. Your father was a good man, Ken."

Frank was not only a Korean War veteran, but during WWII, was with Merrill's Marauders and experienced combat on Saipan.

My wife and I became good friends with Frank and Myla as they lived in the same small town as us, Canby. They invited us over for dinner a few times for my favorite dinner that my mom would make me on my birthdays growing up. It was fried pork chops with mashed potatoes and white gravy.

Myla's version was great, but she always apologized and said, "You just can't buy pork chops like the old days. Today pork is too lean, back then they were full of fat, and they tasted so much better, even the gravy tasted better." To me, hers still tasted great.

Frank was very proud of his service in WWII and the Korean War. I once asked him, "So you fought in the South Pacific where it was extremely hot and humid and in North Korea where it was bitter cold. Which one was the worst?"

He didn't even pause to think about it and immediately responded in a raised stern voice, "The South Pacific was a walk in the park compared to the Chosin, and it's not even close." He's another good man I miss.

Frank Kyser passed away at the age of 81 in September of 2006.

TAD NEILSON   Marines
                               Wife- Evelyn

Tad's three older brothers Otis (Army) Neal (Marines) and Keith (Marines) all fought in WWII, and the youngest brother Larry (Navy) served during the Korean War. Tad joined the Marines to follow in the footsteps of his older brothers.

All five graduated from Pendleton High School, and at the school's first Living History Day on March 12, 2003, Principal Jim Gadberry, a Vietnam Army veteran, recognized the brothers in attendance, Tad,

Keith, and Larry during the Assembly of Honor. The students responded with a loud standing ovation.

Tad attended all of our events with his Chosin Few buddies until he passed but would never talk about his experiences with anyone.

The only thing he would tell me was, "Before the Korean War, I was a Pendleton Police Officer." Tad loved telling me this story even though I had heard it from him a few times, he just thought it was funny.

"Downtown Pendleton had underground tunnels that were all connected from City Hall, the Police Station, and many businesses to the town brothel. Every big shot and politician in town were frequent visitors and even big shots and big-time politicians from out of town and Salem always visited the brothel when in town. Many business deals were made in that place."

Tad would always laugh after finishing this story. Tad only shared one Chosin experience with his wife Evelyn that she later told me.

"Walking out of the Chosin, it was so bitterly cold and snowing, but I'll never forget how heartbroken I was leaving behind our dead. I can't get it out of my mind."

She added, "He always had nightmares but refused to talk about it."

While editing Tad's Chapter in February of '21, I decided to track down and call one of his children to see if they had more to add. I talked over the phone with one of his sons, Fred, a Marine and Vietnam veteran.

"My father never talked about it, but I still remember as a little kid, he would have breakdowns and have to be hospitalized sometimes for several weeks. Mom would farm us out to different families to stay with.

"As a little boy, I never understood this and was never told why. Financially, this was really rough on our family and without the help of local Mormons who paid our mortgage and groceries, we wouldn't have made it as we were very destitute.

"Dad grew up in a Mormon family and of course they don't drink, or smoke and he didn't either. He was badly wounded in Korea and suffering from physical and emotional pain back home, and he took classes teaching how to deal with all the pain.

"The class's number one technique to help reduce pain and stress was teaching them how to properly smoke a cigarette, how to slowly suck in the smoke, hold it for a moment, and then blow it out slowly to relax. He was addicted the rest of his whole life and could never give up smoking. We never attended church because he felt his smoking made him not worthy of going to church.

"When I was a Junior in high school, I started attending a Mormon church. After graduating, I went on a two-year mission, and then I don't know why, but I joined the Marines. And in the Marines, I learned how to work, set goals, and attended college on the GI bill. My brother Bill served in the Air Force during the Vietnam War.

"Only once did I ever hear my dad talk about Korea. He started telling a pretty intense story to my children, but I stopped him immediately. To this day, I don't understand why he did that."

Next, I called his older sister, Candy. She was expecting my call as her brother had just called her to warn her. She answered and immediately said, "When I was born my dad got to hold me before he was sent to Korea."

She then stopped and started crying and apologized to me. With her voice breaking while crying she then said, "My dad carried a baby picture of me with him in Korea and told me he looked at it several times a day to help him get through Korea.

"When he first came home, he found his wife hanging clothes on a line outside. He was so excited to finally see me he ran into the house. I saw him, threw both arms up, and yelled, 'Daddy.' But my mom told me I called every man daddy.

"I was now a toddler and when my mom introduced him as my real daddy, I hid behind her. This hurt my father's feelings at the time, but we would become extremely close. He was always there for me and very protective, and I miss him all the time."

As with every Chosin Few veteran I've known, Tad tried to get help from the VA for frostbite benefits but was always refused. Most of these veterans would pass before receiving frostbite benefits.

Tad Neilson passed away at the age of 84 in September of 2011.

★ ⭐ ★

RICHARD 'DICK' BAUTCH

Marines
Wife- Dottie

Dick joined the Marines because his cousin served during WWII in the South Pacific as a Marine Tank driver. Donald survived two tanks being taken out during combat. I really looked up to him, so I couldn't wait to join. I joined the reserves at seventeen in '47 and graduated from Central Catholic HS in '48. I worked full time, two summers in a row and had to train at Camp Pendleton.

"Soon after the North Koreans invaded South Korea, along with all of the other Portland Marine reservists, we got orders to report to Camp Pendleton immediately and a couple days later we were shipped out."

While on the ship crossing, Dick was assigned guard duty in the head. "I watched Marines throw up all the time for sea sickness, but I never got sick until we sailed right into a typhoon close to Japan."

"I'm interested in your experiences with the severe cold," I said. Dick laughed and shook his head saying, "They issued us the wrong boots with felt liners. The liners soaked up the sweat, ruined our socks, and our feet were always cold. The first time I was able to change my socks, they pulled the skin off."

"I've heard you couldn't shower or shave for three weeks?"

Dick responded, "That's true, we looked and smelled like hell. The British Marines were ordered to shave every day with a dry razor. It was difficult to sleep during that time because the Chinese would attack in the middle of the night. My father mailed a 22-caliber pistol which I held while trying to sleep."

Dick was part of a demolition team that blew up many bridges and they also defused hundreds of pounds of Chinese bombs strapped to a bridge before the Chinese could blow it up.

"Before we could work on defusing the bombs, me and another Marine had to climb a steep hill to place a 30 Caliber machine gun. It was dark when we got set up and then a Chinese flare went off. We were all alone and scared, but nothing ever happened. The next morning, we saw smoke coming from the canyon below us. We looked down and saw a Chinese soldier, naked and drying his uniform over a fire. We fired the machine gun, and I don't think he ever knew what hit him.

"Another time we found another Chinese soldier, who was wounded, sitting in the bottom of a fox-hole with his whole lower body completely frozen in solid ice. He begged us to shoot him, and we did. Very sad. But I want it known that I never did anything that I would be ashamed of afterwards.

"I'll never understand watching some of our own tanks chase down the Chinese wounded and running them over." The tone in Dick's voice was with disgust as he shook his head.

"A good friend of mine lost all his fingers from a mortar explosion and crawled for over twenty hours across the frozen reservoir to reach us. He survived the war and was Seattle's Superintendent of Parks, and I can't remember his name. He just passed away a few years ago, and I attended his funeral."

I then asked, "How have you dealt with the memories?"

"The only nightmares I have had are seeing the starving, sickly little children digging through garbage for food, and begging for food. We gave them whatever we could, and seeing what war does to children, I just can't get it out of my mind.

"Another nightmare I still have - We had just finished mining a road to slow down the advancing Chinese. As we finished, an old man was walking and leading an ox pulling a cart of children. We waved and yelled, but he just waved back and kept walking towards us. Sure enough, the Ox stepped on a mine killing the ox instantly and wounding the old man and children. We were finally able to reach them and carry the wounded children to a first aid station for help."

"Anything else you want remembered, Dick?"

Teary eyed Dick said, "Yes, when we finally broke out and reached safety, many of us attended a Christmas Eve Mass. In came a choir of Korean children and they sang 'Silent Night' in their Korean language. It was very emotional for us."

Dick Bautch is still living at the age of 91.

KEN VAN KURIN   Marines
                                 Wife- Carolyn

I met Ken and his wife over twenty years ago in Canby at a local church. They never attended any Chosin Few events, but once after a church service, I learned he was a Marine during the Korean War and was at the Chosin Reservoir.

My wife and I would run into them many times over the years in Canby. They were super friendly. Several times I invited them to Chosin Few gatherings, but they were unable to attend.

During December of 2019, we sat next to them at a local restaurant for breakfast. "What did you both do for a career?" I asked.

"We were missionaries," they both said at the same time. "We lived in Indonesia, lived in the jungle with no running water or electricity." Carolyn beamed with pride after she stated that.

"Did you have children and raise them there?"

"Oh yes, we had two children and we lived there for thirty-seven years."

"Wow, that is amazing."

I then told them about my *Remembrance Volume I* and *Volume II* books I was writing. I also said to them, "The second volume includes many Chosin Few's personal stories, and I would be honored to include your story, and it will include the how and why you became missionaries."

"We can do it right now," Ken enthusiastically responded and started talking. "I was the sixth child out of seventeen siblings and grew up on my family's farm in Corning, New York. I left home at sixteen years of age and joined the Marines. I don't know if they missed me or not." Both began laughing.

"Did you lie and forge the paperwork?"

"No, they never asked."

I then asked, "Why the Marines?"

And then without any hesitation Ken said laughing, "What else is there?"

"Boot camp was at Parris Island with the 2nd Marine Division. After that we shipped out to Kobi, Japan, and we were all assigned to the 1st Marine Division."

"Were you in on the Inchon landing?"

"Yes, it was very scary and very rough waters. Thankfully we had practiced landing on the beaches of North Carolina."

"Is there anything you want remembered about that battle?

"No, I've never talked about it."

"What about the Chosin? Pretend that it is one hundred years from now and your great, great, great-grandchildren are reading about you. What do want them to know?"

"Well, I've tried very hard to forget it all. We were in summer uniforms in the fall of 1950 and didn't receive winter gear until after the weather turned cold. I always remember the cold. It was tough. After a cease fire, we were overrun. I played dead when a Chinese soldier rolled me over. Then and there, I prayed to God, 'If you get me out of here, I will devote my life to serving the lord.'"

"Wow, that answers one of my questions about why you became a missionary. You must have gone to church as a child?"

"Nope, how do you get seventeen kids ready at the same time? We were raised with no faith. I did pray once as a child though, I asked God to help me find my lost baseball," Ken laughed.

"In Korea, I noticed there was a difference between all the Marines. There were Marines who never cussed and attended weekly church services. I started to attend out of curiosity and to learn how to pray.

"When I came home from Korea, my three older brothers who had all found God serving during WWII, took me to church. That's where I met Carolyn, and we both attended Nyack Christian College in New York to become missionaries. We got married as students."

Carolyn then added, "I was born into a missionary family in Thailand and attended boarding school in Vietnam, so I knew as a young girl I wanted to be a missionary."

Ken then continued, "Every Friday night the college would have a missionary from around the world speak to all. It was very inspiring, and they were heroes to me."

"How did you end up in Indonesia?"

"We were ordered there and came back to Oregon thirty-seven years later."

"Weren't you concerned for your safety?"

"Nope, no fear. We traveled up and down a river and spread the word to every village. We also built airstrips in the villages. We never experienced any issues as I believe the Natives had never seen white people before and were fascinated with us."

"Were there any miracles you witnessed?"

"Oh, many. Once someone tried to poison our dinner at a large gathering. It didn't look very tasty, so I threw it out a window. Sadly, a dog ate it and died.

"I wanted everyone to know God and to also know that God is always with us. I always say find out what God wants you to do and do it. We have no regrets.

"Lastly, write Ken Van Kurin won the Korean War," laughing again. "Just kidding."

Ken Van Kurin is still living at the age of 90.

Additional Members
Chesley Yahtin Sr., Army, Medic, Warm Springs Native American - read about in Native Americans

David Dowdakin, Marines, Wife- Ruth, Also WWII, Saipan, Tarawa, Okinawa - read about in Volume I, WWII Marines

Ken Reusser, Marines, Wife-Trudy, WWII also, Korea, Vietnam, Marines most decorated aviator - read about in Volume I, WWII Marines

Other Chosin Few veterans who attended our events

Vic Saraceno, photographer	James Whitcomb
Bud Bergman, Wife- Lucy	James McNaughton
Art Wilson, Wife- Viola	Don Pullen
Keith Richardson, Wife- Linda	Robert Katelhut
George Russelli, Wife- Roseanne	Floyd Kogle
Harold Smith, Wife- Betty	Joseph Curley
Joseph Stokes	Tom Curran
Gail Matthews, Wife- Grace	Doug Creelman
Clarence Coles, Wife- Mae Baxter	Thomas Satchell

Clay Brace, Wife- Liz   Shirley Laird
Albert Hodgin, Wife- Beverly   Clifford Towner
Don Meisenbach   Jay Feeback, Wife- Pauline
*Bill Smith

*I only met Bill one time as he passed away shortly after, but within a few weeks of meeting him, he sent me a beautiful hand carved walking stick with my father's name and 'Marines' etched on it.

NATIVE AMERICAN VETERANS

There is a camaraderie that transcends ethnicity when you serve your country overseas in wartime.

~ Senator Ben Nighthorse Campbell, Northern Cheyenne

There is a long history of Native American veterans' military service, and according to the U.S. Department of Veterans Affairs, more than 10,000 Native Americans served during the Korean War. One of the most notable were Vice Admiral Joseph 'Jocko' Clark, a Cherokee, the first Native to graduate the Naval Academy and commander of the Navy's 7th fleet during the war.

> Native Americans and Alaska Natives serve in the Armed Forces at five times the national average and have served with distinction in every major conflict for over 200 years. Considering the population of the U.S. is approximately 1.4 percent Native and the military is 1.7 percent Native (not including those that did not disclose their identity), Native people have the highest per-capita involvement of any population to serve in the U.S. military.
>
> ~The National Indian Council on Aging, Inc. (NICOA), 2019

CHESLEY YAHTIN SR.

Warm Springs Tribe
Army Medic

Chesley was a Native American from The Warm Springs tribe and was an Army Medic at the Chosin. He was a very quiet, dignified, proud man. After learning his story from Bill Chisholm, I felt it was too important and needed to be remembered.

After joining the Oregon Chosin Few, Chesley only attended the summer potluck picnic with his family mostly because he lived on the Warm Springs Indian Reservation a couple of hours drive from Portland. He would bring several freshly caught salmon and barbecue them over an open campfire.

The salmon was always great and very popular with everyone. Every year I would try to talk to him, but he was very quiet and just not a talker.

I could never get him to attend a Living History Day until we honored all of the Native American Veterans at Milwaukie High School in 2008. He agreed to attend and represent his tribe but did not want to talk to students or be assigned a classroom.

I learned later that he followed fellow Chosin Few veterans Ray Goody and Pete Cummings into their assigned classroom to listen to them speak. During lunch, the teacher assigned to the classroom literally ran up to me all excited and said, "Ken, I have to tell you about an extraordinary experience that happened in my classroom."

"One of the Chosin Few Veterans, Pete Cummings, told the students that the only reason he is alive today is because of Chesley Yahtin who saved his life. He said he was badly wounded and Chesley stopped the bleeding and carried him back to safety."

Chesley is a large, big man, so I thought about him easily doing it. The teacher continued with, "Chesley started sobbing uncontrollably, and then Ray Goody and Pete Cummings went over to him to comfort him. Then several high school girls got up and gathered around him for a group hug. I started crying and I looked around and everyone in the class was crying. It was unbelievable."

I learned later from Bill Chisholm and Art Wilson that Chesley had a difficult experience from his military service. He joined the Army because he felt that he needed to learn and understand the white man's ways, but learned right away that he would never be accepted by his fellow soldiers, NCOs, and officers as he experienced racist remarks daily. He was called 'Big Crazy Indian' and 'Indian Medic'.

I also learned that he was wounded badly and froze to the ground in his own blood. Despite this, he was returned to the front and served in four major combat actions while in Korea and earned eight commendations.

Chesley put in numerous requests for leave to visit his home on the Warm Springs Reservation when he returned home stateside, but his requests were always denied. Then one night when he saw a chance he returned home to the reservation. When he returned, he was punished for being AWOL by being dishonorably discharged without even a hearing from the military.

I later heard that he said he always felt it was because he was a Native American and because of how horribly the majority of the NCOs and officers treated him.

In 2003, Bill Chisholm and Art Wilson approached Chesley when he attended a Chosin Few event to tell him the Chosin Few would help to overturn his discharge and return his medals. At the time Chesley had no interest, but his daughters were interested.

Their cause was greatly helped when The Oregonian Newspaper ran a big story on Chesley's injustice. Senator Ron Wyden saw the story and joined the cause. Now, with the powerful help of a senator, and the

Chosin Few Korean War veterans, 58 years later, in 2005, a review of his case was started. The inquiry found that Chesley was court martialed for minor offenses and that his service had been involuntarily extended even after numerous medals and combat wounds.

His discharge from dishonorable was then changed to honorable and all medals awarded were returned and he was able to access much-needed veteran's benefits.

Chesley Yahtin Sr. passed away at the age of 78 in June of 2009.

DON LOUDNER

Sioux

Army

I met Don during the trip to Washington DC with the Blackfeet Veterans Honor Guard in 2010. Don, just like all the Native American veterans I have come to know, is very proud of his Native heritage and his military service. And he also has a great sense of humor and is always cracking jokes.

One of the first jokes he told me was, "If you ever come to visit me in South Dakota, I'll take you to the best fried chicken restaurant on the reservation. The white tourists love it, but they don't know it's prairie dog they're eating...Just kidding," as he laughed.

Every time he spoke to high school students in Oregon, he always opened with this question, "What was this country called before it was called the United States?" The students always looked perplexed and never answered. Don would say in a loud voice, "OURS" and then laugh.

Don earned the name 'Tomahawk' during boot camp because he was the only soldier to accurately hit the target by throwing a hand grenade. The Drill Instructor asked, "How did you get so good at throwing and hitting a target?" Don responded, "By throwing tomahawks at white people." Again laughing.

I asked about his childhood growing up on a poor reservation. "My family was so poor growing up that I slept on the floor till my senior year in high school as we didn't own any beds. I never thought anything of it and that's not a joke. We had over 80% unemployment on our reservation and the drug and alcohol addiction was just as high. There was no hope."

Don's presentations to students were always very educational. He would bring a short DVD documentary about Native American veterans from several tribes who were code talkers, the Choctaws during WWII in the European Theater, and the Comanche, Hopi, Meskwaki- Sac and Fox, the Chippewa-Oneida, and of course the Navajo in the Pacific theater.

It was amazing that students and teachers, including a majority of veterans, did not know this history as most only knew about the famous Navajo Code Talkers.

Don had many stories of racism from in the military to when he returned home. I remember him telling me about when he came back to the states from Korea, he and his Army buddies went into a local tavern in California to have a beer. The bartender approached Don and said in a loud voice, "We don't serve Indians here, you need to leave now."

Well, Don, with his quick sense of humor answered, "What makes you think I'm an Indian. I'm Mexican."

The bartender backed down after Don's Army buddies jumped in to support Don's fib and poured him a beer. Don would tell the students, "Serving alcohol to Indians was still against the law and in 1953 the U.S.

Congress repealed the legislative law passed in 1832 that banned the sale of alcohol to Indians.

"In fact, Native Americans, until 1924, were not citizens of the United States. We still have separate nations within the U.S. on our reservation land."

During our annual Goodbye Dinner in November of 2017, Don got up to tell everyone about his amazing find in the Black Hills from the previous year. His great-grandfather had buried many Sioux Buffalo arrowheads wrapped in a Buffalo hide. Then he showed his son where it was buried, and this was repeated until it was also shown to Don.

Don was showing one of the arrowheads to all of us as he spoke. "I had some of them packed in my carry-on bag, but security took them away and told me the process I would have to go through to get them back."

I asked, "So how did you get that one through security?"

Don says, "I put a couple of them in my shoes." Then he then pulls out of his pocket two beautiful hand-made necklaces with colorful beads and one of the arrowheads tied to each.

Don pauses and then says "Rodney Forni (see acknowledgments) and Ken Buckles, these are for you."

"Wow," I immediately stated. I was blown away. It was a very emotional moment for everyone there. What an amazing gift!

Don Loudner is still living at 89 years of age.

AL LANE   Marines
                            WWII
                            Yakama Warrior
                            Wife- Shirley

Al was a member of The Chosin Few and said to me that it was an honor to gather with his fellow Marines and their wives to remember their fallen brothers and the price they paid. He also told me that he was a proud member of the Marines and an honorary member of the Marines of L-3-5 on Guadalcanal and a Yakama Warrior.

I'll never forget the first time I met Al. I sat next to him at a Chosin Few luncheon in 1996, and he asked me where I lived. I responded, "Canby." He laughed and said, "Ah, General Canby. My great, great-grandfather Captain Jack killed General Canby. The whites say it was an ambush, but it was a fair fight."

This was in 1996, and I did not know it at the time, but this was to be my first introduction to Native American humor. I later spoke with a friend who is also a Modoc and a historian on Captain Jack and General Canby.

He said to me, "Have you ever heard of Native humor before? Because most Natives in Oregon claim they are related to Captain Jack." After he said this to me, I remembered Al laughing the whole time after telling me. I think Al got me pretty good because I believed it and even told people what he had said to me for a number of years.

Al Lane passed away at the age of 80 in April of 2008.

PURPLE HEART ASSOCIATION OF OREGON

KEITH KINGSLEY   Army
                                 WWII
                                 Korea

I visited Keith at his retirement home apartment months before he passed. He was his humorous, funny self. Before I started asking questions, Keith said, "I've decided to give you my two books, and please use whatever you would like for your book. At this point in my life, I just don't feel like going there anymore. I just want to live out the rest of my life happy."

I was able to use Keith's own writing from his two short books *Armored Cav, Stateside, France, Germany, Austria, 1943- 1946*, and *As I Lived It*. With all due respect to Keith's WWII experiences, I have only included a few stories from his first book primarily focusing on his Korean War experiences.

Keith in his first book wrote that he was in a Recon outfit in General Patton's Third Army. Standing just ten feet away from Patton who was giving a pep talk.

> I remember being surprised at the high pitch of General Patton's voice and he used a lot of cuss words. But, he got my attention.
>
> We were moving through Germany, and someone complained, "What is that smell?" I replied, "That is the smell of death." We soon came upon Ordorf Work Camp. It was shocking.
>
> Soon after us, General Eisenhauer and General Patton arrived and toured the camp. Eisenhauer ordered all of the people who lived in Ordorf to come see this horrific death camp.

Keith earned the Bronze Star in Austria when they were attacked one night. He volunteered to stay and repel the attack with machine gun fire while everyone retreated.

> It was very sad having to fight the 'Hitler Jung Soldiers' who were 13-15 years old. Many refused to surrender and kept fighting to the end. The SS troops were ruthless.

Even when Keith was back home his experiences from the war never really left him. At a large family gathering in the evening, when Keith first got back home, this happened:

> My father was standing in the middle of a lighted doorway. I just reacted. I grabbed my father and pushed him, yelling "Keep the hell out of a lighted doorway."

The following is from his second book *Armored Cav, Korea, September 1950-1951, As I Lived It.*

> I made the mistake of joining the Armored Cavalry Reserve. In September of '50, I received a letter ordering me to report for duty in thirty days. And I was married with a six-month-old son.

> We were shipped to Pusan and put on a train and sent to the front. I reported to the Command tent and a Sergeant yelled, "I want Kingsley, we need WWII guys like him."

> So, I was assigned to 7th Recon troop and in command of a Mortar Section. Recon gathers information for the division five to eight miles ahead of our positions. Our mission is to find the enemy and radio the information back to Division. Most of the time we got into a firefight, so the enemy found us just as easily as we found them. We also covered retreats and plugged holes in the main line of resistance when the enemy broke through.

> One night, moving through mountain passes on dangerous icy roads, one of our tanks slid off the road into rocks and the tank's front sprocket wheel broke. Our platoon Sergeant orders

everyone to keep moving, leaving behind ten men. The five tankers and five scouts to repair the tank.

I protested angrily, "This is not the Recon way. During WWII in Europe, Recon never left anyone behind, we were always a team." My protest was to no avail.

A short time later, we arrived down the mountain side to the small town Chechon. Within minutes, we hear the sounds of a firefight. Many of us raced back up to find all were dead. The five tankers were shot while still in their tanks. The five scouts were all shot in the back of the head missing their shoes, jackets, and hats.

I was so angry, and I let everyone know. They heard me loud and clear...

At the start of my third week in Korea, early in the morning, we heard bugles and whistles. Across the valley is the largest number of Chinese I've ever seen running as fast as they can towards us yelling, "Americans you die." They try to surround us, but our firepower was just too much for them.

We had to be on guard 24/7 as it was always dangerous. Just to smoke a cigarette, one man would throw a blanket over you and then you would switch places. It's amazing how alert you could be with very little or no sleep.

...Once we were finally able to build a fire to heat up our C rations. Because we had gasoline, it was not difficult starting the fire in such cold. I reached down to grab my can when I noticed a new guy staring at my feet in shock. I looked down and all of the snow around the fire had melted and I was standing on the face of a dead North Korean soldier."

"I pulled the new guy aside and said, "Welcome to the bloody Korean War."

I earned my Purple Heart when a large mortar round exploded near us. One piece of shrapnel knocked out my three front teeth and a second larger piece tore into my upper right thigh. It was a bad deep seven inch long wound.

I remember waking up with a doctor checking on me and I asked, "What about my family jewels?" He responded, "One is just nicked but you will heal up good as new."

"Doc, you just made my day!"

The healing took a long three months. The Doctor told me, "The leg wound is looking Ok, but you will never walk again." I was furious and yelled, "I'll walk in a month."

My right leg was immobile and rigged in a contraception device slightly raised off the bed and had drainage tubes from the wound. When shrapnel enters into the body, the risk for infection and gangrene is high and my doctor was very concerned.

I assumed and everyone else told him, "This wound is your ticket home."

...After healing I was sent back to Pusan and ordered to report to my new CO. The CO's tent had an American and Confederate Flag flying over it. I walked in and said, "I'm Yankee Born and raised in Wisconsin. We whipped the Rebels once. Do we have to do it again?"

The CO said, "You have a new job commanding the Scouting section which will make you a Staff Sergeant today. I like WWII Cavalry scouts even if they do not like rebels."

In the spring of '51, the Chinese went on the offensive again, and Keith and his men were involved in more firefights, but I decided to end his Korean War experience with a little humor.

We slept whenever we could and always on the ground. I told some new guys, do not carry any hard candy in your front field jacket pockets. Of course, they didn't listen to me but were awakened early in the morning with rats on their chests eating their candy. One of the guys completely lost it.

...In September of '51, I finally received orders to go back to the states. Reporting to Fort Lewis, I was offered a promotion to Master Sergeant if I stayed in the Army. "No, I'm now behind four years in my life, and I would like to catch up to my wife and now 18-month-old son who was six months old when I was recalled."

I learned that Keith was nicknamed the Silver Fox, but I never found out why. He was a fun character and all the veterans loved being around him. I still get asked to this day, "Ken, Remember the Silver Fox? He was such a character." I will always miss him.

Keith Kingsley passed away at the age of 91 in August of 2015.

---

* ★ *

DALE ALBEE   Army
                             WWII

Dale Albee and Keith Kingsley were best friends and always spoke together as a team at every Living History Day at high schools around Oregon until Dale passed away in 2007. Their classroom sessions were stand-up comedy routines at its best. They were hilarious, and the students loved them.

They would barely touch on their World War II experiences, just telling students that they did dangerous and scary recon behind German lines. Dale was wounded in World War II, and Keith was wounded in Korea. They made it a point to tell students only the funny stories from their experiences in the Army.

Keith would open his talk to the students, "I'm a retired high school woodshop teacher." Then he would hold up both hands and said, "And look. I still have all my fingers."

They would greet every student with handshakes for the guys and hugs for the girls. Dale and CJ Lindsey, another World War II veteran, were responsible for holding up the charter bus from leaving Pendleton High School's Living History Day because they were both hugging every single teenage girl in the hallway.

They were so much fun, especially at the Purple Heart Oregon State Conventions. Dale required everyone to hug each other when greeting. They were always smiling, cracking jokes, pulling pranks, kidding, and making sure everyone was having a good time.

Dale enlisted in the horse cavalry, but the 11th Horse Cavalry was later mechanized as part of the 10th Armored Tank Division. I learned more about Dale from speaking to Robert Haltiner, Army, Vietnam, and who was also a fellow member of the Purple Heart Association.

Robert said to me, "Dale never talked to anyone about his war experiences, not even us Purple Heart recipients. When he suddenly died of cancer, not even his children or best friends knew he had cancer. I didn't know and we were very close.

"Dale landed in Normandy after D-Day and fought from Northern France to Czechoslovakia and was in the Battle of the Bulge and the Siegfried Line. He was one of only a few men to earn a battlefield commission going from platoon sergeant to second lieutenant.

"Dale told me he was color blind, that he failed the first eye test when he enlisted but was able to get the color-blind test and memorize it. He said to me, 'I passed, but probably shouldn't have made it in because I really was color blind.'

"He also told me that they were sent to Europe with their horse but once there, the Army took the horse away and assigned them tanks. Dale was furious and protested to no avail. As he was in Recon, he said a horse could sneak up to German positions and not be detected, but a tank could be heard for miles. He was still angry when telling me this."

Dale Albee passed away at 87 in May of 2007.

KOREAN WAR VETERANS ASSOCIATION
OREGON TRAIL CHAPTER

The Oregon Trail Chapter of the Korean War Veterans Association (KWVA) have supported and attended our Living History Days for over twenty years. And yes, every one of them were a great group of veterans and spouses.

DON BARTON   Army
                                    Ex-POW

Don helped start the Oregon Trail Chapter with Don Cohen. Mr. Barton served in the Army and was captured by the Chinese Army. He was a POW for 28 months, and I heard his story was powerful, so I went into the classroom he was assigned to back in 1997 with several other Ex-POWs. He was speaking when I entered, and the riveting look on the students' faces while he was speaking was priceless. You could have heard a pin drop.

I was given permission from Don's wife Daisy to use his own personal account of his experience in Korea.

On February 26, 1951, I sailed from San Francisco aboard the General Nelson M. Walker, headed for Korea. As the ship pulled away, a band standing on the pier was playing, "Farewell to Thee."

After being at sea for twelve days we finally arrived at Yokohama, Japan. From there we were taken to Camp Drake, which was near Tokyo, for processing. A week later, we boarded a train bound for Sasebo, and then from there we took an overnight ferry ride to Pusan, Korea. As we docked in Pusan, on the 16th of March, a phonograph at the dock was playing, "If I knew you were coming, I would have baked a cake."

I would be assigned as a medic to I Company, 23rd Infantry Regiment, 2nd Infantry Division. Most of my time in Korea was spent working out of the 3rd Battalion aid station. Our main area of responsibility was from Wonju to Inje, including the Soyang River.

On the 16th of May, the Chinese Communist Forces (CCF) started their spring offensive. The Tenth Corps called it the Battle of the Soyang River. Later it would be known as the "May Massacre." Six Chinese divisions attacked along a twenty-five mile front, overwhelming us. As Item Company withdrew, I was ordered to stay behind and help evacuate the wounded.

The Chinese had set up a roadblock cutting off the Hongchon-Inje Highway, just north of the village of Hangye. Vehicles from both the 2nd and 3rd Battalions were trapped, and the wounded had to be evacuated overland from the valley floor. This had to be done by going up a hill and through the position held by Item Company.

When word came down for the 3rd BN to withdraw, Item Company was the last to receive the orders. We medics watched as the company withdrew and waited for the arrival of the wounded. After what seemed like an eternity, but in reality was probably only thirty minutes, they finally arrived. Drivers of the vehicles that were trapped behind the roadblock quickly dismounted and started destroying their vehicles by placing white phosphorus grenades on the engines; these burned through the blocks. Four aircraft dropping napalm were called in to finish the job.

With four men to a litter, we carried the wounded along a ridge line the 3rd BN rifle companies had taken less than an hour earlier. There was a parallel ridge, about three-hundred yards south of our ridge. We hadn't traveled very far when we noticed a group of men, wearing OD rain gear, moving toward us on the parallel ridge. A short distance ahead, both ridges merged into a single trail. As we neared this point, these men began to yell as us. Thinking they were Americans, and happy to see friendly forces, we yelled back. Shortly afterwards, they opened fire up on us with burp guns, almost cutting one of our wounded soldiers in half. For the next two hours, we engaged in a firefight. However, being outnumbered, cut-off, out of ammo, and badly shot up, our group of approximately fifty-six men surrendered. On May 18, 1951—I became a Prisoner of War.

A week later on the 25th, around 3:00 AM, as our group of about three-hundred POWs marched north in two columns on either side of the road, an artillery shell exploded in the middle of the columns killing or wounding several POWs, along with several Chinese guards. A piece of shrapnel hit me in the right shoulder knocking me to the ground. Another POW cried out, "Help, help. Someone give me a tourniquet; my leg is off." Men were yelling, screaming, and crying out in pain. In the pitch black darkness, it was utter chaos.

Fearing more explosions, my main concern was to get the hell away from there as fast as I could. I yelled at a buddy, who was walking behind me, and told him what I was planning to do and for him to follow me. So, we took off running leaving the sounds of the wounded behind. In the process I also left men from Item Company behind; I never saw them again until the end of the war. My buddy and I were found the next morning by a Chinese artillery officer, who spoke broken English. He told us to walk north and we would not be killed. That night, around dark, we were recaptured by the Chinese infantry.

A piece of shrapnel from my right shoulder caused a steady stream of blood to run down my body and fill up my combat boot. A Chinese medic bandaged my wound with the shrapnel still sticking up through the top of my shoulder bone.

For the next few days, we continued walking north and collected small groups of POWs as we went, until we arrived at a POW collecting station—called the Pines. While here, another Chinese medic pulled the piece of shrapnel from my shoulder with a pair of pliers; shattering and splintering a lot of bone in the process. We were here only a few days and our numbers swelled to between two-hundred fifty and three-hundred men.

One morning, the Chinese singled out a small group of ten-to-twelve wounded men, placing the most serious ones on an ox-cart with the others walking behind. In this fashion, we moved from one primitive hospital to another—I was in this group. During this time, we were turned over to the North Korean Army. We traveled through Wonson—on the east coast—west to Yong Dock, finally reaching the NKPA's 39th Field Hospital in Pyongyang.

Within days of arriving, blow flies had worked their way underneath my bandages and maggots had begun to eat the infection. I was taken to surgery where two female North Korean doctors, under the supervision of Russian or Czech civilian doctors, operated on me—without the use of anesthetic. They removed shrapnel, and bone fragments, during two surgeries. For the next three months I carried my right arm between the second and third buttons of my fatigue jacket. Finally, the drainage stopped and the wound healed.

During this time frame, the group of wounded men who left the Pines with me died one-by-one. Those who became too weak to travel were left behind, in filthy hospital rooms, to die later. We were thrown out of the 39th Field Hospital by a North Korean general, after a large U.S. bombing raid almost leveled the city of Pyongyang on August 20, 1951. We then had to walk twenty miles to another prison at Kang Dong, which had been built by the Japanese during their occupation of Korea. It was surrounded by barbed wire, and had guard shacks at fifty-to-seventy feet intervals. Here I was thrown in with a room full of ROK prisoners. I protested, and that night one of them stole my shoes—I was now barefooted.

On the 10th of September, we received word that we would soon be moving; some of the ROK prisoners had already been sent north. Around noon on the fifteenth, a group of one-hundred ten GI's, British, and Turk POWs moved out on foot, on a march that lasted thirty days—and covered two-hundred and twenty miles. Being without shoes, I reminded a North Korean officer that he had promised to find me a pair of shoes for the march. He furnished me with a pair of thongs that had a coarse rope, which formed the upper part of the shoe. The rope rubbed against the side of my feet as I walked, grinding into my feet like sandpaper.

The first day out we marched most of the night—over rocky mountain trails—to avoid being spotted by U.S. Planes. My feet had become a bloody, blistered mess. Finally, I just kicked off the thongs and continued barefooted. I thought to myself, "What a way to start a long march."

The next morning, I went to the officer and showed him my feet. He told me not to worry that he would get me a good pair of shoes. Shortly afterwards, they carried a dead GI out of a room, and I noticed that he too was barefooted. A short time later, the officer brought me a pair of high-top tennis shoes.

Two dozen or more Americans died on the march due to their wounds, dysentery, malnutrition, and just plain fatigue. Some even predicted their own deaths; others got a death stare, which everyone recognized. When one got the stare, he would be dead by morning.

Approximately two weeks into the march we stopped at another Japanese built prison camp, which the Koreans called "Camp DeSoto." It had log walls and enclosed buildings that resembled an old American fort. During our week stay there, seven more

GI's died. We placed their bodies in rice sacks and buried them on a hill outside the compound.

Leaving Camp DeSoto, we marched for another seven days, reaching the Suiho Dam on the Yalu River. Once again, a small group of sick and wounded prisoners, including myself, were separated from the main group. We were told we would travel by boat to a hospital at POW Camp #3, which was run by the Chinese. It was here that the North Korean Army turned us back over to the Chinese; we waited for three days for the boat to arrive. On our last day there, a North Korean guard murdered a British prisoner. Finally, the boat arrived, and we took a one-day boat ride to Camp #3. Here we stayed for nearly two years—it was October 15, 1951, when we arrived.

In late November we were released from the hospital and joined the company, which was housed in an old schoolhouse, in a Korean village a few miles from the hospital.

In December 1951, an agreement was reached with the Communists at Panmunjom to exchange a list of the POWs held by each side. The list of Americans being held was rushed to the U.S. where each name, and hometown, was announced on the radio. This is how many mothers, fathers, wives, sisters, and brothers found out for the first time their loved ones were alive. Some of those captured early in the war were listed as MIA (missing-in-action) for as long as eighteen months before their families learned they were alive.

In the spring of 1952, the companies at Camp #3 were reorganized and moved. Black soldiers, Brits and Turks, and all ranks above corporal were sent to other camps. Second Company moved around an inlet, in the Yalu River, to a different location about four road miles away. At the new location we were joined by a company of POWs known as "Tiger Survivors," so named because a North Korean officer in charge executed several of their group, and ordered his guards to shoot stragglers on their march north. This group of soldiers from the 24th Infantry Division, and some civilians, were captured in July of 1950.

There were originally seven-hundred fifty-eight in the group, but five-hundred of them died—or were murdered—during the winter of 1950-51. The name of each POW who died was put on a list made by an eighteen year prisoner by the name of Wayne "Johnnie" Johnson. When the war ended, he smuggled the list out in a hollowed out toothpaste tube.

In June of 1952, the power generating turbines at Suiho Dam were bombed and knocked out of service—permanently. However, this eliminated what little lighting that was available in the barrack we occupied. From then on, until the end of the war, our only light at night was in the form of a small bowl of oil and a cotton wick placed in only one room of the house. When lit, it threw off a low flickering light that was inadequate for reading, but bright enough to find your way in and out of the room.

Life had become monotonous in the camp. Our hopes of being released skyrocketed in June of 1951, when negotiations with the Chinese began in Kaesong; in fact our Chinese guards told us the war was over. However, more than a year later, it appeared the negotiations would drag on indefinitely. We followed the progress of the negotiations in Communist publications like the "New York Daily Worker."

Winters were especially hard. Everything froze with the temperatures dipping to thirty and forty degrees below zero. Ice on the river was several feet thick, and there was little heat in the rooms of houses we occupied. The heat came from an evening fire built under the "kang" (cooking pot) in the kitchen, which was always at one end of the house. The heat traveled from the kitchen through a flue under the floor to a chimney at the opposite end; thereby heating the floor as it passed through. Sleeping on mats, on the floor, which was the custom, you were either roasting hot or by early morning—freezing cold.

On and off, for nearly two years, POWs were exposed to Chinese "brainwashing" or political indoctrination. The first phase of the indoctrination was the study of life in the Soviet Union. There was a daily lecture by a Chinese person, who we were instructed to address as "instructor so-and-so." After the study of the Soviet lifestyle, we studied the American economy—this was nothing more than criticism of the U.S. Government. Every bit of corruption, in the history of the American political system, was exaggerated by the Chinese instructor. After a time, some GI's began to muster up the courage to argue with the instructors, and to voice opposing opinions the Chinese did not want to hear. These men were labeled "reactionaries" and soon began to disappear from the company—sometimes in the middle of the night.

The Chinese set up a hard labor camp, where those who disagreed with them were sent. Others were court-martialed and given prison sentences. One GI received two years for conducting religious services that the Chinese viewed as sabotage. Another one received a one year sentence for refusing to attend a Chinese sponsored sporting event. However, a few GI's began to cooperate with the Chinese; these men were given separate rooms instead of sleeping five-or-six to a small room. They ate better, were given Chinese made cigarettes, and given positions of authority within the company.

Near the end of the war these men formed a voluntary study group, even after the Chinese had given up on converting the vast majority. This group continued to meet daily to study communism. Towards the end of the war, it became known throughout the camp that this small group of men would refuse repatriation when the war ended. When the war did end, twenty-three Americans refused repatriation, although twenty-one actually stayed with the Chinese; four were in Second Company. They had been our friends; now they were shunned.

In early June of 1953, several men were transferred to Second Company from the hard labor camp that was located up the river. The Chinese were breaking it up and shutting it down. One day as I was walking down the main street—of the company—I came face-to-face with Willard Ward. Willard was an Item Company soldier who was standing next to me—on the hill—when we were captured twenty-eight months earlier.

As we looked at each other, he said, "You're dead." I told him my story of escaping during the confusion when the group was shelled that night some two years earlier. He then explained those who I had known in Item Company believed I had been killed when the artillery shell exploded. He went on to say the column regrouped and moved north to POW Camp #1, taking only a couple of months to reach it. It had taken me five months to reach Camp #3, which was only twenty road miles from Camp #1. We became close friends as the end of the war neared.

The exchange of sick and wounded POWs, from each side, took place in April of 1953. Now rumors were beginning to run wild that the rest of us would be liberated. Everyone thought the war would be over any day.

The Chinese anticipated there would be retribution against the GI's who played ball with them for special treatment. That is why—I believe—when the war ended, a small number of prisoners from each camp, including myself, were singled out, accused, and tried for war crimes; we were all given prison sentences. There were five permanent camps—for American Prisoners of War—with as many as seven companies per camp. They were located along a fifty mile stretch of the Yalu River. This group of twenty or more prisoners convicted at trials, were a reminder to other prisoners to not start any trouble; or receive the same punishment as the progressives.

My trial took place the day the announcement was made that the war was over. Later that day my sentence of one-year of hard labor was read over the camp's public address system.

Those convicted of various crimes were of course segregated from the prisoners. They were moved, under heavy guard, to a central location in a camp that previously housed ROK soldiers; they had long since been moved south for repatriation. The senior American officer, with our small group, was a Lt. Colonel who commanded a combat engineering battalion prior to his capture—in December of 1950 at Kunu-ri. He told us to do, or say, whatever the Chinese demanded that would help our case for release.

Some weeks later, after appropriate confessions and apologies were made to the Chinese officials that were holding us; we were taken to the rail head at Antung, North Korea, and put aboard a train bound for Kaesong—which was located on the north side of the demilitarized zone (DMZ). Arriving at Kaesong, the group was put on display at a ceremony that had been arranged by the Chinese for the benefit of their foreign press. Reporters and photographers from all the Soviet Bloc countries were present to document the occasion. The Chinese said we were the worst war criminals from all the Americans they had captured. However, in keeping with their policy of lenient treatment, and after our confessions, they would pardon our crimes and return us to our home country.

When the U.S. and UN military brass at Panmunjom were informed the Chinese would be holding the twenty Americans in our group as war criminals, a senior American official threatened to immediately stop the prisoner exchange. He also said that thousands of Communist prisoners would be held indefinitely until they released, and repatriated, all American prisoners— they released us immediately.

Afterwards we were transported to a tent city where all POWs waiting release were assembled. We again waited for several days before being put on trucks and driven across the four kilometer wide DMZ, to our release point in Panmunjom.

Following our release, on September 3, 1953, at the exchange point in the Joint Security Area, we POWs were taken to Freedom Village. Here we each received a shower, light meal, a new uniform, and a medical evaluation. Then we were flown, by helicopter, to Inchon.

The USNS General A.W. Brewster lay at anchor in the Inchon Harbor. That evening we would board her for our trip home, but first, there was the matter of the Army's inquisition—officially called a counter intelligence debriefing.

Once the Brewster was underway, the Army's CIC officers lost no time in calling each POW into a small room to debrief them. A forty page counter intelligence questionnaire, designed by G-2 experts to determine whether or not a soldier had succumbed to Communist indoctrination, was completed and all answers recorded. Then there were another thirty-seven pages of questions that covered the enemy's military capabilities, and infra-structure. The answers given by the POWs during this questioning, were then classified as SECRET SECURITY INFORMATION.

When the debriefings were over, the Army had a large file on every POW. A typical file was as thick as an unabridged dictionary, and some were two feet thick. My own dossier, declassified and released to me in April of 1994, runs two-hundred and seventy-seven pages.

We knew there would be investigations into the conduct of individual POWs who were guilty of making propaganda speeches, and other acts of collaboration with the Chinese. However, no American POWs in the history of our country has ever undergone the level of interrogation as those released at Panmunjom in August and September of 1953.

Returning home from Korea, in November of 1953 I re-enlisted in the Army; with duty at the Presidio in San Francisco, California. That same month, in a ceremony in Tahlequah, Oklahoma, I married Daisy Battenfield. My best man—Willard Ward.

In January of 1957, I retired from military service at Letterman Army Hospital, for reasons of physical disability—a shoulder that Army doctors couldn't fix.

I recently spoke with Don's wife Daisy, and she told me.

"Don was badly wounded with shrapnel and could not use his right arm. They were forced to walk for thirty days. His boot was filled with his blood. He was a medic and was able to take care of himself. It took five guys to hold him down as they took the shrapnel out of his wounds with no antiseptic. He was 19 years old.

"My husband was the driving force behind getting the Korean War Memorial built in Wilsonville. Without him, it never would have been built. He wrote many, many letters, phones calls. He also took two trips to South Korea to ask for donations. It took him six years. He was the kind of guy who put his all into causes. He gave it his all.

"Right before Don passed, he spent 59 days in the hospital and only one veteran from the KWVA came to visit him, Don Cohen. He was really hurt about that."

Don Barton passed away at the age of 78 in May of 2010.

FRED LIDDELL   Army
                                Ex-POW

Fred came to our Living History Days at Milwaukie High School with the KWVA. He was a great guy and always had a smile and infectious laugh, but I had lost track of him because he had moved to Alabama in 2002. However, thanks to Daisy Barton, I reconnected with Fred when she informed me that he was living with his son in Tacoma, Washington.

I called him on August 13, 2021, and after catching up, I started by asking only a couple of questions, and then he got on a roll. Fred has a great memory, with names and dates. He is something else.

"Where and when were you born?" I asked

"I was born in Seattle on October 20, 1928."

"Tell me about your father and mother."

"Well, my father, Fred, served in France in the Canadian Army. His older brother was in the same unit. My mom was a stay-at-home mom, her name was Clara.

"I flunked every class as a freshman in high school, so I dropped out and got a job making fifty cents an hour. That was good money back then. There were men raising a family on that pay. Why go to school if I could make good money? My parents sent me to a military academy in Portland up on Rocky Butte. At the end of my junior year, my mom got me and brought me home because she needed help with my father who had a debilitating cerebral hemorrhage.

"After six months he started to improve, so I joined the Army in January of '47. I was stationed in Japan assigned to the Signal Corps, heavy construction. I was sent back home and decided to reenlist as there was no work to be found. Back at Fort Lewis, I was moved to the 2nd Division repair crew. I was now a Staff Sergeant and had a three-man crew.

"I needed a driver and the PFC I wanted was already on a ship at Okinawa getting ready to ship home. I picked him. I got hepatitis with jaundice and spent about two months recovering. After that, I was reassigned as a squad leader. I had one more year to go. We started out with 210 men and were down to 85.

"We were ordered to get up a hill when a Dutch soldier walking down told us, 'There's a lot of Chinese over this hill.' Soon after we made it up, all hell broke loose. It was dark, I grabbed a sniper rifle, but it kept jamming. I grabbed a carbine rifle and used that until running out of ammo. Then I helped reload my BAR man with magazines.

"The worst was being hit by artillery rockets by the Marines. There was a wounded soldier on a stretcher, we gave him a pistol and several hand grenades and left him. The Chinese were firing everywhere. We had to get the hell out of there running towards the Marines.

"We then joined another group and followed them. They accidentally took us back to where we were. Then we walked into an area with about 200 American soldiers, and we asked who they were with. One yells, "Get the hell out of here, we are POWs.

"We go inside a hut which was filled with the wounded. I open a back flap and tell my buddy, Henry, 'Let's get out of here, the clouds are covering the moon.' But just then Chinese soldiers came into the tent and caught us. One of the guards wanted my gold wedding band. I got married right before leaving, but he didn't get it.

"We were moved to an open field with machine guns in every corner aimed at us. After a while, they then ordered us to start walking. We walked all day until dark for ten days in a row on trails with very little food and water. Dysentery went through us fast.

"If you couldn't keep up during the march, the Chinese bayoneted or shot you. We could hear the screams and shots from behind us. When you had to relieve yourself, we would run up to the front of the line, go, and then fall back into place.

"The Chinese would always ask us questions like, 'Why did you start this war?' We learned right away to keep your mouth shut. The last two days, Obie Wickersham and I took turns carrying a buddy, Pat J. Arthur, on our backs. We were marched 500 miles to a prison camp in Suan, southeast of Pyongyang. It was a mining camp. We started this forced march on May 18 and finished on July 3.

"We asked if we could clean up Pat, they said no and ordered us to take him to the hospital. We soon learned it was not a hospital, but a death camp. We wanted so badly to save him but buried him on July 8. We buried our dead daily on a hill.

"About thirty years after, the North Koreans returned a bunch of remains and a lab in Hawaii identified most of his bones. We buried him at Arlington National Cemetery."

"Wow, that must have been emotional."

"Yes, it was very emotional."

"What happened next?" I asked.

"We were moved to a collecting place to send us further north. One guy tried to escape. They caught him, tied his arms behind his back until his elbows were touching, and hung him up over a wall overnight. He survived and had scars on his arms. Now we walked only at night about ten to twelve miles a day. We were put in small huts in a small village. A couple of days later we were cluster bombed by our own Air Force.

"Every day we had re-education classes, nothing but propaganda. Once they were lecturing us on how racist America was. One of my friends, a fellow POW, was a black guy, Turner Johnson. He yelled out, 'That's all not true. Where I live, I can go into stores, restaurants, and bars.' The Chinese were so flustered, they didn't know what to do as all they knew was what was on the paper given to them by the Communist party.

"In February of '51, I was interrogated. It was so cold, it was hell. During the interrogation, it was amazing how much the Chinese knew about you. If you didn't share enough information, you were sent away never to be seen again. They kept asking me what kind of weapons training I had. I kept answering that I was in construction, no weapons.

"I wasn't telling them what they wanted to hear, so they made me stand in a corner all day and my feet were freezing cold. The last thing they said to me was, 'I hope you remember your story?' I yelled, 'It's not a story, it's the truth.' When I got back with my squad. A buddy warmed my feet up by sticking them under his armpits.

"While in camp, I finally received the first letter from my wife. We had a daughter. She found out she was pregnant after I was shipped out. I got to write her back. We wrote each other many times. I have them all saved in a box. My wife, Donna, died of cancer in 1995 and is buried at Willamette National Cemetery waiting for me." Fred became emotional telling me this.

After a short silence, he continued.

"One day the Chinese decided to have an Olympics and required us to enter the games holding the Chinese Flag. We said, 'No thank you.' We were told, 'Then you will not get dinner.' The next day they said, 'OK, you don't have to carry our flag in, but you must carry a red banner.' Again, we said, 'No, thank you.' And they said the same thing, 'Then you will not get dinner.'

"On the day of the Olympics, they told us we didn't have to carry the banner but just march in together. As we march into the open field, one of us starts singing, 'God Bless America'. Soon we all were singing at the top of our lungs.

"As soon as we were done another one of our guys starts chanting loudly, 'Mao Tse Tung will you let us live? Or will you shoot us dead?' He says it two times and then we all march out of the area. The Chinese were furious. But, at that point, we did not give a damn anymore.

"They had these cages made from wooden slats like a picket fence that were very small. They would force a POW in there as punishment. They were so small you had to sit with your legs straight. I knew of two POWs who were put in there.

"I never witnessed any horrible atrocities, just mistreatment. I am always asked about atrocities, and they never wanted to talk about anything else. I didn't witness any myself. But the Chinese were as bad to themselves as us. Once a Chinese guard was caught having sex with a prostitute. He was executed and she was sent to a re-education camp.

"One day, I was given a letter from my wife. She had taped a religious medal to a letter to me. When I opened the letter, the medal was gone. I could see the imprint of the medal on the letter. I went to the Chinese office building and protested the theft. Bad idea. I was punished by being made to stand against a wall with my arms out holding my arms up.

"A little later, I hear all this yelling, and another POW was thrown through a door down the hall. It was Clarence- a U.S. soldier of Chinese descent. Clarence was beaten and hurting pretty bad.

"They put him right next to me. Now I've got somebody where I can put my arm down on his head. Finally, the guard goes to sleep, and I ask Clarence what they got all mad about. He says, 'I told them the only smart thing my grandma ever did was get the hell out of China.' They were trying to recruit him to join their army, but he wouldn't do it.

"We had become so angry and bold; we took rocks the size of baseballs and covered them with snow. They became hard as ice. We waited until a bunch of Chinese soldiers were marching on the other side of a building and a row of huts. and we threw them over the building and the huts." Fred laughed afterward.

I quickly asked, "Didn't you get in trouble?"

"No, they investigated, but we got away with it."

"On August 8, 1952, we were moved again. We were first loaded on cattle cars standing, packed like sardines. It was pouring down rain and a bridge was washed out. A Chinese guard tried to cross the Yalu River but was washed down river. So, we walked up the banks of the river until we came upon a scaffolding bridge where we all crossed hand over hand."

I decided to ask him, "Can you tell me about your liberation?"

"It started out with just a few at a time, being called out to go to what we called 'freedom'. I was with the last bunch on the last day. They took us to a temple, and they wanted to serve us a steak dinner for our last meal. We responded, 'Go to Hell.'

"The next morning, we were loaded on a truck and after riding in the back for a while, I lifted up the back flap because I was sitting in the rear. I saw a United States Marine. Then when we came to a stop, the Chinese interpreter told us to remain seated on the truck. A Marine came up to the truck and shoved the interpreter out of the way and said, 'They are in our hands now, you guys can get out now.

"Then we walk up to a building, and General Ridgway is at the front door greeting every one of us. It was something I'll never forget."

I then asked, "Tell me about your first reunion with your wife, parents, and seeing your daughter for the first time." Fred gets really emotional, and although I can't see him, I hear him sniffle over the phone and assume he must have some tears.

"She was the most beautiful thing I've ever seen in my life," his voice cracks. Then after a short pause, "My wife never looked better, and my parents were there also. It was very emotional."

Fred had a difficult time upon his return to America. During the entire time of his captivity, he was only allowed to claim three months' pay. Fred told me, "I wrote many letters for years to Congressmen and heard nothing."

According to Fred, all American troops in Korea received combat pay yet for one group, the Korean War POW-MIAs, the supplemental compensation was capped at three months, regardless of their entire time in captivity. Fred said to me, "I was told that it was too late. And to this day, I've never received anything."

I told Fred just how sorry I was to hear that. Then his voice changed to a different, less serious tone, and he continued by saying, "So I have a funny story for you.

"We could never get clean. But once, we were taken to a small lake and ordered to strip naked and clean up in the lake. There were a bunch of Chinese photographers taking pictures. So, we grabbed our privates and started waving them at the photographers until they got frustrated and walked away," Fred laughs.

"This is another amazing story. When one of my buddies, Pops, died, I put one of his dog tags in his mouth and we buried him. I kept the other, but a Chinese guard took it away. Decades later, I was visiting the DNA lab in Hawaii and Pops' dog tag was on display. I found that out when his remains were sent to Hawaii, his dog tag was still in his mouth, in the skull remains."

I said, "That's incredible," and continued with, "after you returned how did you deal with the memories?"

"Going to all of the POW reunions was very helpful because we could talk to each other. I really believed and still do that you have to talk it out, get it out. My first therapist was Dr. Vern Summers of the VA and he helped me greatly.

"Two of our reunions were held in Portland. At one of them, we were all seated to eat dinner when a friend came to our table to tell me that my friend Rubin "Teddy" Tibor had a heart attack and was at a local hospital. I went to the hospital, and he was still sitting in the waiting area of the ER. I let the front desk know this was unacceptable. Have you ever heard of Medal of Honor recipient Rubin Tibor, Ken?"

I answered, "No, I haven't."

"He was a Hungarian Jew who survived the Holocaust, and Mauthausen concentration camp. He came to America and joined the Army, was in the First Cav, and was captured. He was captured because the white southern sergeant volunteered Rubin for the most dangerous patrols and missions in hopes of getting him killed. On one assignment Rubin was attacked and fought until captured.

"Almost every evening, Rubin would sneak out to steal food. He shared the food with everyone. He also took care of POWs and even carried them to the latrines. He was very religious and helping his fellow men was the most important thing to him. Rubin should have received the Medal of Honor but never did because he was a Jew. But in 1993 they found Rubin had been discriminated against because of his religion, and then in 2005, he received the Medal of Honor from Bush.

"Bigotry makes me so mad. I became friends with several black American POWs, and they were all damn good men. Back in the states, we were being processed out when another white sergeant told a friend of mine next to me, who happened to be black, that they couldn't find any paperwork on him, and it would take a few days to find them.

"The sergeant thought it was funny. I stood up and told him to shut up and said, 'This guy right here has spent more time as a POW than you have in the Army.' We were both discharged on October 28, 1953. Then on the 5th of November, I was hired by Pacific Northwest Bell, as a cable splicer."

Fred suddenly stopped talking and asked, "Ken, was your father's name Gordon?"

Surprised, I said, "Yes, and he was a cable splicer for Pacific Northwest Bell in Portland too."

I could hear the pride in Fred's voice as he said, "I'll be damned, I worked with him until I was transferred to sales."

Fred then asked me when *Remembrance: Volume II* would be available and if I had thought about doing an audiobook. As Fred became older, he lost most of his sight, so he wanted a spoken version of the book.

I told him, "Yes, I am planning on one, however, I'm not in a financial position to make that happen now."

Fred shot right back, "How much does it cost?"

I replied, "About $1500."

He immediately responded, "I'll cover it." I was speechless.

Fred Liddell is still living at the age of 93.

DON COHEN   Army
                             Bronze Star

Don always spoke his mind and never minced his words. When the KWVA Oregon Chapter wanted to build a Korean War Memorial in a park in Wilsonville, Oregon, a suburb of Portland, they needed to raise about $500,000 dollars. On a fundraising trip, Don flew to South Korea for a meeting with some impressive CEOs of large South Korean Corporations including Hyundai, as well as the President of South Korea.

Don was asked to make the presentations and to ask for donations. In the packed board room, Don approached the podium and spoke with a raised voice and stated, "Well, none of you would be here today if it wasn't for me and all my buddies." He then walked back to his chair and sat down. They all donated a combined $400,000 dollars.

Years ago, Don Cohen invited me to his PTSD Korean War veterans support group. He felt that attending a session would help me understand how PTSD affected their lives. He told me, "If it was not for this group, I would have ended my life years before. Do not judge or be angry with your father because everyone in his group understands what your father was living with."

There were about 10 Korean War veterans and a psychiatrist, and all agreed to let me attend a session. After I was introduced to all, Don Cohen again spoke to me, "You need to know Ken, that when we talked to the Milwaukie High students, we only opened up this much." He then held up his hand with the thumb and index finger almost touching each other. I couldn't see any gap between his thumb and finger.

Then he said, "And to you, we will only open up a little bit more," again holding up his hand with his thumb and finger almost touching again. "But you probably know more about us than our spouses and children know. We only open up around each other. You will probably never hear any horrible details from us."

Every veteran then told me how much the support group meant to them. Some of them got pretty emotional. It was very powerful and therapeutic, and I'm still very grateful for that opportunity.

In March of 2018, I called Don in to ask him a few questions so I could include him in this book. I knew questions about his experiences in Korea were off limits, but I was shocked at what happened next.

For as long as I've known Don, he has never shared anything about his experiences during the Korean War and has numerous times declined to be interviewed for this book, but I wanted him remembered, so I asked again.

Well, to my complete shock, over the phone Don tells me, "Ken, my two best friends were killed right next to me. We were pinned down by heavy machine gun fire and artillery shells exploding everywhere. One of the shells hits to the right of us and the explosion tears my friend's body apart. Immediately after that, my friend to the left is shot in the head.

"We were ordered to grab canteens from the dead and retreat. We were being overrun. My buddy, Don Barton, was on the other side of the hill from me when he was captured.

I was stunned and didn't know what to say. Don then said, "That's enough." And that is all he ever shared with me.

Don Cohen passed away at the age of 87 in August of 2020.

BOB GIFFORD   Army

I heard Bob speak for just a few minutes in a classroom because, as was always the case, I had to suddenly leave because someone was looking for me to ask a question. I called it 'putting out fires', so I had to leave his classroom presentation as he was speaking.

I did hear him say, "It was so cold, freezing cold, and on top of that the wind made it worse. All of a sudden, we hear the sound of bugles blowing and cymbals clanging. Then across a huge field frozen with ice and snow, thousands of little dots start moving towards us getting bigger and bigger. It was thousands of Chinese soldiers running towards us.

"We all opened up with machine gun fire. The first wave of Chinese soldiers had no weapons, coats, or shoes, the next wave had weapons, and the third wave had no weapons. The soldiers in the third wave would grab dead soldiers' rifles and continue to charge us.

"The dead and wounded covered the entire frozen field and the Chinese would just run over their bodies. When we finally repulsed the attack, dead and wounded Chinese soldiers were stacked on top of each other three and four high."

Bob stopped talking and started to get choked up. The students were glued to him. Just then the classroom door opened, and a student asked if I could solve an issue. I apologized and left the classroom.

Bob was a wonderful, kind gentleman and his lovely wife Mary Gifford is still heavily involved with the KWVA Oregon Chapter.

Bob Gifford passed away at the age of 82 in December of 2012.

* ★ *

HENRY BENDINELLI
Army Air Corps
Air Force WWII
Korean War

Henry was a real character, a great guy who was always extremely positive and enthusiastic. First, Henry was very proud of his Italian heritage, and he also loved to ski, something he did for over seventy years. We became friends the first time he attended our Living History Days. He took me to lunch soon after that day to personally thank me, and of course it was an Italian restaurant.

He loved talking to high school students about his military experiences. Henry was an Aerial Navigator in the U.S. Army Air Corps, flying B-29s on bombing missions over Japan towards the end of WWII.

He always told the students, "I was under fire 72 times during two wars." And he also always said, "But being part of the flying missions to West Berlin during the famous Marshall plan and Berlin Airlift were my proudest moments of my service."

When the Korean War broke out, Henry was called back and again served as a Navigator, flying many missions in Korea. During another lunch date, I told him, "You have never told me about your experiences during the Korean War."

Without pausing, Henry took out a piece of paper and a pen from his briefcase and started drawing. When finished, he stated, "This is the coastline and mountain ranges in North Korea." He joked that he was not a good drawer. About halfway up a mountain in the drawing, he drew several large squares.

"These were steel walls that would open, and anti-aircraft guns would roll out, fire as many rounds as possible, and then quickly roll back into the mountain with the steel walls closing behind them. We bombed the side of those mountains for days with zero impact to the steel walls and everything inside.

"We came up with a plan. A single bomber flew in north of the target and at very low elevation, zigzagging to avoid being detected. While it came in from behind the mountain range, the rest of us came in from the front. We timed it so when the wall opened and the guns rolled out, the bomber from behind flew over and dropped their bombs."

He laughed and said, "That solved our problem."

I learned later that Henry loved to ski in Japan during the war. Over the years, I have learned from many veterans that military personnel when in Japan on R&R (Rest and Relaxation) during the Korean War called it I&I (Intercourse and Intoxication) or A&A (Ass and Alcohol). Henry, however, had nothing to do with this, for whenever he took his R&R in Japan, he could be found on the slopes of a mountain skiing to relieve the stress of war.

Henry was very proud of being an avid skier, even skiing still at 90 years old. He was a member of the Mt. Hood Ski Patrol for decades. Henry's nickname was 'Mr. Timberline' because he had been skiing Oregon's Mount Hood longer than its landmark Timberline Lodge had stood.

Henry Bendinelli passed away at the age of 91 in October of 2015.

EUGENE EVERS   Air Force
                                EX-POW

"I was put in a hole in the ground for seven months, solitary confinement. But I survived, and it's something I really don't like talking about."

This was the only thing Gene would say when he stood up in front of the students in a Milwaukie High School classroom with other Ex-POWs in 1998. It wasn't until 2018 when I was able to finally get Gene to eventually open up and share his story with me.

Gene was very proud of his family's history. They moved from San Francisco, California to Forest Grove, Oregon in 1860, and it was in 1880 when they built their farmhouse using just three trees. "I was born in that home and was in the middle of eleven boys and four girls. Only our last sibling was born in a hospital."

The house is still standing and is now designated as a Century Farm. The very same house was only a few hundred yards from the old farmhouse where my interview with Gene took place.

"We had to milk the cows and do our chores every morning at five and then ride our bikes the four and a half miles to school, then back home to do more chores. At fourteen years of age, I got to drive our Model A Ford occasionally to school.

"After graduating high school in '49, I enrolled at OSU (Oregon State University) to major in Agriculture and only attended for one term when my money ran out. I was disappointed because I knew more than the professors.

"My older brother, Ed, an Army Medic with the Oregon National Guard was sent to Korea. He wrote home and said, 'Gene, we need help over here.' So, I decided to join the Air Force. After boot camp, I was sent to photo school in Denver. While there, a friend said to me, 'Hey let's volunteer to go to Korea to install cameras on planes.' We ended up in Tokyo, Japan working as camera inspectors at a camera factory that did contract work for the US Air Force and Navy.

"One day an RB-29 pilot (a B-29 outfitted for reconnaissance with only defensive weapons), Ted Harris, came to us and told us that the camera on his B-29 only worked on the ground and not in the air. I volunteered to go with them on an eight-hour reconnaissance flight over China and North Korea to help with the camera.

"Well, we were hit bad and shot down by a Russian MIG. I was knocked out. When I came to, everyone was gone except for two dead crewmen, and the plane was going down fast. I received no parachute training from the Air Force, but because I took some flight lessons back in Oregon and was taught how to use a parachute, the lessons saved my life. Luckily, I was in the rear of the plane and parachuted out.

"The wind carried me for miles, and I floated over a river. I tried to land in it, but the wind carried me too far. I landed face first in a muddy rice paddy. I was hit with shrapnel and had burns, but I could walk. It was July 4, 1952, and my parents received a telegram that I was KIA.

"Two days later, they received a second telegram listing me as MIA. This was very confusing for my parents. My brother Ed had just visited me as he was on his way home from front line duty with the 3rd Division in North Korea, and they all thought I had a safe job in Tokyo.

"None of our crew was ever listed as POWs. Because it was a spy plane, I was not listed as a crew member, and only the pilot, Ted Harris, knew I was on his plane.

"I left my parachute in the mud. I heard some talking getting closer to me and a banging sound. I laid down on my back to hide in deep mud and covered my body with mud. Chinese officers walked right by me as I could see one of the officers had a wooden holster and the gun would bang against it when he walked.

"For two days I stayed there and laid in the mud. I saw a cow and went to milk her, but I was discovered by some farmers who held me down till the Chinese Army came and got me.

"I spent the first seven months in a hole under eaves from a bamboo hut. It was terribly cold, I researched years later that it was at least minus twenty degrees, and I slept on rocks with one thin cotton quilt. The guards checked on me regularly as I was forced to sit and keep my eyes open.

"After the first seven months, I was moved north. They gave me my watch, identification card, and wallet back. I was put in a Russian jeep blindfolded, handcuffed, and feet tied together. I was forced to sit with my head between my legs while they sat on my back. And this broke my neck.

"I was practically frozen for the 28-hour drive on rough roads to Mukden, China- presently Shenyang. About every ten minutes, the jeep stops and a soldier fires off a round to get the OK to move forward. I wanted to die.

"We stopped and my blindfold was taken off and I see a big building. Then I passed out. When I opened my eyes, I'm inside and in a small hole, with the light on all the time. I sat on a door with a blanket. It was built by the Japanese during WWII and smelled of Ammonia. It was used for hot and cold torture. They only gave me a book. It was unbearable.

"I complained about the shrapnel in my legs. One day they took me out, walked me three to four miles to a little hut where a Chinese doctor trained in Japan removed the shrapnel. He was very nice to me, and we could communicate a little because I had learned a bit of Japanese while in Tokyo.

"Once a day, they would let me out for potty. I had diarrhea, and I was damn filthy. I had long bright red hair and a long red beard down to my belly. I never saw another POW. The Chinese thought I was a spy and always accused me of having a radio or gun hidden somewhere. One mean SOB loved to yell at me, 'You die, Spy!' They tried hard to brainwash me.

"On Easter Sunday, I saw Chinese Catholic nuns. With a Russian officer present, I was asked to confess. I yelled out, 'I want Mass!' 'What is a Mass?' one of them yells. "The Chinese are mad at me. I just want to get out of here. I was given some rice to eat though."

In 1996, Gene and the surviving RB-29 crew members were contacted by military historian Paul M. Cole. Doing research in Moscow, he found the transcripts of Gene's court martial in China, conducted by Russians. Gene was found guilty and sentenced to die by hard labor in the mines.

"I went fourteen months with no bath or shower. I received one cup of water per day, one bowl of rice gruel in the morning and one bowl of watery rice with vegetables in the evening, no meat, and the vegetables were always rotten.

"On Christmas, Chinese Christians gave me a small bird leg to eat, and I have no idea what kind of bird it was, but it was good as I was hungry. On New Year's Eve, I was given a cooked pig tit and it was good too. I learned later that Christians serving in the Chinese Army made this happen.

"After liberation in Manchuria, they started to feed me more, gave me a bath, a haircut, shaved my beard with a straight razor, a new clean uniform, and matches with a carton of Chinese cigarettes. I smoked them all just to have something to do.

"The day Stalin died; all of the guards wore blue patches on their arms. We were loaded on a train with two other POWs. Of course, we all started talking to each other, but were told, 'Shut Up.' I recognized Kenneth Bass, our tail Gunner.

"After a couple of days, we were loaded on trucks with Chinese guards. Again, one of the guards yelled, 'You must not talk.' Someone yelled back, 'You try to stop us,' with several obscenities included. He was Sam Strieby, our co-pilot. The guards just ignored him.

"I noticed on the same truck with us was Bill Koski, one of the gunners. He says to me, 'Evers, I saved your life. They were going to shoot you for being a spy, but I told them you were an ABC expert.' I replied, 'You bastard, that was on September 18, wasn't it? That was the day they beat the hell out of me.' The Chinese thought ABC was Atomic, Biological, and Chemical.

"When they unloaded us at Panmunjom, we were given ice cream as members of the Polish press took pictures of us. We were ordered to walk across a bridge at the DMZ and on the other side were American MP's wearing chrome helmets. They looked ten feet tall. An officer with a clipboard couldn't find our names and yells out, 'Who the hell are you guys? But, welcome back.'

"Ted Harris, our pilot, was held back over an hour from the rest of us because he refused to sign the statement presented to just him by the Chinese.

"Ken, I want you to know that during my fourteen months and being tortured, I almost gave up and just wanted to die. I was told constantly, 'You are never going back home.' But now I was elated at how great it felt. I thought to myself, 'I'm going to win!'

"After we were in American custody, we were given new American uniforms. I was concerned because there were Ex-POWs who did not believe I was a POW probably because I was in solitary confinement and no one else saw me. So, I went back and grabbed my POW uniform from the pile as proof. It is now on display at the National Prisoner of War Museum in Andersonville, Georgia.

"I visited our B-29 pilot Ted Harris' hospital room and told him, 'Thanks for the airplane ride, but you didn't tell me we weren't coming back!'

"Back home, my own doctor told me I was crazy and didn't believe me. I had read in Stars and Stripes that after three months of solitary confinement you become crazy. It took fifteen years to prove to VA that my neck was broken.

"In the late 70s, I realized I needed help bad and got counseling. I want Linda Gilliams of the VA acknowledged as she saved my life."

Gene's daughter Lynn said, "Dad would scream at night, we had to be careful all the time, no noise, no fireworks."

Gene said, "My first wife thought I was crazy."

"How did you get through it," I asked.

"I prayed all the time, I learned to say the rosary with my hands behind my back. I remembered stories of hard times during the depression and Mom feeding hobos.

"Back in Oregon at the Oregon State Fair while my father had his prized Holsteins in the show ring, they announced over the loudspeaker, 'Bert, Gene Evers has returned!' Then he announced that I had been released as a POW. The cows were spooked as the applause and cheers were deafening.

"I lost over 80 pounds during captivity, but while in a Hospital in Seattle, I gained it all back." Gene laughed. "I have eight children, six girls and two boys whom I'm all very proud of."

The interview ended and Gene gave me a bottle of his homemade dandelion wine. "I learned how to make this as a ten-year-old and still make it."

As we ended our talk, I thought to myself how beautiful his farm was and that I could have sat there for hours watching the hundreds of different birds, especially Hummingbirds eating at his many bird feeders. It was non-stop.

Eugene Evers is still living at 90 and still drinking his wonderful dandelion wine.

* ★ *

JIM MARTINEZ   Marines

Jim attended many of our events for over 20 years. What is amazing about his family that needs to be remembered is all eight Martinez brothers joined the Marine Corps - Ernie served in WWII, Bud, Jim, and Bob served in the Korean War, Leroy and Joe served during the Cold War, Dennis served during the Cuban Missile Crisis, and Louie served in the Vietnam War.

The only thing he told me was "I always told my mother I was stationed way behind the front and was safe, but it was not the truth." He did not want to share any of his personal experiences.

Jim Martinez is still living at 88.

Other KWVA members who attended our events

Chuck Lusardi, Army	Richard Johnston, Army
Bob Wickman, Navy	Bruce Wickward, Army
Carlos Manrriquez, Army	Leo Adams, Army
Richard Frazee, Navy	Rudolph Tietz, Navy
Jerry Lyons, Navy	Alan Lertzman, Army
Robert Kuenzli, Army	Hollis Hess, Navy
Ray Guimary, Army	William Lundell, Navy

Additional Korean War POWs Who Attended LHDs

George Keen, Navy

* ★ *

ADDITIONAL KOREAN WAR VETERANS

HARRY WOODRUFF

Army
All-Black 24th Infantry Regiment
Vietnam
Two Bronze Stars

I met Harry at the Memorial Service for Tuskegee Airman Ed Drummond Jr. in Tacoma, Washington in August of 2014. After learning that he was a veteran of the Korean War, I got his contact information and invited him to Oregon for our annual LHDs in November.

Harry served in the Army's 25th Division and in one of the three black infantry regiments of the 24th Infantry, the largest black unit to serve in Korea. Because of this I told him that he deserved to be recognized and honored.

Harry told me upfront, "I have never talked about my experiences to anyone, not even my wife. And I'm not going to start now."

I responded, "That's perfectly okay as there are other veterans who attend but don't speak either. I feel that you are an important part of our country's military history. The students will learn that you served in the last segregated Division in American Military History."

Harry accepted our invitation, attended, and had a great time, but due to some health issues, he was unable to come back until November 2018. Since that time, my wife and I have twice visited Harry and his 'Georgia Peach' wife, Greta, and although he has shared some of his experiences, he still says, "I will never talk about it, I saw too many close friends killed." He also admitted that he still has nightmares.

Harry was born in a small town in Jacksonville, Alabama, and attended segregated schools. I asked him, "Did you do any sports?"

"Yes, and I was a good high school running back, and a good baseball player. Every summer, I worked at Fort McClellan and even wanted to join the Army as a young teenager.

"There were no job opportunities for young black men anyway, so I joined the Army at 18 in 1948. We had mostly white officers, but there were some black officers as well. The base was segregated, but we trained together and there were no problems."

"When did you meet your wife?" I asked.

"After I was wounded in Korea, I spent six months in different hospitals. The last was at Fort Benning in Georgia and I met her there. We got married in December of '52, and I was sent back to Korea for a 2nd tour the next month in January of '53."

"Wow, that must have gone over well with your new wife?" I responded.

"Yeah, she was not too happy, and we had just found out she was pregnant. But that wasn't the first time we received new orders. We were sitting down to eat dinner in '64 when I received a call ordering me to Vietnam."

"When you were ordered to Vietnam, how did that go over?"

"It was really tough as my eleven-year-old daughter was really upset. In fact, when I was ordered back to Vietnam a second time in '69, my daughter had a nervous breakdown. I decided then it was time to get out."

Harry then gave me some pamphlets on the 24th Infantry Regimental Combat Team Association from past reunions. "I'm going again this summer so I need to get new documents from my doctor so I can get through security." He laughed and said, "I still have shrapnel in my body."

"Where is it?" I asked.

"From the back of my head all the way down my body to my calves. There is a big piece in my right shoulder. And I spent six months in the hospital recovering."

Harry then showed me, with pride, his medals, A Bronze Star earned in Korea plus a Purple Heart and two Bronze Stars earned in Vietnam. He was so humble and a class act. I was hoping maybe he would share a little bit more, but it was not to be.

As we ended our interview, he handed me a book, *With a Black Platoon in Combat, A Year in Korea* by the platoon's white officer, Lyle Rishell. He looked at me with a stern look and said, "I'll never talk about it, but read this and you will learn what we went through."

After reading the book, I was shocked to learn that the North Korean Army had come close to wiping our troops out in 1950. They had pushed us to the end of the Pusan Perimeter with our backs to the sea. At home, the press was saying it was going to be another Bataan.

The tenacious fighting by our American troops stopped the advance and we started to counter-attack, but then the tide changed greatly from General MacArthur's Inchon Landing, which cut off the North Koreans' supplies.

The tide had turned and the 24th was credited with the first Allied victory at Yechon. The Allies pushed the North Koreans all the way north to the border of China. Then the Chinese Army entered in great numbers and our troops, surrounded by the enemy, were almost wiped out again. It was during this Chinese attack that Harry was seriously wounded a second time.

I'm very grateful for all Harry was able to share.

Harry Woodruff is still living at 91.

---⋆ ★ ⋆---

CLARK 'DOC' HICKMAN   Marines
                               Korean War Era Drill Instructor

One meeting with Doc and it's obvious that he was an instructor of something. He stands upright and tall at 6 foot 4 inches, and he is still in good shape at 88 years of age. When I learned he was a Marine DI, a Gunny, I was not surprised at all.

I first met Doc as a toddler, although I have no memory of that. Doc, my father, and a couple other Marines started a Drum & Bugle Corps and came up with the name 'The Leathernecks' in 1957. I'm not surprised at the choice of name either.

My father and Doc became good friends, and he spent a lot of time at our house when I was young. He would eat dinner with us, and then my dad and he would go to the Leathernecks' weekly practice. After my dad retired from the Leathernecks in '65, I would not see Doc until 30 years later.

Doc surprised me at a Milwaukie High School Living History Day and has been supporting our events ever since with his super friendly wife, Linda.

About three years ago at a small gathering of veterans, Doc told me a story about my father. "Your father probably holds the record for stealing a bottle of whiskey from behind every bar we ever visited in the state of Oregon. He would drop them into a wastebasket and retrieve them a little later. Once a bartender chased after him and your dad stuck it up a drainpipe and came back to get it later."

Doc was born in 1932 in Seattle, Washington, and his family moved to Beaverton, Oregon a few years later. I asked him, "So, you graduated from Beaverton High School?"

"Yes, and you'll find this hard to believe, but my senior year I had a job driving the school bus for a dollar a day," Doc laughed.

"I was drafted the next year and decided to join the Marines right away. Fifty-three other draftees joined the same day. Only three were declared 4-F."

"How did you end up becoming a Drill instructor"?

"It's unbelievable, but right after boot camp, I was promoted to Drill Instructor, maybe because I was a squad leader and tall." Doc laughed again.

"Was there a shortage of DI's because of the Korean War?"

"I never looked into that, but that was probably a big reason."

"I believe I know one possible answer is because Doc, you are an imposing man even at eighty-eight years of age. You must have been a physical specimen as a young man?" Doc just laughed.

Doc was the drum major of The Leathernecks, and as a child, I remember how impressive he looked in front of the Drum & Bugle Corps at parades. "Oh, I should add I was put in charge of the Color Guard for Graduation also."

"How long were you a DI?"

"One year. I was then transferred to Japan and assigned to the 3rd Marine Division's Rifle Team for a year, then to Hawaii and then back to the States assigned to Camp Pendleton's Color Guard."

"What a great assignment?"

"Yes, it was, and one of my best memories was driving Lieutenant General Robert H. Pepper to inspect Marine Corps Reserve units. I first met the General when he inspected our rifle team in Japan. When I presented arms to him, he looked impressed and asked me, 'Where did you learn that technique Marine?'

"I told him I was in Camp Pendleton's Color Guard. One year later back at Camp Pendleton, General Pepper remembered me from the inspection in Japan, and requested me to be his personal driver.

"Mostly we did lots of ceremonies, funerals, and parades. It was great. We even presented the colors for the Grand Opening of Disneyland in California in 1955. I have some pictures to prove it at home. I'll have to show you sometime."

We set a date in February and Doc came to my home to share his pictures but before that, I searched the internet for the Grand Opening of Disneyland. On YouTube was the entire event that was shown nationwide on ABC.

As soon as Doc sat down in our living room, "I said I have a surprise for you." I then started the program on our big screen television. The Marine Corps Color Guard was right up front behind Walt Disney, who was welcoming the TV audience to Disneyland.

Doc did not move or talk and had a look of complete shock. After a couple minutes, Doc said, "I've never seen this," as his eyes moistened, still looking stunned.

"I have one more surprise for you today." I then played some YouTube footage of Portland's Grand Floral Parade from 1963. The Leathernecks were asked to be part of a five city blocks long tribute to the movie

Cleopatra. Everyone was dressed in Roman Soldier uniforms that were on loan from Hollywood.

Leading everyone was Doc Hickman, then the color guard, followed by the Drum & Bugle Corps playing 'The Parade of the Charioteers' from the movie *Ben Hur*. -Please, search for this music on the internet because it's awesome!

Following them were one hundred Oregon National Guard Soldiers dressed as Roman Soldiers marching in formation with their large shields, spears, and swords. Bringing up the rear was a beautiful float with a lion, a tiger, and a bear in separate cages and many Gladiators guarding them. Then about twenty Egyptian slaves were pulling another absolutely beautiful float with Cleopatra sitting above everyone on her throne.

I was eight years old sitting on a curb with my mom, sister, and brother. I saw my mom crying and asked, "What's wrong Mommy?" She said, "I'm fine son, these are tears of happiness and pride."

After we finished watching the video, Doc was again shocked, "Wow, I've never seen this either." That was an incredibly special moment my beautiful wife Malinda and I shared with Doc. He was so grateful.

When the video was finished, he also told me, "I was able to do a lot of fun stuff then. I remember one time I got stationed at an audience award show where Eddie Fisher sang the 'Star Spangled Banner', and Grace Kelly was in the audience. When we finished, an actor named George Gobel walked up to us and said, 'Let's go off to the bar boys,' and we all went."

While visiting Doc in January of 2021, Doc blurted out, "I have another funny story about the Drum Corps that I forgot to tell you. We were asked to perform at the Dallas Cowboys vs. Los Angeles Rams football game which was played in Pendleton, Oregon. It was the Cowboys first season.

"We were practicing the day before when one of the Rams football players accidentally walked into our practice. One of our guys ran up to him and yelled, 'Hey get your big black ass out of the way!'

"Just as he finished saying it another one of our guys ran up and grabbed our fellow Leatherneck by his shirt and pulled him back around and forced him to walk away fast. He told him 'Are you an idiot? That's Rosie Grier of the famous Fearsome Foursome.'" Rosie was a 6-foot-5-inch (196 cm) 284 pound (129 kg), All-Pro Defensive Tackle.

Doc is still living at 89.

ED WILKINS   Marines

Ed was the Athletic Director at Milwaukie High School when I started teaching and coaching there in the fall of 1982. He retired in '88, but his strong stance on who would become Milwaukie's next head football coach after the most successful football coach in MHS history, Jerry Harn, retired in 1987, will always mean a lot to me.

We had a new principal who felt the job should go to an outsider because another Milwaukie teacher/coach and I both wanted the job. They narrowed the finalists to three coaches, me, my fellow coaching buddy, who had been at Milwaukie for two years, and the outsider, a coach from our archrivals at Putnam High School. The principal voted to give the job to the outsider.

Well, Ed Wilkins was angry. He told the committee, "Ken Buckles is the new head coach! Why? First, he's a Mustang, and second, he has been here teaching and coaching the longest, he's paid his dues, the kids love him, and I believe in loyalty. I will raise holy hell around here if you give it to someone else."

Thanks, Ed, I got the job because of you.

When I finally got around to talking to him about his war experiences, he agreed to be interviewed just a month before he passed away.

I started off by asking him, "I've learned that you had three older brothers who served in WWII?"

"Yes, that's true. My father was a 12-year Navy veteran and also a WWI veteran. My oldest brother, Bob, was a Navy Corpsman attached to the Marines in the South Pacific. I know he was at Bougainville, but I was never told anything else.

"My next brother was Dale, Navy, who served on a minesweeper in the South Pacific." Dale attended several MHS Living History Days and was a real character.

"I remember Dale, he would get high school girls to dance with him when our jazz band played any Glen Miller songs. Once he got up on stage at the end, grabbed the microphone, and yelled out to the students 'You have restored my faith in America!'"

Ed told me the next day, "Don't ever let him do that again, you'll never get the mike back," while laughing. "Charles, my third brother, was with the Army, and he parachuted into Normandy on D-Day. He earned the Silver Star and a Purple Heart when a shell hit his rifle and he lost his hand. He never talked about it, in fact, none of my brothers ever talked about the war. Charles just threw his medals into a drawer and left them there."

"Your parents must have been a mess?"

"Yes, my mother was always stressed out and refused to answer the door. I was nine years old when an Army car pulled up in front of our house. Mom was so nervous she literally couldn't open the door, so an uncle opened the door and thank God, their message was just telling us he was wounded but OK."

"So, you joined the Marines, why?"

"My best friend Bob Cassidy and I graduated from Central Catholic in 1950, and we joined the Marines together. My father was not happy about it (wanted me to join the Navy), but I told him, 'I don't want to be like the rest of you,'" Ed laughed.

"You should know Ken; it was a different world back then. The Korean War had just broken out and I felt it was my turn. I felt a strong obligation and that's just the way it was."

"How was Boot Camp?"

"I learned a big lesson right away: Just say 'Yes, Sir' and 'No, Sir'. I got in trouble once though. I was caught sneaking and smoking a cigarette. My punishment was sleeping with five M-1s in my bed.

"After boot camp, I was sent to El Toro and assigned to a Close Air Support outfit, and we were sent to Korea in early 1952. We were responsible for looking for the enemy and reporting the location to Air Support and they would be taken care of. We were three miles from the 38th Parallel when the war ended."

"Any experiences you would like to share?"

There was a pause, "It's just best not to talk about it." Ed paused again and then said in an excited voice, "But I ran into Bob Cassidy over there. What were the odds?

"One of my highlights over there was while I was waiting for my flight to Japan for two weeks of R&R. I watched one of our planes fly in on fire and land doing a wheels-up belly landing, then skid down the tarmac sparks flying to finally come to a stop. The pilot was Baseball Hall of Famer, Ted Williams."

"Any story you want to share about your R&R time in Japan?"

"No comment," Ed laughed.

"After the war, I was sent to Seattle. And was stationed there but came home every weekend to see my parents and brothers. Sadly, both of my parents passed while I was stationed there.

"When I got out of the Marines, I enrolled at Vanport College, which is Portland State now, on the GI bill, then transferred to the University of Portland. I married my next-door neighbor, Aileen, and we were married for 60 years. I taught English, Journalism, and school newspaper at Valsetz High School for two years, then to Clackamas High School for 17 years, and then on to Milwaukie High School for the next 11 years as Athletic Director."

I'll never forget something about Ed that always irritated all of us coaches. After Friday night football games, we would all meet at someone's home with our wives for an after-game party. Ed loved his beer warm and left his cases of beer out in his garage. In September, the garage was always hot so his beer would be very warm.

As soon as anyone complained, Ed would always say, "Hey, go get your own beer if you don't like it." Then he would smile and say, "But you're welcome to drink as much of my beer as you like," and he'd laugh again.

Just another stubborn Marine!

Ed Wilkins passed away at the age of 89 in March of 2021.

BOB CASSIDY   Marines

I met Bob and his lovely wife Nikki years ago when he was the president of the Oregon Trail Chapter of the Korean War Veterans Association (KWVA). They were such a sweet and kind couple, and Bob always had a beautiful smile.

When he learned that I had taught and coached at Milwaukie High School, he asked, "Did you know the Athletic Director Ed Wilkins?"

"Yes, he was instrumental in me getting the head football job."

"Well, we were best friends in high school." When I interviewed Ed over the phone during the covid shutdown, he told me that Bob and he joined the Marines together.

"I graduated in 1950 from Central Catholic High School where I played baseball and football. I played halfback in the single wing offense and was good enough to play in the Shrine All-Star game my senior year. But baseball was my game. I'm not bragging, but I had a cannon for an arm. I played catcher and no one ever stole a base on me my senior year.

"I enrolled at OSU and played football on the Frosh team, but I was just screwing around too much and not taking school serious enough. Ed told me he was joining the Marines, so I decided I'd join with him. We were in the same platoon during boot camp."

"How was boot camp for you, tough?"

Bob smiled, "Easy peasy, I was already in great shape, and I had joined the Jr. Marines in high school and learned a lot with them, that helped prepare me for boot camp.

"One experience really terrified me though. The DI was ordering us one at a time to jump in the pool at the deep end. Ed was ordered to jump but he does not know how to swim. I rushed to the pool. Big mistake, DI jumps all over me and orders me back in line. Ed is struggling and going under water. Finally, another DI jumps in the water and saves him.

"My MOS (Military Occupational Specialty) was to be a flight radio operator as I went through morse code school in El Toro. You had to type twenty words a minute, all short words that never made any sense to me.

"I flunked out and then they told me I was color blind. I wasn't but oh well. So, I played football and baseball for our El Toro base. There was a league with teams from every base on the West Coast. It was fun.

"They needed bodies in Korea, so I volunteered. I was hand-picked for a radio job on a channel used only by Colonels and Majors. My job was to record their conversations. One time I was on the plane when a Marine officer stepped on board, and I saw he had a Medal of Honor ribbon on his chest. It was a WWII Ace!

"Here I was, an eighteen-year-old PFC, and I sat just a few feet from him doing my job. After we landed, he said to me, 'Cassidy, you did a hell of a job. I'm going to recommend you for a merit badge.' It never happened," he said laughing.

"Then we were shipped to Japan, and I didn't get seasick. The Pacific was calm, smooth sailing all the way. From Japan, we were flown to an old Japanese airfield in Po Huang, South Korea. At first, I was with a construction battalion. They were hardcore. They built an ice machine that created sheets of ice, and we were the only enlisted club with ice for cold beer.

"A couple months later, I was assigned a radar outfit and about two months later, Ed joined us. Whenever Ed and I had time off it was a heavy beer drinking night. Man, he could drink a lot of beer," he said laughing. "Our job with the radar squadron was mostly ordering air strikes.

"We were shipped back home when the war ended in '53. Then it was back to El Toro. I played football and baseball for the last three years of my time. I'm glad I joined the Marines, it provided me mental and physical discipline.

"It was way different than I thought it would be. I learned a lot of great lessons: honor, duty, you got a job to do, do it right, no excuses. I came home, got married, had five kids, worked full time, and attended University of Portland carrying a full load. Graduated in three years. Bob laughed saying, "Ed went to UP also."

"Wow, you must be smart?" I said quickly.

Bob smiled and said, "Ah shucks. Well, yes, I was pretty smart," laughing even more.

My lovely wife Malinda had dropped me off at Bob and his wife Nikki's home and had just returned to pick me up and came inside to say hello. They both were so happy to see her and asked if she had been singing. She said yes and offered to sing, 'I'll be Seeing You'. Both had tears in their eyes as she sang that popular WWII era song.

As soon as she was finished, Bob asked, "Have you ever heard the song 'Stella by Starlight?' Before any of us could answer, Bob starts singing the song, and he has a beautiful voice. When he finished, I responded, "Wow, a great athlete, a smart student, and a great singing voice. You must have been a real ladies' man." Bob just laughed.

Bob is still living at 89.

★

'The Schonz' was the beloved play-by-play announcer for the Portland Trail Blazers for almost three decades, from the team's start in 1970 until 1998. I didn't know Bill was a Marine until attending a Blazer game a couple of years ago where I was honored as a Hometown Hero.

Before the game, my wife and I were invited into a lounge designated for former Blazers, major sponsors, and local celebrities. I noticed Mr. Schonely sitting at the bar, and I approached and introduced myself and why I was there. He shook my hand and said, "I know who you are, and thank you for what you do for us veterans. Did you know I was a Marine?"

I immediately invited him to MC our next big event at the Oregon Military Department Camp Withycombe. He accepted and was a great hit with all the veterans. After I introduced him to a standing ovation, Bill stood at attention, saluted the crowd, and said, "Bill Schonely, United States Marine Corps, reporting for duty." He received another standing ovation.

After hearing that he was a former Marine, I called Bill and set an appointment to interview him over the phone, and we set a date. When I called him back, he answered, "Hello Ken, let's get going. I was born on June 1, 1929, in Norristown, Pennsylvania, the firstborn son of Walter and Juanita Schonely. My two younger brothers were Richard and James. My father served in the Navy at the end of WWI on the USS Pennsylvania and also on President Wilson's yacht."

As I was writing notes, I had to interrupt him many times during this interview because he was on a roll, just like when he was announcing at a basketball game.

"After serving, my father married his high school sweetheart and became heavily involved in the American Legion and church. After church, we would go out to eat for brunch. One Sunday after we finished eating and got in the car, my father started the engine, and the radio was on.

"It was President Roosevelt talking about the surprise attack at Pearl Harbor. My father told us to be quiet and turned the volume up. After a couple of minutes, he turned off the radio and said to my mother, 'June, first thing tomorrow morning, I'm going down to the Navy recruiting office and re-enlisting.'

"My mother responded, 'If you believe that's best, go right ahead.' That next morning, he put on his old uniform and re-enlisted. He was shipped out, and my mother continued to raise us three boys. During the depression and the war years, I remember my mother giving food away to struggling families from all walks of life. She would always say, 'It's just the right thing to do.' My father ended up serving a total of twenty-five years in the Navy.

"I was a stutterer as a child growing up, and it took a lot of work to overcome. I took vocal lessons and loved to sing. Ken, you know stutterers can sing beautifully?" Without pausing for my answer, Bill kept speaking.

"While in high school, I worked on a weekly high school informational radio show on WNAR in Norristown, Pennsylvania, and started dating Dottie. Dottie loved singing, loved music, and played the piano and the organ.

"After graduating from high school, Dottie and I broke up, and I didn't know what to do. A good friend of mine who happened to be a Marine Corps recruiter talked me into joining the Marines. My father was furious at first, 'How could you join the Marines over the Navy?' He soon became very proud of me though.

"I was sent to Parris Island, South Carolina for boot camp and that experience made a man out of me. My head was now on straight. It was the best thing I ever did in my life, joining the Marines.

"We were sent to Treasure Island in San Francisco and then shipped to China, but when we arrived in Hawaii, our orders were changed. My outfit was shipped to Guam, and I was stationed there for three and a half years."

I will never forget Bill's amazing voice that I had been listening to for the last twenty minutes but suddenly his voice changed to one I had never heard from the 'Mr. Rip City' before. Bill paused and he became very emotional and said, "This next experience is something I'll never forget. On Guam, the WWII war crime trials were being held. I attended and watched all the trials.

"The people of Guam hated the Japanese from all of the atrocities they committed during the war. The stockades had to be guarded at all times, and I was assigned to the execution detail. I was ordered to stand at parade rest right beneath the trap door of the hanging platform. And I didn't know why.

"Soon a Japanese General walked up the stairs, a hood was placed over his head, the trap door opened, and his body dropped, swinging right in front of me." Bill got quiet for a moment. "Next was a Japanese Admiral who broke down emotionally and would not go up the stairs. Two Marines had to force him up and put on the hood and he was dropped."

Bill stopped talking. I was stunned and the only thing I could think to say was "I'm so sorry."

"I've tried hard to get that out of my mind," he said after a long silence.

"Have you ever told anyone this?" I asked.

"No, not really," he said again with a long silence afterward.

When Bill started speaking again his famous voice had returned.

"A lot of us servicemen from every branch took correspondence courses and believe it or not, many of the Japanese POWs helped, mentoring us with our studies.

"Oh, and while stationed in Guam, I formed a Drum and Bugle corps. I was the lead drummer. We performed at many different functions weekly and would greet Navy ships when they came to Guam. I also formed a six-piece dance band and a choir of Marines for church. I wanted to whet my appetite.

"Then, I was transferred to the Armed Forces Radio and became a disc jockey and did the news, sports, and interviews. I also did my first play-by-play, calling military football and baseball games.

"When the North Koreans invaded South Korea, we were all ordered to pack up and report to the dock where they told us, 'You're all going to Korea.' As they read each Marine's name off, he would walk up the plank."

Then Bill's emotional tone of his voice returned again. "My name was not called, and all my buddies were. This happened to me three times during the next month. Even to this day, I have no idea why my name was not called." Bill paused even longer this time before he said, "My buddies never made it back home."

After a few moments, he started off again with his famous voice, "In 1951, I'm reassigned to Quantico, Virginia and I worked under General Clifton B. Cates. We became good friends. I was only a sergeant, but we would spend hours just talking.

"I worked on the weekly base newspaper, emceed military events, and parades. And I also escorted military celebrities to New York City, Washington, D.C., and Philadelphia for radio and TV interviews.

"Sadly, the bodies of the men were coming home, and I attended many funerals. I also was responsible for interviewing Marines who had fought in Korea. I was being wined and dined as they wanted me to stay in the Marines, but I told them five and half years was enough.

"Just before I was out a major approached me and said, 'I have a good friend who just bought a TV station in Baton Rouge, LA. I'll give him a call if you are interested.' I told him yes, and got on a greyhound bus from Quantico, Virginia, and went all the way to Baton Rouge where I was offered a job and was told it would be waiting for me as soon as I got out of the Marines. Once there, I did all sports, even rodeo, but mostly baseball and many LSU sporting events.

"Then in 1955, I'm offered a job in Seattle, Washington, doing Husky football games, hockey, and then the play-by-play man for Seattle's new Major League Baseball team, the Totems. Well, they moved to Milwaukee and changed their name to the Brewers. I could have gone, but I fell in love with the Pacific Northwest.

"Then my good friend Harry Glickman calls me and says- "Bill imitates Harry's very deep voice, 'We're starting an NBA basketball team in Portland, we would like you to be our play-by-play guy.'

"And the rest, as they say, is history," Bill laughs

During his career with the Portland Trail Blazers, Bill coined many phrases during the Blazermania phenomenon. Some of his most memorable were, 'Rip City,' 'Bingo Bango Bongo,' 'Lickety brindle up the middle,' 'Climb the golden ladder,' and 'You've got to make your free throws.'

He was so awesome that I know people who would turn down the volume when the Blazers played on TV so they could listen to him on the radio. He was the best at giving listeners a visual of where the players were on the court. I remember him saying things like, 'moving left to right on your radio dial, 'through the cyclops at midcourt,' and my favorite, 'ocean to ocean.'

Schonely blurted out his best-known phrase 'Rip City' during a game against the Lakers in 1970. The phrase stuck with Blazers basketball and even became a nickname for Portland itself. I will always remember how for every broadcast he opened with, "Good evening basketball fans, wherever you may be…"

The final question I asked him was, "What do you remember most from your wonderful life?" He said without even a pause, "When I decided to track down Dottie, my high school sweetheart, and call her. We went out and have been married 29 years."

Bill Schonely is still living at 92.

PAUL KNAULS   Air Force

I met Paul many years ago at a meeting of the Portland Chapter of the National Association of Black Veterans (NABVETS), but I already knew who he was since the 70s.

In the early 1970s, Paul was the first African American to have courtside season tickets at a National Basketball Association (NBA) game. As this was so noticeable to all, many of the league's black players would come over to where he was sitting and talk with him.

He was also able to become friends with many of the Portland Trail Blazers players as well as the legendary Trail Blazers broadcaster Bill Schonely. He told me, "Bill and I are real good buddies."

Paul told me, "You didn't see blacks anywhere in the country in the front row. People would always ask, 'Who's that black guy sitting in the front row?' I'd tell them I was the mayor of NE Portland.

"Once back then, a white man approached my wife and I during a time out at a Blazers game and with an ugly tone in his voice he asked, 'How can you afford these expensive tickets?' My wife yelled at him to get the hell out of here," Paul said laughing hard.

Paul is well known for his infectious smile and laugh and for being such a great guy. His nickname is 'The Mayor of Northeast Portland' as the area of Portland was for over fifty years a predominately African American community with many black owned businesses.

Everyone started calling him that in the 1960s. At that time, Paul owned several businesses in the heart of Black nightlife in Portland. His most famous was the jazz bar the Cotton Club named after the famous nightspot in New York. It was so famous that the likes of Etta James, Cab Calloway, Duke Ellington, and Sammy Davis Jr. went there.

He sold the club years later but started other businesses which also became popular over the years. Gentrification has drastically changed the area in the last twenty years, however Paul, until this year, stayed in the area to show support for black owners.

Paul said to me, "I was just interviewed for four days by National Geographic about this. There were over a hundred black owned businesses in Northeast Portland and today there are only three and they are all gone for good."

Paul grew up in Arkansas, the middle of seven children, and six girls. His father died of black lung at the age of fifty-one from working in the coal mines. His mother was a homemaker who also worked cleaning and cooking for white families. Paul attended segregated schools from elementary through high school.

He told me, "The first time in my life I was ever around whites was as a sixteen-year-old. I got a job shining shoes at a country club. I made the varsity basketball team as a freshman. And started three years for Lincoln High School in Fort Smith, Arkansas."

"Why did you join the military?" I asked.

"There were no good jobs available to blacks back in '49, so I joined the Air Force because they were one of the first branches to integrate. I thought about the Army, but the Secretary of the Army under President Truman said, 'Integration will not happen on my watch,' and the Army was the last to integrate. I reported to boot camp seven days after graduating from high school."

"How were you treated in boot camp?" I asked.

"It worked out okay for me as I'd been around whites quite a bit working at the country club. But for most of the guys from the inner cities who had never been around white people they had a rough time. This was the first time the barracks were integrated, and the blacks couldn't handle being next to white people, and the whites couldn't handle being next to us.

"It wasn't always good for me. I got in trouble too. The sergeant would be calling everybody names saying we were lower than snakes. But I'd start laughing because I thought it was funny. He'd get in my face and yell and spit and then make me scrub the barrack steps with a toothbrush. When I finished, he would inspect my job but step in mud and then step on the cleaned steps and then say, 'You missed a spot.'"

"How often did you get in trouble?" I asked.

"About three or four times a week," he said laughing. "I was the sound off guy when we were marching and once, I started a chant, 'Sergeant Kapers got a three-day pass, his girlfriend told him to kiss his ass.... Sound Off 1, 2.' Sarge was so pissed he grabbed me and cussed me out and shoved me, but I never reported him, and we eventually ended up becoming good friends."

"Were there any other times when you felt uneasy," I asked.

"One day I was called into my superior's office and told that since President Truman had desegregated the army, there was an Air Force base near Spokane, Washington that needed to have the first negro airman. And because of my wonderful personality, I would be the one to have that assignment. I left on a train from Texas and arrived in Spokane at midnight. The next morning, bright as sunshine, I walked into the mess hall to the surprise of everyone."

Did you have any trouble there?" I asked.

"Not much because I was such a good pool player, I always had people asking me to play a game of pool," which he finished with his famous laugh.

Paul was ultimately promoted to staff sergeant. "In those days, that was big. They didn't promote blacks like that. You might get two stripes, but not four. That was just the system then. No African Americans were going to be above the whites, and that's the way it was."

I then asked him, "What would you tell high school students today about the military?"

"I would tell them to join. To learn a trade or a skill that will land you a job when you get out. And it will teach you discipline, like getting up early to go to work."

Paul Knauls is still living at 90 years of age.

* ★ *

DARREL 'MOUSE' DAVIS   Navy

If you are a fan of American football for the past fifty years, you have heard about Mouse Davis and his contributions to the game.

My good friend, All-American quarterback at Portland State University, former NFL player, and head football coach at both the professional and college levels June Jones, always said it best, "Mouse Davis is credited for revolutionizing the passing game of football at the high school, college, and professional levels."

In *Remembrance Volume I*, I wrote that I played for Coach Davis and was one of the offensive linemen who blocked for June Jones. For you readers who don't know any of this, please do an internet search on Mouse Davis and his 50-year football coaching career to get an understanding of just how impressive he was during his career.

Mouse was the youngest of five siblings, with two brothers and two sisters. His father was a truck driver, and a heavy drinker. His mother was strict and treated him just as tough as his older brothers. He told me, "I was kind of a Momma's boy, but she wouldn't allow it." Mouse laughed and Coach has a great laugh.

"Where did you get your intense competitiveness from?" I asked.

"My brothers were all athletes too and we competed hard against each other in everything. My oldest brother Gale who also coached college football was just as competitive as me."

Of course, I had to ask, "When did you earn the nickname "Mouse"?

"When I was a freshman in high school, I was playing varsity baseball. Even though I was smaller than most of the guys, my dad used to always call me 'Boar Mouse'. That's what he called me 'Boar Mouse'. I have no idea why he said boar, maybe he thought I was wild and small like a mouse.

"One day, I was playing second base and my brother was catching, and he throws me the ball and I dropped it. So, he yells, 'Nice hands Mouse!' and from that point on, all my teammates called me Mouse. By the end of high school, none of the teachers knew my real name.

"Even when I went to college, they still called me it. Then when I went into the Navy, I thought I was finally going to lose that nickname. Turns out that when I showed up for military training, I looked around and saw a bunch of guys that I'd just been playing against in college. I knew right then and there I was Mouse, so I just accepted it. Been with me ever since."

"How did you enter the Navy?" I asked.

"Right after graduating from OCE, Oregon College of Education, now Western Oregon University, I landed a teaching job at a grade school but was also drafted. Back in the 50s, if you were drafted, they allowed you to prioritize which branch you wanted to enlist in. I wrote down number one as Army, number two Air Force, number three Marines, and number four Navy. They put me in the Navy," Coach laughed. "I served twenty-one months on the Aircraft carrier the mighty USS Lexington."

Anyone who knows Coach will get a kick out of this next story.

"I made our carrier's All-Star basketball team, and we got to play in a big game against the Army's All-Star basketball team in Japan. Both team's rosters were filled with former Division I basketball players. On the Army's team was some hotshot named Beard from Kentucky.

"I demanded to cover him because he was a cocky little piss ant, kind of like me," laughing again. Mouse's voice rose with the same intensity I remember as my football coach when telling me this but ended it by laughing.

"How did you do against him?" I asked.

"I battled him tough the entire time, never backed down. I don't remember who won though, Hell, Kenneth, that was a long time ago," laughing again.

After our interview, I searched on my computer and found out who this Army soldier Beard was. Ralph Beard, was a two-time All-American guard, playing for Coach Adolph Rupp, University of Kentucky, and won two NCAA National Championships and a Gold medal in the '48 Olympics.

I also found that Beard played two seasons in the NBA until he was banned from the sport after it was discovered he accepted bribes from gamblers to affect the outcome of Kentucky games.

I told Mouse that I remember watching him play in a pick-up basketball game in PSU's lower gym. Many of us football players were in the weight room when another teammate runs in and yells, 'Hey guys, Coach is playing basketball.' We all ran out and into the gym to see. We were in awe with how quick he was and what a great ball handler too.

He would drive in the paint and dish off to an open teammate. I remember his intense competitiveness and how focused he was playing, and he never even noticed about twenty of his football players on the side mesmerized by our coach.

After Coach stopped laughing, I asked, "Do you have any memories of the Navy you would like to share?"

"Yes, and it still pisses me off to this day," laughing. "We were sailing to Australia, and we were given the opportunity to attend the '56 Olympics. The Navy gave us reduced-price tickets to whatever events you signed up for.

"Then there was some flare-up in the South China Sea, and our orders were changed, and we had to sail around the South China Sea just flipping off the Chinese. I was so pissed. I wanted to go to the Olympics and had already picked the sports I wanted to watch.

"After twenty-one months in the Navy, I was allowed to be discharged three months early because I was going into education to be a teacher."

"Who influenced you the most as an athlete and as a coach?" I asked next.

"My football and boxing coach from Independence High School, John Mathis. He was a great guy, and we had a close relationship. In college it was Mac." -the late NAIA Hall of Fame coach Bill McArthur, Western Oregon's all-time winningest football coach, and WWII Army veteran.

"I was his quarterback, and we became very good buddies. He'd even let me smoke cigarettes with him in his car while driving somewhere. It's hard to believe, but everybody smoked back then," He said laughing again.

"But he was crazy and lost his leg playing football, it became infected with gangrene and had to be amputated. That didn't stop him though as he was one hell of a handball player."

Mouse starts laughing and then says, "But me being an asshole, when I played handball against him, I would make him have to run all over the court. One time, Mac stops our game and yells at me, 'Hey asshole, keep doing that and I'll shove this ball up your ass'. He would have too," Mouse laughs again.

"When did you know you wanted to coach football?" I asked.

"I really wanted to play pro football but realized as a senior in high school that I would never be big enough. Even printed in our high school yearbook from me was, 'I want to be a football coach.'

Coach Davis would become not just a football coach, but a legendary football coach who touched the lives of many people all over the world and I am one of them and extremely grateful.

I'm also grateful for him speaking at several of our events including emceeing one of our Oregon Military Hall of Fame events. We inducted the Oregon Chapter of the famous 442nd Japanese American Army soldiers who served in WWII. There were about ten of them who came up on the stage and shook Mouse's hand.

They were all about the same height as him and Mouse started cracking jokes. "Wow, we are all the same height. I can look straight into everyone's eyes." Mouse had every one of them and the entire audience laughing. "We all inherited the same height genes." He was hilarious.

Darrel 'Mouse' Davis is still living at 89.

* ★ *

UNITED MEXICAN AMERICAN VETERANS' ASSOCIATION OF ORANGE COUNTY CALIFORNIA

For over ten years, this close-knit veteran organization has sent many veterans to Oregon to join us in speaking to high school students. I'm so grateful for their support.

FRANK RAMIREZ

Army
Korean War
Silver Star
Bronze Star

Frank was from Central California, just north of Bakersfield. After school and on Saturdays he picked cotton and potatoes as a kid to help his parents with the bills. In seventh grade, school was only half days as all the kids were expected to work in the fields for the rest of the day. He dropped out of school in eighth grade to work full time.

It took me several years to get Frank to open up to me. But when he finally did, I listened to his every word. I started out by asking him about how he felt about dropping out of school.

"Why go to school when I could make more money by picking crops in the fields?" Frank said. "I was drafted at 18 years of age, but never knew about it because I never got any of the letters. My grandmother just threw the letters away." Frank laughed.

He went to sign up with the Army and they told him he was in trouble for not reporting to them after being drafted. They accused him of being a draft dodger. He told them, "I never received any letters, so they resent the letter and a week later I signed up.

"I wanted to be a paratrooper, but they told me they needed truck drivers, but I turned it down. Basic Training was not very long, as we were all shipped off to Korea as soon as possible. Once there, they lined all of us up and said, 'We need ten soldiers to volunteer to be medics, and anyone interested step forward now.'

"Schmidty, a friend of mine, turned to me and said, 'Come on Frank, step forward, let's be Medics.' So, I stepped forward. None of us had any experience and there was no training. They just showed us the pack we would carry, the bandages, and the morphine. They said, 'Just stop the bleeding and give them a shot of morphine. That's all you need to know; besides you can't do much more than that when you're being shot at too.'"

Frank was assigned to the 23rd Infantry Regiment, 2nd Infantry Division, Easy Company. In September of '51, his division was ordered to take Hill 931, after which a fierce and intense battle started. The ensuing one-month battle, which included two other hills, 894 and 851, would famously become the Battle of Heartbreak Ridge. Frank's 23rd Regiment suffered heavy casualties with over six hundred killed in action and over three thousand wounded in action.

"Every day was spent trying to save the wounded and it was so bad I grabbed a gun to protect myself and was told to not use it and to just focus on the wounded."

Frank became very frustrated as he told me, "Every night that first week I was in the same fox hole with a buddy, Saville, from Basic Training. All night, wounded soldiers would yell out, 'Medic!' But nobody helped them but me because nobody would leave their foxholes. My buddy Saville kept trying to talk me out of going out to save the wounded, but I told him I had to try. Saville told me he was going to recommend me for a Silver Star.

"After a week of not making much progress, we were ordered to advance. Well, they started shelling us as I was going to help the wounded, I ran into a buddy from picking crops in California. He came up to me limping with his foot bloody, so I started to try to stop the bleeding when he says to me, 'Don't worry about me, go over that small hill and save the others.'

"I ran over the small hill, and I'm shocked to see so many dead and wounded. Anyone that moved, I stopped the bleeding and gave them a shot of morphine. And then started to try and get them out of there and back to the aid station.

"The next morning, they ordered us to continue the assault on Hill 931. Everywhere there were just too many wounded, and I was told that all of the other medics were killed. I was the last one alive.

"During the assault still trying to take the Hill 931," Frank pauses and becomes very frustrated again. "There's just too many wounded and the mortars keep coming in and then I get hit. I'm badly wounded. Someone yells, 'Doc, are you hit?' and I yell, 'Yes, I'm hit.'

"I have shrapnel wounds in my thigh, my buttocks, and my foot. The guy who yelled takes off and leaves me alone. I bandaged myself and started heading back to safety. Another soldier helps me back to a bunker with some officers in it, and he re-bandages me to stop the bleeding again and I'm evacuated to a field hospital.

"After several days, even though I'm still limping, they ordered me back to my company. I had no choice. I was assigned a new rifle platoon and they are in on the taking of Hill 931. We make it to the top but get fired on by heavy machine gun fire and the bullets go right between my legs and wound the soldier next to me. I only assisted him with his wound because everyone else around us was dead.

"We dug in and soon after the mortars started again. I asked for help bringing back the wounded in the area but again nobody wanted to leave their fox holes. The mortar fire became very heavy, I ran and dove into a foxhole and found my good friend, Saville, but he was dead." Frank stops talking and tears form in his eyes.

"There was an unopened box of hand grenades in the foxhole, but we don't open the box because it might have been boobytrapped.

"Other soldiers try to stop me from leaving the foxhole to save more wounded. But I had to keep trying to save them. I prayed a lot. I prayed, please don't let me go home without a leg or an arm.

"We heard this frightening sound coming towards us in the air. It was a big round, flew right overhead, and there was a huge explosion. I was ordered to go help the wounded. That night the shelling stopped. It was so dark you could hardly see anything."

Frank walked the ridge by himself and in a low voice kept saying, "Medic from Easy Company," over and over again. Every once in a while, someone would yell from a fox hole, 'Halt who goes there?' He'd tell them who he was, and they would say, 'Come on in Doc.'

"I walked around for hours looking for wounded and helping them when I could and separating the dead from the wounded. Then I found my friend from Basic Training, Arnold Perry, I bandaged him up and got him back to safety. After the war, we became close friends and would see each other a couple of times a year until he passed away."

"How did you earn the Silver Star?" I asked.

"When I was wounded, and I stopped my bleeding, I just kept helping other wounded. I just had a job to do and felt I needed to save as many as possible."

Over the years, Frank met many men he had saved on Hill 931. Every one of them felt he should have been awarded the Medal of Honor.

Then in an expression of helplessness and a very sad tone, Frank said, "I've always felt I could have saved more. So many died in my arms. My friends died in my arms. Some would die with their eyes open. I would always close their eyes before leaving them."

One time when Frank was going up the hill to the aid station, he was told to go help tag the bodies of the soldiers because there were too many stacking up.

"I would search the bodies for dog tags or letters for some kind of identification. The bodies I couldn't identify, I would just sign KIA and put them in a bag, and zip it up. Some were badly decomposed with maggots coming out of their chests, and the smell was horrible.

"There were so many I got Korean house boys to help. Every morning trucks would come for the dead and they would stack the bodies on top of each other. At the time I didn't think anything about it. I just did my job. But now I have to talk to a doctor and take pills to clear my mind."

Finally, after thirty days of hard combat, 'Operation Touchdown' as it was initially called, was over when troops stormed Hill 931's peak and it was in the possession of the 23rd Infantry.

"Why was it called Heartbreak Ridge?" I asked.

"Someone in the back of the front asked, 'How is it up there?' and a soldier answered, 'It's a heart break up there.'"

Frank was later awarded the Silver Star for gallantry in action against an enemy. His official citation read:

> The President of the United States of America, authorized by Act of Congress July 9, 1918, takes pleasure in presenting the Silver Star to Corporal Frank Ramirez (ASN: US-56147662), United States Army, for gallantry in action as a member of the Medical Company, 23d Infantry Regiment, 2d Infantry Division, in action against an armed enemy on 24 September 1951 in the vicinity of Satae-ri, Korea. On this date Corporal Ramirez, an aidman, was

attached to a friendly unit during its assault against the well fortified enemy positions on Hill 931. During the ensuing action, Corporal Ramirez observed a wounded comrade lying helpless in a forward position under intense hostile fire. Without hesitating, he left his covered emplacement and proceeded over the fire-swept area to the wounded man. In the course of this act, he was painfully wounded but, completely ignoring his own safety, tenaciously continued on. Upon reaching his destination, Corporal Ramirez immediately administered first aid to his comrade and, after placing him in a defilade position, fearlessly crossed the hazardous terrain to secure a litter team for the evacuation of his comrade. Corporal Ramirez's example of individual bravery instilled confidence and security among the friendly soldiers and aided immeasurably to the success of their operation on Heartbreak Ridge. The gallantry in action and selfless devotion to duty demonstrated by Corporal Ramirez will live forever in the hearts of his comrades.

After Heartbreak Ridge, Frank was then transferred to a tank company and volunteered to go out on night patrols. Frank paused and then said, "I took a small camera with me and took lots of pictures and a friend developed them for me. The pictures were always a hit at reunions."

When the movie *Hacksaw Ridge* about Army medic Desmond Doss came out, I asked Frank if he knew the story. He knew the story but had no desire to see it. When I told him it was the most realistic and explicit war movie I had ever seen. Frank said, "There is no way a movie will ever be able to help you understand the experience of war. The very loud sounds of all of the explosions are unbelievable, the dirt constantly raining down on you, the intense fear, and all while trying to help the wounded. The smells are overpowering, and the smell of the blood on my hands never go away."

Frank was 22 years old when he came home and got a job at a gas station. One day, two pretty teenage girls stopped and got gas. They were sisters and he really liked the sister named Alice. Frank gave her a ride home a few times as she had a job close to the gas station.

"I asked her to go on a date and she said yes but said her mom's rule was her sister had to go with us. Her sister did not approve of me seeing Alice. She said, 'Frank is a playboy, and all of the girls are after him.'"

They had only gone on two dates when he asked Alice to go to Las Vegas to marry him. She said, 'The man who marries me must ask my mother and agree to a big wedding.'

"The next week I asked her mother and she said yes. We got married with a big, beautiful wedding 65 years ago after she turned 18 and graduated from high school. We had two boys, one girl, and adopted Alice's brother's daughter." Frank and Alice are still happily married.

Frank is still living at the age of 90.

SALVADOR LUJAN   Army

Yvonne (Sal's daughter) and other members of UMAVA pressured Sal to come up to Oregon. He did not talk about his experiences with students or any of the rest of us for that matter, but I was happy that he attended.

Several of the UMVA veterans told me, "Sal went through some real tough stuff in Korea and doesn't talk about it, but we all felt this experience up here in Oregon with the high school students would be good for him and we pressured him into going."

On his first trip to Oregon, Sal was very quiet all the time, and I assumed he was not having a good time. Sal would not return until four years later.

Even though Sal rarely came up to Oregon, my beautiful wife Malinda and I saw him every time we traveled down to Orange County. The first time we traveled for pleasure, however, the second and third times were for the funerals of Antonio Mendez and then Ed Romero.

After Ed Romero's service, Sal approached me in 2018 and promised me, "I'm going to come back up to Oregon this next November. I wanted to sooner, but it's just too emotional for me, but that first experience provided me some healing."

After the first day of talking to McMinnville high school students at Evergreen Aviation & Space Museum and the evening's dinner, many of us went to a hotel lounge across the street where we were all staying. I sat next to the only available chair, which luckily happened to be next to Sal.

We were all having a great time visiting for over an hour when Sal leaned towards me and said, "Ken, I have something I need to tell you. I've been wanting to tell you for several years but just couldn't do it. I feel safe telling you because you understand what us veterans have gone through."

I just sat there stunned again and thought to myself, why me? But what an honor it is that he is sharing his story with me. We were all discussing the issue of the NFL players taking a knee to protest during the playing of the National Anthem. It was this discussion that triggered Sal and motivated him to share his thoughts.

"First of all, it upset me very much when the pro football players did that, and I'll tell you why. In my platoon were seven black soldiers, many Hispanic soldiers, many Native American soldiers, and some white soldiers. All of us came from severe poverty.

"I became very close friends with one of the black soldiers named Smitty. We were assigned to each other in our foxhole. Because I was friends with Smitty, I became close to the other black soldiers too. They were all a great bunch of guys."

Sal became teary-eyed and apologized, "I'm sorry Ken, but I think about these guys every day and when I hear the National Anthem, I see their faces.

"I would ask Smitty every day, 'Smitty, will you stay with me, never leave me?' Smitty would always answer, 'I'll never leave you; I'll stay with you. Don't you worry, Sal, when we get home, you're going to come home to Baltimore with me and we will open a hotdog stand.' We would laugh about that. Hell, we were just kids.

"One night, an artillery attack on us started, and soon Chinese soldiers attacked by the hundreds and were overrunning us. As we were defending ourselves, I personally saw six of the black soldiers killed right in front of me. When we finally reached safety and the attack was repulsed, I asked 'Where's Smitty?'

"Another soldier looked at me and said, 'He didn't make it'. I broke down and cried."

Sal choked up telling me and stopped talking and looked away. After a few minutes, he looked at me and said, "We were on the front for eight months. When we were finally relieved and sent to Japan for some R&R, there were only 13 left out of 133 from my rifle company."

Sal paused again and then raised his voice and stated with pride, "But you want to know something Ken, in spite of what happened, I would do it again tomorrow if needed."

Thank you, Mr. Lujan.

Salvador Lujan passed away at the age of 90 in April of 2021.

--- ★ ---

LEO OUELLETTE   Air Force

My lovely wife Malinda and I got to know Leo and his wonderful wife Esther when they offered us to stay at their home when we came down to Orange County for Tony Mendez's funeral in June of 2017. They both had come to Oregon a couple of times and were very friendly, but we had no idea just how very generous and giving these two wonderful people were.

Esther would cook and put out a buffet for every meal as there were many choices. It was unbelievable. They picked us up at the airport, drove us everywhere, and even took us out to dinner at their favorite restaurant 'The Chili Pepper'. In April of 2018, we came down again for the funeral of Ed Romero and they offered us to stay with them again. Such great, wonderful people.

Leo is originally from Maine and grew up very poor, but he learned the value of hard work as a child. He told me, "We were so poor that once my father went to the grocery store and debated with himself to buy cigarettes or milk for the family. He bought the milk.

"If we wanted anything, we had to work for the money and buy it ourselves. I had to work as a kid to pay for my schooling and clothes as I attended a private school. And I had no say in the matter because I was the one attending that school and had to pay for it. I paid for it by picking pears, apples, and beans, and also had a paper route at nine years old."

He moved to California to live with an uncle at age sixteen because his sister told him California schools were better than Maine schools. When he finished high school, they told him he needed to move out, and his only choice was to move back home to Maine with his parents.

"I didn't want to move back home so I joined the Air Force. I was first stationed in England, then Norway to train Norwegian soldiers. Then I was transferred to Turkey. I was working with the Turks and the Greeks, and man, did they hate each other! The Turks would deport the Greeks every opportunity they could. I also was a disc jockey for the American Forces Radio.

"While in Turkey, I visited Ephesus, an old Greek city and international tourist attraction. It was built in the 10th century BC and the city came under the control of the Roman Empire in 129 BC. While there, I found a Roman coin and it was against the law to take anything from a site, but I took it back to the states with me and had it made into a beautiful ring.

"The ring was stolen, and I feel it was Karma because I shouldn't have taken it in the first place. I hope something bad doesn't happen to the person who stole it from me."

I found out later that Leo was a lover of military history and was the founder and curator of the Leo Ouellette Military Museum in American Legion Orange Post 132. When I visited Leo, he gave me a personal tour that I will always remember both for his knowledge of military history and the wonderful stories he shared with me.

Leo Ouellette passed away at the age of 88 in August of 2021.

VETERANS OF UNDERAGE MILITARY SERVICE

The VUMS organization has been supporting me through donations and attending every event we have organized for over fifteen years. Another great bunch of veterans and spouses that I was asked to speak to, and Malinda sang to, at their annual reunion in Laughlin, Nevada years ago.

The National Commander at the time was a retired judge, Hal Pershall. I'll never forget how he opened up the very first meeting I attended.

"Welcome fellow liars to our VUMS annual reunion." He and everyone else laughed.

I learned that the majority of these veterans lied about their ages to join the military because of the extreme poverty their families faced. Most sent the money they made while serving back home to their parents. Another large percent was given a choice by a judge of 'Jail or the Military, what will it be?'

Every single VUMS veteran I came to know personally told me, "The Military saved my life, or the Military turned my life around." Not once have I ever heard a veteran say, "It was a mistake" or "I regret joining." Never!

One of the most shocking and humbling thrills of that reunion for me was meeting and shaking the hand of an elderly veteran who earned the Silver Star at The Battle of the Bulge during WWII at the age of 12 years old. He had the biggest grin and an expression of pride after shaking my hand.

I was blown away by the number of veterans who joined at 12, 13, 14, 15, and 16 years of age. All said they would do it again. For the last ten years, many of these VUMS and their wives would fly to Oregon and join us in going to high schools to speak to students.

WILLIE PARADISE   Navy (16 Years old)

Willie is the Past National Vice-President, Past Oregon President of VUMS. Willie and his wife, Phyllis, an Air Force veteran, have been the driving force organizing VUMS support of all of our veteran related events. We have become good friends.

His childhood story is something else and inspiring. Willie was born in Edinburg, Texas, a small town close to the Mexican border. His father was a WWI veteran who married Juanita, from Mexico and they had six children. They were extremely poor.

Willie was nine years old when his father, James passed away and he had to start working full time before and after school to help out his mother.

"I went to work after he died, picking cotton, cleaning school rooms, and earned $8 a month. Then I started working in restaurants at thirteen, washing dishes and clearing tables. The pay was better at $12 a week.

"I averaged 70 hours a week working at the restaurant. I would jog to the restaurant about half a mile from home to open up the place and start the coffee, work for a couple of hours and then jog to school, eat lunch run back to the restaurant, work the lunch break, then back to school, and as soon as school was out, back to the restaurant till closing time at ten o'clock."

Willie joined the National Guard at 16 years of age following his older brother Charlie's example who joined at 15, was kicked out and went back when he was 17.

"How did you get away with getting in at 16?" I asked.

"When the Sergeant asked me for my birth certificate, I lied and told him I laid it on his desk then I got really upset and accused them of losing it. I told them my mom is going to kill me if I don't bring it back home. So, the Sergeant signed me up.

"While in boot camp, for some reason, my platoon sergeant didn't like me and was on me all the time. I was turning 17 less than two weeks from the end of basic training, so on my birthday, I decided to tell my Sergeant, "Today is my birthday, I'm 17 now.' Man, he was so mad he said, 'You mean I couldn't break a 16-year-old.'"

After completing boot camp, Willie joined the Navy. "Why did you and your brothers join at such young ages?" I asked.

"So, we could send money home to help out our mother. We grew up in a two-room house, one room was a small kitchen, and the second room was where we all slept. We had electricity just before my dad died. It had no running water and we had to carry buckets of water to our house from my grandparents' home who lived next door. We also used their outhouse because we did not have a toilet. The place had cracks in the wall, and the only heater was propane that rarely worked.

"We would start a fire outside then take the hot coals and put them on top of some sand in a big tub. We would bring the tub inside and the heat would last about an hour and a half."

Willie loved telling this story to students, "My mother was washing clothes in a laundry mat when a county sheriff and a couple of immigration officials pulled up in a bus. They ordered all of the Mexican women in the laundry mat to get on the bus to be deported right away.

"My mom walked up to the sheriff and said, 'If you are going to deport me that's fine, but could you please get my two sons so they can go with me? My oldest son is in the Army fighting in Korea, and my middle son is in the Air Force stationed in Japan.'

"She then got on the bus and a few minutes later the sheriff came on the bus and told her to get off."

Willie loved the Navy and served for five years and six months. "They made me a first-class seaman and since I just went through Army basic, I was told by my CO that I didn't have to go through training since I received it in the Army. I did have to take swimming and knot tying lessons though," he said laughing.

"I loved the Navy and traveled a whole lot. The first four years was on the West Coast and when I re-enlisted, I was transferred to the East Coast. The end of my military career ended sadly for me. I got real sick eating the ship's chow and asked for a transfer. They sent me to another ship, and I got really sick again.

"Then, I was sent to the hospital in Norfolk, Virginia, and the doctor noticed that I kept turning my head to hear better. He asked if I was losing my hearing and would I take a hearing test. I did and they said, 'You are out of the Navy.' I tried fighting it, but I was discharged with a disability rating. I was heartbroken."

One Navy story Willie loved telling was, "Once while we were sailing to Korea, the captain gave us permission to swim. I dove but didn't time the roll of the ship and I came up under the ship. When I came up, I found I had dived farther away from our ship and then the current quickly swept me and another sailor away.

"We could see our ship was getting smaller and smaller. We finally saw a boat coming towards us full of men with guns. After they got us on board, they had us look over the side. There were four sharks about the size of Greyhound buses."

Willie Paradise is still living at the age of 83.

* ★ *

ROBERT FORSEY   Army (16 years old)

"I've never met or known a more generous and giving man than Robert. He helped out many friends and relatives with financial help over the years."   ~Robert Forsey's lovely wife Lola.

Robert came up from Arizona for several years from 2015 thru 2019. Both were super friendly. I had talked with Robert many times during his visits and heard lots of his stories and they were all fascinating. I didn't have to ask questions as he was quite the storyteller.

I started out by asking him, "Tell me about your upbringing."

"I was born in 1929 in Seattle, Washington. My father was a WWI veteran from the country of Newfoundland, and he was wounded during the great Battle of the Somme."

Surprised, I said, "I didn't know Newfoundland had troops in WWI?"

"Well, it's quite a story, Canada was still a colony of Great Britain, and every colony around the world was ordered to contribute men to the cause. Newfoundland had no military, so the government put out a notice asking for volunteers. My father was 16 years old and was issued number 10 serial number. Do you understand what that meant?"

"No, I'm sorry, I don't." I quickly replied.

"He was the tenth man to sign up. They were told that the war would be over in a couple of months, and he thought it would be a great adventure to see the world. He was sent to Gallipoli, Turkey with the Brits.

"It was bad, the Turks had them pinned down on the beach and it would have been a total slaughter, but the Turks ran out of ammunition. So, they were able to evacuate to Egypt, then back to Scotland, and then sent to France.

"At the Somme, they were ordered to charge across 'No- Man's Land' and he was hit in the shoulder by German machine gun fire. He laid at the bottom of a muddy and wet shell hole overnight hiding from German flares. The Germans were killing all the wounded they could find but before daylight, he had crawled back to safety, He was sent to a hospital in England where he was surprised to reunite with one of his sisters. She was one of his nurses."

I later found out that the Battle of Somme lasted only approximately thirty minutes and his father's regiment was all but wiped out. I also learned that Newfoundland at the time had a population of only about a quarter of a million, and over 5,000 men went overseas. Nearly 1,500 were killed and 2,300 wounded.

I did not have to ask any questions about Newfoundland because Robert just kept talking. "On the trip back home on the ship, many men died from the Spanish Flu and a lot got it, but my father was lucky. When he returned there was no work to be found in Newfoundland, so he moved to Seattle, Washington sponsored by his brother who was living there.

"So, as you know, I was born there. I attended Roosevelt High School, but I was a terrible student. My junior year, my buddy and I decided to skip school and ride the city bus downtown to watch a movie, but the theater was closed. Next door was a Navy recruiting station and I yell to my buddy, 'Hey let's join the Navy.' We go in and because my friend was a big guy, they gave him the papers to take home but told me I was too young. So, my buddy gives the papers back and says, 'I'm not joining then.'

"Right next door was the Army, and they gave us both the papers to take home to fill out and have our parents sign. I told my buddy that my parents won't sign, and I can't forge their signatures.

"Well, my buddy's mom worked in the Federal Building, so we went to see her. She filled out both of our forms and forged my mother's signature. We were able to get a copy of my birth certificate and doctored it up too," Robert said laughing.

"The next day we turned everything in, got a physical from a doctor who was a friend of my buddy. Then we were put on a bus to Fort Lewis. As soon as we get there, we are issued Army clothes and shoes. I noticed that guys were issued either low shoes or combat boots. When I go to the front of the line, I said, 'I'll take the low shoes.' The sergeant yells, 'You're getting combat boots.'

"After being assigned our barracks, I called my mother. She started panicking and yelling at me. Even though it was 1946 and the war had ended, we were still in a clean-up operation in the South Pacific because many Japanese soldiers had refused to surrender and were hiding in the jungles.

"My mother called my dad at work and screamed at him over the phone, 'Bobby is only 16, he's not old enough and he can't be in the Army. You need to fix this now.' My father told her, 'He made his bed and he'll have to sleep in it. Maybe he'll learn something.'

"Well, I'll never forget we had very little work details to do during boot camp because German POWs did all the work. I was shocked that every German spoke very good English.

"After boot camp, we were all put on a troop train to Chicago. It was the last time I ever saw my buddy. I requested to be stationed in the Caribbean but that was denied, and I was sent to Aberdeen Proving Grounds near Baltimore.

"Because I had worked on cars at a gas station, I wanted to be a mechanic. I became a special vehicle operator learning how to drive all types of Army Military vehicles. I had an Army driver's license. It took 16 weeks to finish that training and then I received orders to be shipped out to Germany in January of '47.

"Before leaving, I was given a three-day pass. My parents came to Massachusetts to visit relatives, so I hitchhiked to Worcester, Massachusetts to my uncle's house. In those days, if you wore your uniform, you didn't have to stick your thumb out very long.

"During dinner, I became sick and went out to the outhouse. After an hour, my father came out to check on me. They took me to the nearest hospital, and I had surgery for a ruptured appendix. My dad called the company commander to tell him. I stayed at my uncles' cabin for two weeks recovering.

"The Army paid for a train ticket home. I arrived in New York in the morning, but the train for Baltimore was not until the evening. So, I decided to walk around New York. I met an 18-year-old WAC - Women's Army Corps, and we spent the day together. She had tickets to the Bob Burns Show at Radio City Music Hall.

"They picked five people to be contestants on the quiz show. I was one of the five picked and given a sport jacket as a prize. I told them I couldn't take it with me because I was in the Army. They gave me $25 instead. That was half a month's pay." Robert laughed about that but quickly started talking again.

"When I got back to the train station that evening, I was stopped by Military Police asking for my papers. I had forgotten them at my uncle's cabin. They gave me a free night behind bars.

"In the morning I was given breakfast and ate with many other GI's who were still drunk. They put handcuffs on us and ferried us over to Governor's Island to the Army prison. The prison held three German POWs who were still loyal to the Nazi party, and they had murdered several other German POWs who were following 'The American Way'.

"The following day I was brought before a military judge who didn't believe my story of forgetting my papers at my uncle's. He stated, "No papers to prove it, you're going back to your cell." I then asked to tell him about my surgery and that my outfit knows about. The judge ordered me to the infirmary to have a doctor check out my story.

"The doctor was shocked when he pulled off the tape. It was painful back then because of the kind of tape they used. He retaped me back up and I was sent back to my cell for a week. The only thing they gave me was a spoon. Finally, I was told, "You've been cleared, we are sending you back to Baltimore immediately and there is nothing to discuss.

"My class had already shipped off to Germany and I was ordered to take a new class starting in two weeks. I was put on detail driving a garbage truck. Two black soldiers were assigned to me. You have to understand that this was when the military was still segregated, and Maryland also was very segregated. Being from Seattle, I was very ignorant of racism but was soon to be educated.

"It was a hot day so when we were finished with our route, I said let's go get a coke. I parked the garbage truck, jumped out, and started walking into a grocery store. I look back and the two black soldiers are still sitting in the truck. One of them says to me, 'We can't go in there.' I said, 'What do you mean you can't go in there?' He answered, 'We are Negroes.' That was my first lesson on segregation in the south. I bought them both a coke.

"My next experience with ugly racism was just a few days later. On a day off, I went to a park off our base to just relax. As I'm parking, I see a young white guy beating the hell out of an older black man. As I run over, I yell, "Get off him and why are you doing this?

"He yells, 'Because he's a nigger.' I pull the white guy off and he threatens me and yells, 'I'll be back to take care of you.' I help the black man to his feet and offer to help clean him up. He became very nervous and kept yelling over and over, 'You need to get out of her now.'

"But it was too late because the white guy had come back with the local police. The police grabbed me, shoved me, and yelled at me to get the hell out of their town. Thank God I was wearing my uniform. I don't know whatever happened to the elderly black man.

"Well, I finished the one class and was given a 30 day leave before being shipped out to Germany. I'll never forget my first flight on an airplane. It was a United D-4 from New York to Chicago to Denver to Seattle in twelve hours. That was the fastest commercial flight time from East to West coast in the day.

"Then we were shipped out to Germany by ship, and on the 5th day we got hit by a major storm and that was a frightening experience that I did not like. The bow of the ship would raise up and crash down and would shake violently as if it was going to fall apart.

"All of us were replacements and our assignments were on hold when we arrived because the number one goal was to ship combat troops back home.

"When I finally arrived at my post, I was assigned to a garbage truck again. In our mess hall, there were two different garbage cans labeled - Garbage and Edible Garbage. I would back the truck into a spot off the base and dump the edible garbage on the ground.

"Waiting there were many, many starving German civilians, Old, young, even children fighting for edible garbage. I saw a little boy, maybe five or six years old digging for something when an older man probably in his sixties shoved the boy away. He took what the boy had found and ate it. The same boy picked up a slice of completely moldy bread and shoved it in his mouth.

"Because of my Army driver's license, I was assigned and reassigned outfits all over Germany. Finally, I was assigned to work with the Constabulary, set up in '46. It was like an Army State Police. I'll never forget the devastation of all of the German cities. Everywhere, there were German women working the streets in prostitution just to buy food.

"Once we were moving tanks back to the base and we would have to turn on the siren to get people to move to the side of the road. This scared the bejesus out of a little boy who started running away from his mother and the tanks, suddenly he stops, drops his pants and poops in the street." Robert laughs again.

"I loved Bavaria, it was beautiful, and I loved learning about German history, and I learned to speak German. But we were all getting worried though as the German people were really suffering. Thank God for the Marshall Plan because now they were getting fed.

"I was then assigned maintenance and I hated it. Picking up broken down tanks and then ordered to try and fix them, but most were just junk. Being the youngest, I had to clean the mud off them all.

"It was amazing driving a tank down a narrow rock road built by the Romans through a small town. One time we had to make a ninety-degree turn and there was a flock of geese in the way. By the time the tank came to a halt, two of the geese were killed and a farmer started yelling, '*Danke, Danke, Danke,* we now have something to eat.' German farmers had to get permission to kill animals for food.

"A major problem was trying to get the displaced Germans back to their homes. They knew they would be executed because they had worked for the Nazis during the war.

"But the worst job I had was digging up temporary American graves to send the bodies back home to the states.

"I finally had enough of this work, especially cleaning the mud off the tanks and I was upset all the time. I saw an Army Band recruiting poster. I filled out the proper forms and was offered an audition. I had played the trumpet in high school, but when I went, I couldn't play very well for the audition because my lip had recently healed from a fistfight.

"Luckily, they needed a tuba player, and I spent my last year in Germany traveling all over playing the tuba with the Army band. I finally got out in '49. And just in 2018, I learned that I was classified as a WWII veteran. President Truman did not sign the Peace Treaty until December of '46."

Robert Forsey is still living at 92.

BILL DAVIES   Navy (15 years old)

"My personal feeling is that all young adults should have the opportunity to serve in the military or to enter into civilian programs that allows them to serve one or two years. For most, this experience will assist them to become responsible adults and have a love, not only for their country but for their fellow man," Bill started by telling me.

Bill learned about our annual events from fellow VUMS Willie Paradise and attended for the first time in 2018. He fit in with all immediately as he was very friendly and a first-class gentleman.

"Why did you join the military at 15 years of age?" I asked.

"You know Ken, I had never talked about my childhood before until coming to Portland to join you with all the other veterans. I went into the classrooms to hear them speak and was moved by how all were opening up. It sure feels good to get it all out."

Bill mailed me a copy of his story and gave me permission to use it.

> My father, Shelby Davies, served in the Army, during WWI, and was on the British transport ship, SS Constantia, off the coast of Ireland in the Irish Sea when it was sunk by a German U-Boat (UB-21) on May 5, 1918. The ship was built for 800 troops only, but there were 2000 troops on it when sunk. Two destroyers rescued all of the survivors and over 200 were lost.

My father was assigned to make railroad ties at a Lumber mill in England until the war's end. I remember they held a Survivor's reunion every year in Portland, and it was just a lot of drinking.

He was a jack of all trades and built our family home in 1920 in SE Portland and it's still there.

I'll never forget the last car my father ever owned as they never bought another car. We rolled over a small hill, 1931 Chevy four door sedan and the car stopped upside down. Mom suffered a broken wrist and bumps, and bruises for everyone else.

My parents were in a loveless marriage. We never ate dinner together. My father just stayed in the basement and drank. He was an alcoholic. He would only come upstairs after we had all gone to bed just to get something to eat.

My mother stayed in the marriage just for us kids and left my father when my sister and me moved out. She worked swing shift as an Electrician down at the shipyards, so my older sister by two years and I were pretty much on our own. Because of this, I was a very scared little boy, afraid of the dark and noises.

I was withdrawn and very shy, and I never spoke much. Only advice I remember my father giving me was "Whatever you do, always own up to it. Act like a Man!"

I got in the military at 15 years of age because I was skipping classes in high school and when the grades came out, I received a '5' grade. I don't know why they used numbers then, and a '1' was the highest. I asked the teacher if I started attending regularly and worked hard, could I raise my grade to a '1'? She said, "Of Course." I worked my fanny off, and she gave me a 2. I was so frustrated and told my Dad I wanted to join the Military.

In 1941, the Oregon National Guard was called to active duty, so the Oregon State Guard was formed to replace them. Members were mostly WWI veterans and teenagers. My father was friends with several of the senior officers who were all WWI veterans and they covered for me.

We had to train weekly and use our own firearms. I borrowed my father's deer rifle, a .30-30 Winchester. One weekend a month we patrolled and protected Portland bridges and the Oregon coast.

After I turned 16, I was honorably discharged and joined the Navy. With an altered birth certificate and after passing the physical, I was sworn in and sent to Farragut, Idaho Navy boot camp. Four weeks after boot camp I was ordered to report to duty to become a radio man at the Navy training facility in Millington, Tennessee. We traveled aboard boxcars with no heat and the trip took seven days.

It was there after five weeks, I got really sick and spent twelve weeks in the hospital with pneumonia and malaria. I had to start training all over again.

After graduating, I was sent to gunnery school in Purcell, Oklahoma. From there I was sent to Corpus Christi for training with dive bombers and then Martin PBM Mariners seaplanes. My first night there, one of our squadron's planes hit a buoy while landing and six of the eleven men were lost.

In August of 1945, during a training flight, we were off the coast of Texas about one hundred fifty miles from the base when both engines went out and were forced to land hard on the water. Fortunately, no one was hurt, and the plane was not damaged.

On another flight to Guantanamo Bay, Cuba, we lost radio contact and we did not know our radio trailing antenna had broken off. We had to use Morse code transmit every hour for a position report. We could hear them calling for us. They launched search planes trying to find us. We made it to the Guantanamo Bay Naval Air Station and spent a week there waiting for repairs.

Halfway through our flight training, every other flight crew was cut out and "sat down" and our crew was one of them. We were assigned various odd jobs and basically only worked about an hour of the day. It was very boring.

About two weeks later, a PBM was being serviced (re-fueling of engine oil by a radioman on top of a wing) He lost his balance, fell off the wing and hit hard on the concrete. I immediately took off running about a quarter of a mile to the personnel office and requested I be his replacement. I was asked, "What about the injured man?" I answered, "There were military personal assisting him."

While I waited for confirmation that a radioman was injured, many other radio men also came to volunteer, but I was first in line and got the job. I was back on flight status again and eligible to receive Flight pay again.

After finishing flight training, our crew was scheduled to fly to Hawaii and then on to an undisclosed area in the Pacific to replace a crew to be rotated home. But the orders changed, and our squadron was disbanded, and members were transferred all over. I was offered duty in Panama on a PBM 520 but only if I signed up for four more years. I declined.

Then I was sent to Camp Elliot Marine Base and received orders to fly to Wake Island to replace a radioman. But the Navy discovered that my discharge date was coming up in three and half months. I was given orders to report to the Air Reclassification Center in Coronado, California now known as the U.S. Naval Amphibious Base. I spent two weeks there doing nothing and then was ordered to report to the Naval Air Station at San Pedro, in the Long Beach area of California (that station no longer exists).

I ran into an old buddy from gunnery school and since my flying days were over, he suggested that I join him and volunteer as a telephone operator.

The base phone exchange was manned by civilian workers, working around the clock. The base commander requested that the night shifts be manned by Navy sailors. This was an old-fashioned telephone switchboard used in the 1920s and 1930s. This was a boring job but soon I was ordered to report to the Long Beach Naval base for discharge. The process took two days and my first day was on a Saturday and on Sunday no processing took place.

So, on Sunday, I decided to go swimming at the base swimming pool. During my entire period of my Navy time, I had never really been put in harm's way. That Sunday was different as I developed a severe leg cramp and panic set in. I floundered in the water, yelling for help.

There were three others in the pool, and I guess they initially did not take my yelling for help seriously until after I had gone under water twice. Thank God, they pulled me out to live up to my ripe old age.

In June of '46, my Navel career ended, and I started attending college and joined the Naval Reserve in Portland, Oregon. The only reserve unit was a submarine unit. Talk about a fish out of water that was me and it was dull as the only sub had been decommissioned.

Because of the Korean War, in September of 1950, I received orders to report back to duty in Seattle Washington. After a week of being tested and processed, I was sent to Miramar Naval Air Station (now US Marine Air Station).

We flew from Sand Point Naval Air Station on Lake Washington to San Diego on a double decker aircraft. It was one of three manufactured for the Navy. These four engine planes carried one hundred fifty persons, which was very large for that era. This was a flight from hell.

Over Los Angeles the two starboard engines quit and because parts, equipment, and mechanics were all at Moffit, we turned around and flew to the Bay Area where we had a forced landing. We had to spend the night and then three smaller four engine transports were used to get us down to San Diego.

I was assigned to a VU-3, a utility squadron and had a mission to fly old F-6 fighters by remote control. Drones, we called them birds, (chaser plane) out to sea so that fleet ships could have gunnery practice to shoot down the aircraft. Our second mission was to fly guided missiles, small aircraft with a ten-foot wingspan. We flew both prop and jet aircraft. These were to train ship gunnery crews into shooting down aircraft.

We were not very busy until they moved us to Ream Naval Air Station at Imperial Beach, very close to the Mexican border, because we were flying drones over residential residents out of Miramar.

I became an instructor for the next six months until I was released from active service. I returned to Oregon and got my job back, but in a new city, Eugene, Oregon. I continued to stay in the Naval Reserve as an instructor at Eugene High School's ROTC Program. My final and third discharge was in January of '56 after serving one year in the Oregon State Guard and ten with the U.S. Navy.

"I had many adventures leaving me with many memories, most being great. And I learned a great deal and GREW UP!!!"

Bill Davies is still doing great at 92 years of age.

JIMMY BUNTING   Marines (15 years old)

Jim was another veteran who followed our events and would generously donate even though having not attended. I asked fellow VUMS Willie Paradise to please bring him to one of our Living History Days and I finally met Jim. From then on, he attended just a few of our events until passing

I never heard him speak, but fellow VUMS, Willie Paradise, shared what Jim had told him. "I know he was born in Illinois, and at the age of four, Jim was adopted out of an orphanage by an Illinois farm family. The farmer only wanted him for labor and treated him badly.

"He was forced to start doing chores at five, years of age. When he started school, he had it even rougher for when he finished chores he went to school, then back home, and the chores started all over again until late.

"Jim hated it so much that when he turned fifteen, he went to the farm down the road and asked the farmer to help him. The farmer had a son who was in the Marines and Jim said he wanted to join the military, but he was too young. The neighbor felt sorry for Jim and let Jim bribe him with two bottles of 'Old Yellowstone Whiskey' to take him to the Marine's recruiting office."

Jim's wife Becky told me, "The farmer went with him down to the recruiting station and used his son's birth certificate to say Jim was old enough to join the military. Jim joined the Marines and went off to boot camp. Jim and I traveled back to meet and visit the farmer and I still have a picture of him. Jim was always grateful to him."

"Did your husband ever share his experiences with you?" I asked.

"Not until he joined the VUMS years ago when we moved from California to Oregon. He saw an ad for VUMS and went to a meeting. For most of our marriage, he had nightmares. But I never understood why as he would not talk about them. I know that in Korea, when climbing down the ropes, when getting off a ship, Jim saw a Marine crushed to death between the ship and the landing craft.

"Jim said he worked as a point man in his platoon with two interpreters. Jim was trying to get the enemy to surrender as the war was over.

"One time, both interpreters were killed, and then his platoon was shot at by an enemy machine gun nest. He ran around to the back of the enemy and took the enemy out with two hand grenades." He earned the Bronze Star for that as the grenade killed two and he was forced to shoot the other three. The enemy had killed four Marines.

Willie told me, "After being in Korea for six months, Jim was called before the CO with other Marines where he told them they had all lied and all were underage. Jim's Bronze Star was stripped from him, and he was drummed out of the Corps. They were told that if they ever told anyone they would be sent to prison at Fort Leavenworth."

Becky told me, "It wasn't until 2011 that Jim told me this."

She continued, "But as soon as he turned 17, he joined the Marine Corps again. I know he made the Marine Corps' wrestling team, and during the practice before the Pan-American Games, broke several ribs and could not wrestle.

"Now I know this story is true because I have a book on the atomic bomb tests and Jim's in it. At Desert Rock, Nevada, he witnessed the atomic bomb tests. They were 3,500 yards from three separate atomic bomb blasts in trenches. Even with dark glasses on and arms over his face, he could see the bones in his arm as if it was an X-ray. Of course, it was very hot."

They were ordered to walk towards ground zero, but he said the sand had turned to glass. "It was crunching as we were walking," but finally, the Lieutenant ordered them back.

After Jim's military service, he attended diving and welding schools under the GI Bill to become a certified pipe welder and a nuclear code welder. I also learned that he was the first welder from California to work on the Alaskan Pipeline. He did this for eight years, as well as working in various areas around the country. He was also a commercial diver working as an underwater welder on offshore oil rigs.

His wife Becky also said that Jim was a good husband who was loving, humorous, enjoyed life, and was also a great storyteller. She also wanted me to know that Jim was a generous man who helped many while remaining anonymous.

Jimmy Bunting passed away at the age of 76 in December of 2015.

VUMS Attending Living History Days and Other Veteran Related Events Age When Enlisting Follows Branch Served

Arizona
Hal Pershall, Air Force, 16
Leonard Anderson, Navy, 15
Bob Forsey, Air Force, 16
Bill Cutshaw, National Guard, 16
New Mexico
Ralph Sabroe, Marines, 16
Louisiana
Ralph Kleyla, Marines, 16
Wyoming
Jerry Swan, Air Force, 16
Oregon
John Stobart, Air Force, 16
Jack Lutz, Navy, 16
Dale Halm, Navy, 16
Joe Bello, Army Air Corps, 16
Bill Cooper, Army, 16
Wendell Johnson, Navy, 15
Bob Hanna, Air Force, 16

John Hosey, Army, 16
Bill Chisholm, Army, 16
Richard Demers, Air Force, 16
Ronald Evenson, Air Force, 15
Jim Bunting, Marines, 15
Todd Thomas, Army, 14
Chuck Lasardi, National Guard, 16
Corky Apilado, National Guard, 15
John Sweeney, National Guard, 16
Willie Paradise, National Guard, 16
California
Bill Davies, National Guard, 16
Washington
Joe Champaign, Army, 16
Walter Holy, Army, 16
Shelby Rama, Army, 16
West Virginia
Frank Buckles, Army 16

HOLOCAUST SURVIVORS

LES & EVA AIGNER   Holocaust Survivors

The Aigners attended our MHS Living History Days in the late 90s, speaking to many of our students. When we organized our 'Night of Honor' at Portland's Memorial Coliseum in November of 2000, our art teacher Lori Moe-Burgener had her brightest student artists create oil paintings on large canvas banners. One for WWI, one for WWII, one for Korea, one for Vietnam, and one for Desert Storm. Lori and I then both decided it would be great to include Oregon's Holocaust survivors.

On the day of the event, as each group was announced students holding the banners would then lead the veterans into the arena. Watching the Holocaust Survivors and their families walk into the Coliseum behind their banner was an impressive and emotional sight.

The group was easily over one hundred family members walking together and being greeted with loud applause and lots of tears. For many of the veterans in the crowd who had no idea this would happen, it was quite emotional and very moving.

After everyone had entered, and the Members of the Yakama Warriors Association opened the event by presenting the colors, followed by a 250 strong Oregon high school band representing high schools in the Portland metropolitan area playing the National Anthem.

Then, three WWII veterans, who were our event MCs, took the stage. They were made up of the KGW TV News team for over thirty years, Richard Ross- Marines, Jack Capell- Army, and Doug LaMear- Navy -all three of their stories are in *Remembrance Volume I.*

Richard Ross kicked off things by introducing Les Aigner, who wanted to personally thank all the veterans for his liberation and freedom. In all my 25 years of honoring veterans, this was, and still is, the most powerful and emotional moment I have ever experienced.

Les approached the microphone and began to speak: "It is a great privilege to be here tonight and talk to so many WWII veterans. In the name of the Oregon Holocaust Survivors, I'd like to thank you all for being here today to help pay tribute to the brave men and women who sacrificed so much bringing WWII to an end.

"It was their courage and this great country's fortitude to do what was right that played a major role in bringing one of the world's darkest conflicts and periods to a close.

"I am a Holocaust survivor, and my experiences are much like many of the Holocaust survivors who are here tonight. We all were subjected to starvation, torture, slave labor, and total dehumanization because of our religion.

"At the young age of fifteen, I was taken to the concentration camps, specifically Auschwitz. There I lost my mother and my nine-year-old sister, as well as most of my extended family. Midway through my imprisonment, I was taken to Dachau.

"I had a major injury on my foot that was inflicted by one of the Nazi guards. I was on the brink of survival, just like most of the concentration camp inmates.

"On April 29, 1945, amidst all the despair, the most glorious event happened to us, American troops marched into Dachau Concentration Camps and liberated us, and you have liberated more than 300 concentration camps throughout Europe.

"I can tell you that liberation was the powerful moment, most glorious moment in my life. When I had come so close to death, and now these brave soldiers only a few years older than me, came to our rescue. Not only did the U.S. soldiers free us, they also nursed us back to health.

"A single thank you is not sufficient enough to express the gratitude we all feel toward WWII veterans' efforts and sacrifices. You are in our prayers every day. We thank you for your bravery and humanity. I salute you. God bless you all."

After Les' moving thank you, most everyone in the audience had tears in their eyes. But what happened next had everyone literally crying. Not known to anyone, including me, there was more emotion to come. Doug LaMear said to all, "Mr. Aigner, I'd like you to meet Jack Capell. He was one of your liberators at Dachau."

Les immediately hugged Jack and they both had tears in their eyes. Jack then said, "Mr. Aigner, it was one of the great privileges of my life. A great honor to be able to go into Dachau concentration camp and be a part of liberating those people. A great pleasure to meet you, Mr. Aigner. I probably met you then. You would have been a boy. There were some boys there. Little boys in their striped suits. Something I'll never forget." Jack then broke down sobbing.

A moment I will never forget. I have even been accused many times of setting it all up. However, I assure you, I did not.

I learned in February 2021 from Eva, Les' wife, that Jack Capell reached out to them after the event and invited them up to Seattle to visit. She also said to me, "We visited on three different occasions. We talked over the phone many times and became good friends. He and his wife were such sweet, kind people. And just think Ken, this never would have happened if it weren't for that night."

A few years later, I reconnected with Les and Eva Aigner, this kind, caring and loving couple, at Holocaust Survivor Alter Wiener's funeral - his story is in Volume I.

I'm so grateful they have allowed me to include their stories in this volume as we all can learn so much from them. I did not want to interview them as I learned from Holocaust Survivor Alter Wiener that every time Alter told his story, his nightmares returned for one to two weeks, but he felt it was necessary to teach people the truth.

I asked Eva if they had their stories written down and could I please use them. She shared a video presentation she and Les had given to high school students -Video presentation credit goes to Peter Dutton, sponsored by the Oregon Jewish Museum and Center for Holocaust Education.

Les Aigner spoke first.

"For over 40 years, I never talked about the Holocaust, but in 1989 the deniers started claiming it never happened. I became very angry and have spoken about it ever since. I do not tell you this to make you feel sorry for me, but it happened, and it must be known to all now and in the future. Personally, it is my duty to talk about it.

"In 1939, as a ten-year-old in Czechoslovakia, my father's business license was taken away. Discrimination against Jews was all around us. Nobody was hiring Jews either, so my father moved to the outskirts of Budapest, Hungary, to a town called Csepel. I stayed behind with my grandparents to finish elementary school.

"Jews were not allowed to go to high school, so in 1943, I rejoined my father, my mother, and sisters. My father took me to a machine shop to become a machinist apprentice. Soon after that the Hungarian Nazis, the Arrow Cross Party, came for my father and he was sent to the Russian Front with the German Army for slave labor. The Arrow Cross moved my mother, my sisters, and myself, now alone, to the Jewish Ghetto. My oldest sister was sixteen, and my younger sister was eight. We all were forced to wear the Yellow Star.

"I'll never forget my mother telling me the exciting news "On June 6, 1944, the Americans landed in France, and it won't be long now."

"What an understatement!"

"Then they came for my older sister for slave labor. Soon, we were ordered to pack whatever we could carry and forced onto a truck, and taken to a large, abandoned brick factory packed with several thousand Jews. We were then packed into boxcars. Conditions were so bad, many of the older people died during the trip to our unknown destination.

"We were unloaded at Auschwitz and were separated into two lines, one for men and boys, and the second for women and children. At the front of each line on a platform was the infamous Nazi Officer, Dr. Mengele, who gave the thumb to the right or left which meant life or death.

"It was the last time I ever saw my mother Anna and sister Marika again. My little sister waved goodbye to me, and my mother turned her head to look away.

"We were assigned barracks built for fifty-six horses. There were bunk beds built that were three high and ten to twelve people shared each level. 800 of us were packed into each barrack. There was not enough room for everyone to even stand.

"I noticed four large chimneys with black smoke billowing day and night. I asked another captive if it was the bakery. He said, 'No, it's the crematorium for cremating the dead.'

"About three weeks later, a German guard asked for some volunteers. I raised my hand, and I still don't know why. I was put into the kitchen to chop up cabbage and potatoes and worked there for close to three months.

"One day a German guard yelled at me to shut up, and I didn't stop talking fast enough, so the guard threw a pitchfork at me stabbing my right foot. I was put into the camp hospital for ten days. There was no care or anything to deal with the pain, but at least I was off my feet.

"Days later, Dr. Epstein, a captive himself, came in and pointed to five of us and ordered us back to work. I begged him to be able to stay, but he only said, 'Herraus!! Get out! Go back to your barrack!'

"In pain, I limped out of the hospital. Later that day, we learned that everyone in the hospital was taken to the gas chamber and that Dr. Epstein had saved my life.

"I was always hungry and starving. I was taken to a large bunker factory that required the work of 30,000 slave laborers at all times. Over 15,000 perished there. I worked about five months there doing very hard work, always hoping to be liberated. During our walk back to our barracks, German people would risk their lives throwing some pieces of food to us. All of us had lice the entire time and most got typhoid, including me.

"We were taken to the railroad tracks and loaded on boxcars again. During the trip, the train was shot at by allied planes. Two men standing right next to me were shot in the head. The planes turned around to make a second pass. The German guards went into hiding, but some of the captives opened the doors and we ran into the forest. After it was over the Nazi soldiers hunted us down with dogs, and on gunpoint ordered us back into the boxcars, they didn't even remove the dead bodies. It became known as the death train. I was one of the lucky ones.

"When we arrived, we were unloaded and walked into Dachau Concentration Camp. We were hanging on to each other. I was a 75-pound walking skeleton. On April 29, 1945, the 42nd Rainbow Division entered Dachau and liberated us! I call this my second birthday! Right after being liberated, we were put into a real hospital, with beds and clean white sheets. We cried and laughed at the same time.

"I first went back to our town in Czechoslovakia and found no relatives, so I went to Budapest. I met a man who was able to reunite me with my father and older sister. My sister survived because she jumped from the truck taking them to the railroad tracks onto a trolley car that was passing the truck in the opposite direction. The trolley driver pulled her in and ripped off her yellow star. Another righteous man.

"Eventually, my father remarried, and his stepson, also a survivor, was living in Portland, Oregon. We escaped Communist Hungary in 1956 during the uprising when Soviet tanks entered the city.

"I want you students to know I do not hate the German people and I wanted a home full of love. I did not want to burden my children with my past. I had enough of Ism's- Nazism & Communism, and I am forever grateful for the United States of America for giving me freedom."

Eva Aigner spoke immediately after Les.

"I just wish we could all just accept each other without discrimination and I'm so grateful my children were born in this country.

"I was born in 1937, in a small town in Czechoslovakia. In 1939, discrimination against Jews spread like wildfire, even our neighbors turned on us. My father was a hat maker. My sister was eight years older than me. Before 1939, my family lived in peaceful times.

"The first Nazi law was that Jews could no longer own a business and my father's license was taken away. Because no one would now hire Jews, we moved on the insistence of my father's brothers, to Budapest, Hungary.

"The goodbyes to all of our relatives were sad, and it was the last time I would ever see them. Only one cousin survived Auschwitz.

"With the help of my uncle, we found an apartment. My father got a job, also with my uncle's help, and we thought our life was good again. But in 1943, The Nazis took my father away for forced labor and our lives became very difficult.

"I'll never forget watching my mother cry as she stitched the Star of David yellow patch on our coats, every stitch, a tear rolled down her cheek. Sadly, my father never returned. He was killed during a bombing of the forced labor camp.

"Every time we went out, we were yelled at and had things thrown at us. I was now in first grade, and every morning we and my classmates stood and sang the Hungarian National Prayer. Soon our teacher announced that the Jewish students had to go out in the hall and wait as we were no longer allowed to sing the song. As a six-year-old, I didn't understand.

"A few weeks after that, our apartment became a marked housing, with a yellow star on the front of the building, and we had to share our small apartment with three other families. There was no electricity or heat and many times no running water. Then we were forced to move to a ghetto area and had to share an apartment with twenty other people. We all laid on the floors just on a blanket, as there was just no room enough for anything else," she said.

Someone everyone should learn about is Eva's mother, Gizella, who was beyond a hero. I've never in my life heard such a powerful story about a mother's will and determination to save and protect her daughters. The effort she went through should be immortalized in a movie or documentary.

"The Hungarian Nazis (Arrow Cross Party) took my mother, Gizella, away when I was eight years old, and my sister, Ibolya, was fifteen. She was loaded on a train boxcar filled with other women and the destination was Auschwitz.

"During the trip, the train stopped, and the doors were opened for some water. My mother jumped off the boxcar and ran to escape. A German soldier yelled, 'Halt' and aimed his gun. My mother knew many languages, Slovakian, Hungarian, German, and Yiddish. She grabbed the knees of the soldier and said, 'Please, let me go. My husband has already been killed, and I left two children behind. They will die if I can't get back to them.'

"Then the soldier stopped and said, 'I have a wife and three children waiting for me at home. I can't openly help you, but I'm going to turn around towards the train with my gun. If you can run, run.' She did and it took her ten days on foot to reach Budapest. She snuck into the ghetto at night, and when she started looking for her children, she was told they had been removed from the safe house and taken down to the river to be shot.

"Jews were marched to the banks of the Danube, ordered to take off their shoes, which were valuable in wartime, then shot in groups of 50 or more and pushed into the river to avoid the need for burial. My mother ran to the river, approached a guard, and offered him the last thing she had, her wedding ring, to buy their lives. The guard took the ring and said, 'Jewish children cannot wander around the city.' She recognized our cries, out of all the people. It was a miracle!

"We spent the remainder of the war, until Budapest was liberated by the Soviet Army on Jan. 18, 1945, in the ghetto."

Soon after hearing Eva's story, I called her to tell her how much I was in awe of her.

Eva responded, "My mother is my hero; she was the most courageous and loving mother and grandmother. Nobody could stop her from saving her children. Her bravery and love are an everlasting memory for me and our family."

In the background, Les yelled, "I always called her Mom!"

"Right after marrying Les, I told him I do not want our children born in a country filled with discrimination. We had neighbors who were Nazis and now lived in a Communist country and faced discrimination from them also. We were standing in a bread line and overheard two men talking behind us. They said, 'Let's get rid of the communists first, then we'll get the left-over Jews!'

"I wanted to give birth in a safe, free country, with love.

"Les had a difficult time with the memories. Nightmares every night, crying. In his dreams he was back in the camps and afraid. But when our first child was born, Suzanne, in 1960, at that moment Les' outlook on life changed. Les told me, 'I'll never forget, but now I have a new life.'"

I interviewed both of their children. First was the oldest daughter, Sue.

"I was in middle school, I believe as an eighth grader, when my parents told me they were Holocaust Survivors. Looking back on my childhood, there were many little things that now made sense. They were always very protective. We were told to not talk about being Jewish in public. Keep it private.

"My parents were not as trusting, and it took time for them getting to know someone before trusting them. Eating meals as a family always started on time. Food was like gold, and we were required to eat everything on our plate, no waste. The refrigerator was always full and always with meals already prepared.

"I had a great childhood; our home was filled with love and some of our best friends were Germans and Hungarians who were not Jews. I was taught, 'There are good and bad people in every race and religion. Look for friends with integrity, who are honest, good people.'"

Sue recently retired after 37 years as a nurse. A study about second-generation children of PTSD passed down from Holocaust survivors found that a large majority worked in the medical profession as doctors, nurses, and caregivers.

Les and Eva's son Rob was born in 1964, and as a junior in high school, while taking American History and studying WWII he suddenly had many questions.

"I had an epiphany. I knew my parents were from Hungary, and they never talked about it. I was piecing together the unknown because we were Jewish, and there had to be more to the story.

"That evening, after school, I asked my dad about what he did in WWII, and he told me the truth.

"I felt guilty about asking him. My father did not want us to worry or feel guilty. I remember how private my parents were, especially money, when buying a new car, or family vacations. It was all personal and not to be talked about. They always had fears of authority. I really noticed it when a police car was right behind us or at our side.

"My dad suppressed his feelings very well and was more hardened and maybe callous that bad stuff happens in life. He was not afraid of death. but had a beautiful simplicity about life, really enjoyed the everyday beauty in life. My parents raised a family in a normal life and way healthier than the average family. He never made a big deal out of the small things. If I didn't do well on a school assignment, he would say "I'm glad you care, just try harder next time, it's no big deal.

"Over the years, I've learned a lot about the children of Holocaust survivors. We inherited worrying and anxiety, but we are very resilient also. My parents are my heroes, and their history has given me a much better perspective on gratitude."

Eva, with the support and involvement of Les, was one of the co-chairs of The Oregon Holocaust Memorial in Portland's Washington Park. If you ever have the chance, you must visit there. It is beautiful.

The memorial has a circular cobblestone area similar to a town square. During the Holocaust, Jewish families were rounded up in town squares before being loaded onto trains and taken to concentration camps. You can see bronzes of glasses, a doll, a violin, some shoes, and a suitcase, that represent everyday objects that were left behind by the families.

It also has a cobblestone walkway with bars, simulating railroad tracks, which lead to a wall of panels that give a history of the Holocaust and quotes from Holocaust survivors. At the end of the wall is the soil vault panel. Buried below the panel are interred soil and ash from six killing-center camps of the Holocaust.

Les and Eva, with five other survivors, two Rabbis, and six adult children, including Sue and Rob, traveled to Poland and Germany to collect soil and ash from six different death camps: Auschwitz-Birkenau, Treblinka, Sobibor, Chelmno, Majdanek, and Belzec. The soil and ash were put into six bags and put into homemade traditional Jewish caskets, no nails, all built by Les, and then interred below the panels.

Sue told me, "It was a very painful and healing experience, lots of tears."

Eva also told me they were invited to speak to the WWII veterans of the 42nd Rainbow Division's National reunion years ago. This was one of the units that were in on the liberation of Dachau. She told me that all the veterans were overwhelmed with emotion after Les thanked them.

I asked them if they had ever heard of the great basketball player Kareem Abdul Jabbar and that Kareem's father was in the all-black 761st tank battalion that had taken part in the liberation of the Mauthausen concentration camp, Gunskirchen, on May 5, 1945.

Les responded, "I didn't know that, but the first black men I ever saw were black American soldiers who helped liberate us."

Les and Eva also supported and testified before the Oregon House of Representatives for legislation requiring all Oregon students to learn about the Holocaust and other genocides. The bill was inspired by the Holocaust survivor Alter Wiener. It unanimously passed in 2019.

I will always remember Les and Eva as never complaining, and they always greeted anyone with a smile. They are two wonderful people who will always, for me, embody the meaning of the word 'survivor'.

I also consider Les and Eva Aigner as American heroes and, in their honor, I asked Gracie Goddard, who made the patch for Holocaust Survivor Alter Wiener to make another Star of David patch for Holocaust Survivors Les and Eva. It includes the words 'Love Over Hate' and also has barbed wire in the shape of a heart shape surrounding their names. In their honor, Audrey Rumpakis sewed it on The Jacket.

Les Aigner passed away at the age of 92 in August of 2021.

Eva Aigner, his loving wife for over 65 years, is still living.

Les and Eva gave me a beautiful video birthday message just days before Les passed away. I am forever blessed to have had them in my life.

IMPORTANT ACKNOWLEDGMENTS

BENJAMIN BLAIR (LYTLE)

Co-Author, Editor, Remembrance Volume I, II, & III

Benjamin is an expatriate living in Morioka, Japan, where he has been teaching for over twenty years as an adjunct lecturer at universities. He graduated from Western Oregon University with a Bachelor's in Public Health Education, minoring in Eastern Philosophy. He also earned his Master's in Teaching at Lewis & Clark College in Portland, Oregon.

Benjamin is married to Yukari and has two children, Marina and Leon.

Benjamin is my stepson from my first marriage to his mother, Lorraine. I met him when he was in the fifth grade, and I was lucky to have him as a student for four years in Strength Training at Milwaukie High School. I also coached him in football, wrestling, and track and field.

He was extremely intelligent as a youngster, and was a very gifted athlete, and had a strong work ethic. At Milwaukie High School, he was a three-sport athlete. He did football, wrestling (coach Jim Gadberry pressured him into wrestling his junior and senior years, and he ended up advancing in matches at the State Championships), and track and field (4×400m relay, 4×1600m relay, 200m, and shotput).

It was in football however where he excelled. As a freshman, Benjamin started on special teams and was a backup linebacker. He even scored a touchdown as running back in a varsity game. And all this only as a freshman. He started both ways his sophomore, junior, and senior years. He was a natural leader.

He was not only First Team All-League as an Offensive Guard and Inside Linebacker, but was the Three Rivers League Defensive Player of the Year. He was named to the First Team All-State team on Offense and Defense. He played in Oregon's Shrine All-Star Football game and received a full athletic scholarship to play at Idaho State University. But his most impressive honor was being selected the Three Rivers league's Scholar-Athlete of the Year.

After university, Benjamin decided to spend a year overseas, which led him to live permanently in Japan teaching English. We have always kept in touch over the years, and he has always considered and called me Dad, which means the world to me.

Benjamin offered to help me and Bob Christianson co-author and edit *Remembrance Volume I*, and is the co-author of this *Remembrance Volume II*. He will also be again co-authoring our next book, *Remembrance Volume III: Dear Vietnam Veterans, I'm So Sorry For How You Were Treated When You Came Back Home.*

Benjamin is so thorough with his editing and writing skills and fact-checks everything. I'm very blessed, lucky, and grateful for his devotion and impressive work. I'm also extremely proud of him, and I know his mother, Lorraine, is too.

I love you, son!

KELLY SCHAEFFER

Second-Editor

Kelly is a former Strength Training student of mine at Milwaukie High School and graduated in 1999. She was very involved in sports and activities. She was an All-League softball outfielder, played soccer, and was the class president.

She graduated from Western Oregon University with a Bachelor of Arts in English-Linguistics, minor in business, in 2003, and earned her Master of Arts in Teaching Degree in 2004. She was the Western Oregon Journal Copy Editor from 2001 to 2003. She taught English Language Arts at Scio High School in Scio, Oregon from 2005 to 2008, and then at Newberg High School in Newberg, Oregon from 2008 to 2018.

Kelly is currently a substitute teacher, a tutor, a coach, and an editor.

She is married to Colin Schaeffer, a Milwaukie alum class of 1999, who is currently teaching math there and who was the former head football coach. They have two boys, David and James.

She was heavily involved with our Living History Days at Milwaukie in '96, '97, '98, and worked with her classmates to honor veterans at our high school as well as The Tribute to Veterans at the Veterans Memorial Coliseum in 2000.

As a teacher in Newberg in 2012 and '13, she organized over 800 students and staff from Newberg High School to travel to our Living History Days at Evergreen Aviation and Space Museum.

When I asked Kelly to give me a little background for her to put in the book, she sent me this. It is just something I want to take the opportunity to brag about as she and I are still very proud of her weight room squat record.

"I was Mr. Buckles' student for strength training in my sophomore and junior year-- I ended up being a top female squatter in my class- maxing out at 255 lbs. when I weighed only 120 lbs. I made the weight record wall my senior year for softball- outfield: (Bench 135, Incline 115, and Squat 255 = 505 lbs.) I was so proud of myself!
I don't think you have to write all that, but I thought I would share that with you because it wasn't easy."

No, Kelly, it wasn't easy, but I knew you could do it! I'm very grateful to Kelly for her helpful editing skills and for taking the time on her own to help promote the books.

Kelly's posted review on Amazon:

"I treasure this book! It's my new favorite, and I'm a high school language arts teacher. I am grateful for the stories that Mr. Buckles has immortalized in these pages because they are the true stories of our American Heroes, Our Veterans, written by their trusted friend, Mr. Ken Buckles. It is only because of Ken's vision, his years of dedication and love for these Veterans, for his students, and for history that we are privileged to get to read about and learn from these real, untold stories today. I was one of those lucky students who attended Milwaukie High School for the first 3 Living History Days, and it changed our (the students') outlook on life. It's hard to describe the miracles that we witnessed on those special days-- the people we met, the pride, the honor, the healing, the humanity-- but Ken does an excellent job of capturing that spirit of Milwaukie that made this happen. Thank you to our Veterans, once again, for your vulnerability, courage, and sacrifice so that we may learn from you and live with love for you! You will not be forgotten! Highly Recommended Book!"

MALINDA LETT BUCKLES

Remembering America's Heroes Communications Liaison/Performer

I've been married to Malinda for the past fifteen years. Malinda was a Milwaukie mom and her middle son, Bennie, set us up on a date sixteen years ago.

Bill Call, a former Marine and veteran of WWII and the Korean War, said it best sixteen years ago when Malinda and I were dating, "Ken, bringing Malinda onboard your non-profit is the best move you ever made."

Malinda was born and raised in Atlanta, Georgia, and has lived in Oregon for over 30 years. She has five children, Nick (Air Force veteran), Nikii, Cristal, Bennie, and Moriah, and eight grandchildren, Trinity, Ozias, Delami, Roman, Kahlia, Caussius, Tianna, and Tavion.

She loves dancing, singing, and modeled as a teenager, and also acted in two movies, *Just an Old Sweet Song*, with Cicely Tyson, and *Mr. Holland's Opus*, with Richard Dreyfuss.

Malinda got involved with our Assembly of Honors during Living History Days at Milwaukie High years before we ever dated. One of her great additions to our Tribute to Vietnam Veterans event was when she talked every female teacher at Milwaukie High into wearing a mini skirt, go-go boots, and a blond wig. During the assembly they all danced to 'These Boots are Made for Walking'. Everyone loved it, especially the students and they received a standing ovation.

Once we started dating and married, I had her sing for the majority of our veteran related events, and the veterans love her. She has been asked to sing by veterans more times than I'm asked to speak. She has sung at several national veteran reunions.

In July of 2013, I spoke at a Saturday session at the National Reunion for the USS Indianapolis Survivors Association, and Malinda sang a couple of songs. Afterward, members from the USS Indianapolis Survivors asked her to sing the next day during their annual and emotional Memorial Service to those veterans still at sea.

I'll never forget how many WWII veterans and spouses would break down sobbing or crying whenever she sang 'I'll Be Seeing You'. 100-year-old Alice Bruning, a WWII Nurse on a Red Cross hospital ship, approached Malinda after singing that song. And with tears running down her face she said, "My husband sang that song to me on the docks right before they boarded to be shipped overseas. We were married just the night before. Thank you so much for singing our song."

The most important addition Malinda brought to our mission, she recommended that the veterans' spouses be included in events, and I agreed. This took us to another level as we all became a big family, and all looked forward to seeing each other every year.

I'm so grateful for her passionate support, dedication, commitment, inspiration, and love for all that we do and have done. She deserves a lot of credit for getting on me for several years to write and finish these Volumes.

Malinda, I love you!

* ★ *

ACKNOWLEDGMENTS

Carlos Catala and Safeway

As a child, Carlos grew up in the Japanese occupied Philippines during WWII. I first learned of Carlos when he was the supervisor in charge of shipping and receiving for Safeway's Oregon Distribution Center. He contacted me because he got Safeway to donate over $1000 worth of food for our 1st MHS LHD lunches and $1000 cash. Carlos was able to get Safeway to donate for 12 years in a row. Unfortunately, the donations ended when Carlos retired. I didn't meet him in person until the 3rd year when I asked if I could come to his work. I asked him, "Why do you make these Safeway donations happen?" Carlos said "I was born in the Philippines and as a small child remembered watching Japanese and American planes dogfighting in the sky above. All of the teenage boys and men had to escape to the mountains, and they all joined the 'Guerrilla' movement. The old and the women and children stayed behind during the Japanese soldiers' occupation. It was a brutal time. I make these donations happen because I'll never forget the loud rumbling sound approaching our Barrio one morning. We all ran outside and saw

American tanks with the lead tank flying a large American flag coming down the dirt road. I remember my mother, grandmother, and all the other women falling to their knees crying and thanking the Lord and the Americans. I owe the American Soldiers, and these donations are a small token of my appreciation." Carlos invited me to a couple of the Philippine American Association Oregon Chapter events. The Philippine people were all so friendly and giving. I met a couple of men who were Philippine Guerrillas. I met Jesse Oscilla, who was a US Navy Vietnam veteran, and he was able to convince Alex Deal Rosa, Simeon Mamaril, Florence Gonzales, Marcelina Pilmenta, and Concordia Burja-Mamaril to attend a MHS LHD and speak to students. This was the first time they had ever publicly spoken of their horrible experiences during the Japanese occupation. I knew this was going to be powerful and emotional, so I assigned them to a classroom of seniors. All three women spoke about being raped by Japanese soldiers. All three cried during their presentations and of course, most of the students cried also. It was the only time they agreed to talk to students as Jesse Oscilla could not get them to come back again.

Scott Guptil and PGE

Scott reached out to me right before our first 'Veterans - A Night of Honor' show at the Memorial Coliseum in November of 2000. He was the public relations liaison for Portland General Electric. He handed me a donation from PGE for $3000 and he offered to bring the company's large golf cart that could seat about 10 people. That evening he picked up veterans from the parking lot and shuttled them to the event. The next year when our event moved to the Rose Garden, he was able to get PGE to donate $12,000. For the next 10 years, Scott was able to get PGE to donate $3000 a year. Thanks to Scott Guptil, PGE was our number one financial supporter. I never had to ask or fill out any request applications. Sadly, when he retired, I called the new person in charge to ask what I needed to do to continue receiving donations. I was immediately told, "I don't know how your organization got this kind of money all these years but it's over now. We need to share our funds with other organizations." I asked her, "Do you know what our non-profit does?" But before I could finish speaking, she interrupted me saying, "No, but it doesn't matter, you've gotten enough money from us." I will forever be grateful to Scott Guptil and what he did for us while at PGE for the 12 years of support.

Merrill & Judy Jackson, Oregon Veterans of Foreign Wars - VFW

Merrill was an Air Force Vietnam veteran living in Redmond, Oregon. Both he and his wife were VFW State Commanders. She was the VFW's Auxiliary State Commander. They both attended some of our LHDs at Milwaukie High School in the late nineties and came to our big shows at the Memorial Coliseum and Rose Garden. They were super friendly and would ask me, "If you ever do an LHD at Redmond HS, let us know. We can help with everything." They were the first veterans I called when I told them, "I've got great news, we're doing an LHD at RHS." They were so helpful. They raised money and hosted a welcoming dinner at their local VFW. I wish we had more people like them in every community. They were top-class, and I am forever grateful.

High School Administrators and Teachers

Milwaukie HS - Joyce Henstrand

> Without her giving a very enthusiastic thumbs up in 1995, this journey never would have gotten off the ground. When I asked her for permission and was telling her the plan, Joyce's eyes started to well up. I was taken back and asked, "Did I say something wrong?" She looked up at me smiled and said, "I think it's a wonderful idea. My father was at the beaches of Normandy on D-Day driving a Higgins boat, and he married a young English woman after the war. My mom lost her family on her 16th birthday during a German bombing raid of London."

Redmond HS - Dan Purple
Dayton HS - Dave Fluke
McMinnville HS - Ryan McIrvin
Gervais HS - Mike Martin & Mike Solem
Reynolds HS - Jeff Gilbert, Mike Anderson, Dee Archie
Pendleton HS - Jim Gadberry, Tom Lovell
Chemawa Indian School - Lora Braucher
Nestucca Middle School - Jim Gadberry
Oregon City HS - Ed Burton, Kathy Johnson, Tom Lovell
JROTC Commander Doug Thomas

Thank you to all the other administrators for letting veterans come to their schools.

★

Milwaukie High Teachers, Students, Staff, Cooks, and Parents

Jeff Gilbert
Jeff Linman
MHS Tech Cadre
Pulse Media
Lori Moe-Burger
Greg Van-Winkle
Katri Rainhold
Bill Burdett
Jeff Bjorn
Dustin Erickson
Sandy Bennett
Vera Barrett
Sharon Stutzman
Bill Flechtner
Kathy Farrell
Ivonne Guerra
Graci Evans

Heidi Pullen
Sue Moody-Baker
Clyde Curley
Barb Jenson
Kelly Carlisle
Victoria Wheeler
Elyse Nemes-Gilbert
Barb Hacke
Aina O'Malley
Sue Johnson
Marty Wilkins
John Grant
Pam Owens
Joyce Henstrand
Beth Palmer
Frank Higuera
Sue Roberts

Laurie Drysdale
Ed Belknap
Jim Owens
Joann Hiromura
Linda Reese
Barb Sitz
Bill Zehner
Jennifer McMahon
Diane Richardson
MHS Parents
Linda Palandech
Shelly Rigdon
Lillian Stone
Linda Reese
Katy Spinks
Sarah Landers
Colin Brown

Val Krewson
Karen Sheets
Justin Fieldler
Steve Bishop
Kyle Kelly
Rob Krewson
David Bell
Tara Piner
Leann Flateau
Stephanie King
Malarie Huizar
Chris Keller
Greg Keller
Ashley Keller
Jake Keller
Tony Wright

Amanda Reed
Vickie Carter
Gesica Winship
Vanessa Taylor
Cassandra Smit
Colin Brown
Jessica Rindfesch
Robert Griffin
Joe Deich
Chris Davenport
Ed Butler
Vienne Nguyen
Kelsey Neubauer
Mark Newbauer
CJ Cabral
Carl Loomis

Lindsay Tomac
Lisa Emmons
Stephanie Overton
Mike Reed
Jonathan Fitzpatrick
Brad Stiffler
Randy Schweitz
Adam Phillips
Alicia Tallman
Kelley Tallman
Leslie Hawkins
Ali Townsend

So many more,
please forgive me if I
left anyone off

⋆ ★ ⋆

Performers over the years:

Malinda Lett Buckles
Steve Wasson
Justine Reese
MHS Pony Pipers
MHS Choir
MHS Jazz Band
String of Pearls
    Anne Du Frense
    Lois Lindsay
    Leslie Rohoe
The Kingsmen
    Dennis Mitchell
    Mike Michell
    Dick Peterson

Billy Haugen
Barrie Malcolm
Brian Tierney
Hailey Kilgore
Anthony Armstrong
Paul Greenidge
Julie Emry
Margie Boule
Michael Allen Harrison
Julie Ann Johnson
Pastor Richard Probasco
Allen Delay
Paul Delay
Musical Saw & Father of Jazz

Kim Nicklaus

Steve Peterson

Todd McPherson

The Brown Sisters

   Dorcus

   JoAnna

   Rachel

   Leah

Norman Leyden

Glen Miller Band

Chrisse Roccaro

Maurice Wright

Sojourn Breneiser

Chuck Bolton

Rodney Eichenberger

   Guest Conductor Florida State

Mt. Hood Community College Jazz Band - Susie Jones Director

2 Sisters and a Mr.

   Terry Scott

   Laura Erickson

   David Erickson

   Moriah Taylor

   Ron Silver

Alisha Baker

Bob Coopenrider

Gerutha Greenidge

Scott Anderson

Kamela Davis

Dennis Marcellino

John English

The Hot Shot Tap Dancers

Kells Irish Pipes & Drums

Portland Police Highland Guard

Judy Gregoire & Tap dancers

Jon Mortz

Robert Stull's All-Star rock band (all MHS Alumni)

All-Star Bands from - Benson, Canby, Clackamas, Cleveland, Corbett, Estacada, Glencoe, Grant, Gresham, Milwaukie, Mountain View, Putnam, Barlow, Skyview, Tualatin, and Wilson high schools

Choirs from - Beaverton, Clackamas, Cleveland, Corbett, Estacada, Jefferson, Jesuit, Lake Oswego, Milwaukie, Putnam, Tigard, and Wilson high schools

MCs over the years -
   Coach Darrell 'Mouse' Davis - Navy
   Coach Jerry Glanville
   Bill Schonely - Marines, Voice of the Trail Blazers

Indoor Museum and Outdoor Military Vehicles -
   NW Historical Association
   Military Vehicles Collectors Club of Oregon

Especially Steve Greenburg

Camp Withycomb Military Museum

US Marine Reserves

Andy & Max GI Surplus - Owner MHS Alumni

POW Display -

James Rollison, Army Air Corps, WWII, Ex-POW, Germany

Fred Jossi, Army, WWII, North Africa, Ex-POW.

Mike Myer, 10th Mt. Division

Roddie Tamblyn

US Flags & Dog Tags

Revolutionary War Re-enactors

NW Civil War Re-enactors

WWII Re-enactors

Vietnam Re-enactors

Vietnam Veterans of Oregon Memorial Fund

NW Veterans Motorcycle Association

* ★ *

Hispanic Medal of Honor Heroes Display-

Rodney Forni MHS Class of '72   Roger Forni, MHS Class of '72
          Owners of LaQuinta Inn & Suites Portland Airport.

Great guys and very comedic twin brothers who were classmates and football teammates at Milwaukie. All three of us have the same painful memory of not getting to play in the last game as seniors. The memory is seared in my mind because the three of us had lockers next to each other. All three of us had tears of hurt rolling down our faces as we changed out of our uniforms and into our clothes. Rodney and Roger's generosity the past ten years are a major reason we've been able to keep our mission alive. They have comped hotel rooms for our entire out of state veterans every November, anywhere from 25 to 30 rooms for five nights. Also, they sponsor our Annual 'Goodbye Dinner' at Saylor's Old Country Kitchen steakhouse for 75 people and insist that everyone order whatever they want from the menu. This dinner has become one of the highlights of the week as all have become friends. The veterans every year give gifts of gratitude to the Fornis. Thank you so much! And thank you to your amazing staff at LaQuinta, especially Cami Pollack, Director of Sales, and Marlene Rodriguez, General Manager.

Tech Audio's Randy Summers, MHS Class of '76
>> Sound for many of our events, MHS, Oregon State Fair,
>> Veteran's Tributes and always gave a 50% discount

Galaxy Productions
>> Owner Scott Griffith, MHS Class of '71

COR Accounting, Milwaukie, Oregon
>> Owner Melannie Cormack
>> Amy Bolger-Persad, Account Manager

COR Accounting has been doing R.A.H.'s bookkeeping Pro Bono for the past ten years. Thank you, Melannie and Amy for your amazing support.

Wolf Wise Media, Milwaukie, Oregon
>> Dustin Erickson, MHS Class of '04
>> Carly Taylor
>> Tech support, web design, video recording, video editing, photography, graphics, etc., for the past 15 years for either pro bono or 75% discount.

They were so supportive & awesome. Thanks so much.

Alex Buckles, CPA, daughter-in-law, married to my son Anthony
>> Has prepared R.A.H.'s taxes pro bono for the last two years

Thank you, Alex.

Optimist Club of NE Portland
>> We are very grateful to Scott Keller & the rest of the members for their past three years of support and generous donations.

Chuck Fretwell, FOB Taproom, Owner, Army

Forward Assist, Non-profit helping wounded veterans

John Steinbaugh, Army, Special Forces, Delta Force Medic
>> 3 Purple Hearts, 17 Tours, Bosnia, Afghanistan, Iraq

Dennis Cater, Army, Helicopter Crew Chief, Medevac, Afghanistan

Don Coburn, Army, Crew Chief, Special OPS,
Canby American Legion Vice Commander
Gerald Rowlett, Westlake Development, Street of Dreams builder
Mike Harn, Army, Anlon Development, Street of Dreams builder
Luke Morley, Lakeside Lumber, Owner, Street of Dreams builder
Lt. General Russell and Shirley Davis
Backstop Bar & Grill, Ken & Lori Arrigotti, Owners
Businesses that sponsored tickets for Veterans- An Evening of Honor
in 2018 for their employees who were veterans -
Camp Withycombe
Precision Cast Corp
The Standard
Rich Lane, PSU Vikings Football, Class of MHS '88,
Weston Kia
David Hoopes, PSU Vikings Football
Phoenix Investment Group
Bill Call, Marines, WWII, Iwo Jima, Korea, Inchon, Chosin Reservoir
American Veterans of Intel
Portland General Electric
Nike Military Veterans
Veterans Care Centers of Oregon
Charles Herring, PSU Vikings Football
Korean Society of Oregon
Dignity Memorial - Lincoln Memorial
Bob Sisul, PSU Vikings Basketball
Hunter-Davisson, Inc.
Alliance Steel
Mae Terry, Widow of Roger 'Bill' Terry, Tuskegee Airman
Frank Cutsforth and Cutsforth's Thriftway
Media & Image Consulting, Inc., Beverly Brooks
SP&B Canby Printing, Ginger Graham
Hillsboro VFW
Portland Police Association
Gretchen Pilip

Byung-Moon Lee
Scott Cereghino, MHS Class of '94

———— ⋆ ★ ⋆ ————

R.A.H. Board of Directors Current
      Paul Henderson, Board Chair, Navy, MHS Class of '85
      Jim Gadberry, Army, Vietnam, National Wrestling Coaches
         Hall of Fame
      Rich Lane, MHS Class of '88, PSU Football Hall of Fame
Spearheaded founding of R.A.H.
      Jim Page, Navy Corpsman, Vietnam
      Kathy Page, Nurse, Vietnam Era
Gov. Victor Atiyeh
Rich Campbell, Army, Vietnam
Anne DeFrense
Doug Bomarito, Naval Academy, Navy, Vietnam
Jim Riggle, National Guard
Dick McPike
Bob Palandech, Air Force
Keith Baker
Bob Hammitt
Ron Youngman, Coast Guard, Vietnam
Dream Weaver
Tammy Stevens, MHS Class of '85
Robert Lippi, MHS Class of '84
John Haub, Army, Vietnam, Assistant U.S. Attorney

Advisory Board
      Clint Elsom, Navy, Vietnam Era
      Lt. Gen. Russell Davis, Air Force
      John Steinbaugh, Army, Special Forces, Medic, 13 tours
         Afghanistan and Iraq
      Pastor Richard Probasco, New Song Community Church

Office Managers
       Lillian Stone
       Katie Spinks
       Shelly Palandech
       Linda Palandech West

So, so many more, please forgive me if I left anyone off.

Thank you one and all.

May God bless you and yours.!

ACCOMPLISHMENTS & AWARDS

Raised over $5,000 for various Veterans Causes, Oregon Korean War Memorial, Tuskegee Airmen Scholarship Fund, Navajo Code Talkers Funeral Expenses, Yakima Warriors Veterans Association

Raised $10,000 for WWII Memorial, Washington, D.C., MHS was #1 school in fundraising for Memorial in the U.S with the help of Milwaukie High School students and staff

Recognized and Honored by President Clinton during his speech at for WWII Memorial Groundbreaking Ceremony featured on CNN and C-SPAN

Recognized and Honored by President Clinton and Senator Robert Dole at The White House during breakfast for the top donators to the WWII Memorial June 2000

Recognized by President G. W. Bush by Personal letter Nov. 2001

Recognized by President Barack Obama at the last American WWI Veteran Frank W. Buckles' funeral at Arlington National Cemetery in March 2011

Raised over $475,000 for programs honoring veterans relating to Living History Days and Assembly of Honors

Founded and created Oregon Military Hall of Fame, honoring Oregon's famous and highest decorated veterans 2005, 2006, 2007

Organized Living History Days at 43 high schools over 23 years

Teacher of the Year 2005 Oregon Education Association's Excellence in Education

Military Order of the World Wars, Patrick Henry Gold Medallion

> Only two others were awarded in 2000, Ross Perot 1992 US Presidential Candidate and Speaker of the House Congressman Henry Hyde of Michigan

> Since 1918 the first person from the entire Western Region of The United States to receive this honor

Youth on the Move, Inc.'s International Educators Hall of fame inductee, Los Angeles, CA, Oct. 24, 2015

Portland State University Athletic Department's 1st Annual Legends of the Game Award honoring PSU Alumni Athletes accomplishments to society Sept. 3, 2016

NBA Portland Trailblazers 'Hometown Hero Award,' Mar. 1, 2018

CONVERSATIONS WITH FAMOUS VETERANS

Senator Robert Dole
    Army, 10th Mountain Division, WWII, Bronze Star
Lt. General Hal Moore
    Army, WWII, Korea, Vietnam, Distinguished Service Cross, Bronze Star, co-authored *We Were Soldiers Once... and Young*
Joe Galloway
    Journalist., Vietnam, Bronze Star, co-authored *We Were Soldiers Once... and Young*
Major Bruce 'Snake' Crandall
    Army, Vietnam, Medal of Honor, Distinguished Flying Cross, Bronze Star, Purple Heart, Helicopter gunship pilot
Captain Ed 'Too Tall' Freeman
    Army, WWII, Korea, Vietnam, Medal of Honor, Helicopter pilot

Chuck Yeager

Air Force, WWII, flying ace, test pilot, first pilot to break the speed of sound - I was asked to introduce him to veteran event in Oregon where he was honored and was the speaker. He ordered me to write the introduction down as if I was a private. When I started to introduce him, he interrupted me. He said "You're already screwing up. Sit down. I'll introduce myself."

Louis Zamperini

Army Air Corps, B-24 bombardier, WWII, Ex-POW of the Japanese, Life made famous by *Unbroken* book and movie

Guy Gabaldon

Marines, WWII, Saipan, Tinian, Navy Cross, Purple Heart, at 18 captured or persuaded to surrender over 1,300 Japanese soldiers and civilians during battles for Saipan and Tinian islands in 1944, Life made famous by movie *Hell to Eternity*

Steve Kofron

Army Special Forces, *12 Strong* Movie

Anthony Sadler Jr.

Army, *The 15:17 to Paris* 2018 Movie

Ben N. Skardon

Army, WWII, Bataan Death March Survivor, '60 Minutes'

Hershel Woodrow Williams

Marines, WWII, Iwo Jima, Medal of Honor, 2018 Super Bowl Honorary Captain & Coin Tosser

Chris Spence

Army Special Forces, Movie *12 Strong*

General Siegfried Knappe

German Wehrmacht, WWII, Author of *Soldat: Reflections of a German Soldier* - After reading this book in the early 1990s, I called information and they connected me to his home phone. He was living in Cincinnati, Ohio and we talked for about 45 minutes. He passed away in 2008. The 2004 Oscar nominated film *Downfall* about Hitler is based on his book.

SPEAKING ENGAGEMENTS/ KEYNOTE SPEAKER

1st Marine Division National Reunion and Oregon Chapter events

Tuskegee Airman Association National Reunion

USS Indianapolis Survivors National Reunion

Veterans of Underage Military Service National Reunion and
  Oregon State Reunion

Defenders of Bataan & Corregidor National Reunion

101st Airborne Association National Reunion

Korean War Veterans Association National Reunion

Chinese American Veterans Association National Reunion

USS Cruisers Navy Association National Reunion

Tin Can Sailors National Association of Destroyer Veterans
  Reunion

USS Little Survivors National Reunion

Pearl Harbor Survivors, Oregon Chapter

Military Order of World Wars, Oregon Chapter

Eighth Air Force, Oregon Chapter

Philippine American, Portland Chapter, Women's Stories

Vietnam Veterans of America, Oregon Chapter

442nd Japanese American Veterans, Oregon Chapter

41st Sunset Division 'Jungleers', Oregon Chapter

Purple Heart Association Oregon State Convention

EX-POWS, Willamette Valley and Columbia River, Oregon
  Chapters

National Association of Black Veterans, Washington D.C. Chapter

NABVETS, Oregon Chapter

USS Neville Reunion, WWII LST, Oregon Chapter

American Legion State Convention

VFW State Convention

Chosin Few State Reunion, Oregon Chapter

United Mexican American Veterans Association Reunion, Orange
  County, CA

10th Mountain Division Reunion, Oregon and Washington
    Chapters

Korean War Veterans Association, Oregon and SW Washington
    Chapters

LST Navy Veterans Association Oregon State Reunion

US Naval Academy Alumni Association, Oregon Chapter

US Women Marines Association, Oregon Chapter

Northwest Veterans Motorcycle Association

Oregon State Penitentiary Incarcerated Veterans Club

Walter Reed Medical Hospital Wounded Warriors

Oregon State Fair Veterans Appreciation Day

Tribute to Veterans at The Veterans Memorial Coliseum

Veterans, A Night of Honor at The Rose Garden

Tribute to Veterans at Arlene Schnitzer Concert Hall

50th Anniversary of The Veterans at Memorial Coliseum

Over 50 Veteran Funerals, Memorials, or Celebrations of Life

Other speaking engagements around Oregon, Washington, California, Oklahoma, Montana, Hawaii, Maryland, Nevada, Arizona, West Virginia, Virginia, Indiana, Texas, and Washington D.C. including many small veteran organizations, churches, retirement homes, Rotary Clubs, Lions Clubs, Optimists Clubs, American Legion Posts, VFW Posts, Band of Brothers Clubs, Fire Departments, Police Departments, Howard University, and Lewis & Clark College

Winter of 2002 formed 501(c)(3) non-profit organization Remembering America's Heroes (RAH) to spread the Living History Day experience to schools all over the State of Oregon and United States 1996-2019

Organized Living History Days—Veterans' Classroom Sessions. Spoke to students at the following educational institutions to in-service expectations of a Living History Day

    1996-2010 Milwaukie High School

    1999-2000 Glencoe High School

    2001-2003 Rex Putnam High School

2001-2002 Clackamas High School

2003-2004, 2009 Pendleton High School

2004-2007 Redmond High School

2005-2007 Nestucca Middle School

2008-2011, 2017 Dayton High School

2008-2009, 2018 Oregon City High School

2008-2009 Jesuit High School

2008 LaSalle High School

2009 Barlow High School

2009 Dunbar High School, Balou High School
    Howard University, Washington, D.C.

2010-2019 Gervais High School

2010-2019 Reynolds High School

2012-2013 McMinnville, Newberg, Sheridan, Willamina, Amity, Yamhill-Carlton, Delphian, Dayton, Gervais, St. Helens, Scappoose, Horizon Christian, David Douglas, Roosevelt, Lebanon, McNary, and Oregon City High Schools and Portland Community College

2008-2018 McMinnville High School at Evergreen Aviation and Space Museum

2019 Chemawa Indian School and Oregon City High School

MHS ALUMNI VETERANS

I was absolutely amazed at the number of Milwaukie High Alumni Veterans that attended our 1st Living History Day. For the next several MHS LHDs, the number increased as the word got out. We started this program at MHS because the students, staff, community, and alumni's support were so amazing. The following are the MHS Alumni who attended our Living History Days from '96 - '99:

Paul Shrock
    Class of '29, Army, WWII, Photography, South Pacific
Norris Perkins
    Class of '30, Army, WWII, Tank Officer, North Africa, Sicily
James Perkins
    Class of '33, Army, WWII, Medical Service
Kenneth Ward
    Class of '34, Navy, WWII, USS Neville, Guadalcanal
Waldo Stransky
    Class of '34, Army, WWII, European Theater
Harold Boehi
    Class of '34, Army, WWII, European Theater
Archie Mecklem
    Class of 35, Navy, WWII, Minesweeper, South Pacific
Delmar Westlund
    Class of '35, Army, WWII, Philippines
Eugene Van Gordon
    Class of '35, Army, WWII
Larry Knutson
    Class of '36, Army, WWII, European Theater
Harold Jahn
    Class of '36, Navy, WWII, Pearl Harbor Survivor
Alan Elder
    Class of '36, Air Corps, WWII, C-47, Philippines, Korea, B-29
Philip Walter
    Class of '36, Army, European Theater
Merrily Hewitt
    Class of '36, Waves, WWII, Pearl Harbor Survivor
Melba Searle
    Class of '36, Army, WWII
Virgina Matach
    Class of '36, Waves, WWII
Violet Calhoun
    Class of '36, WWII, Home Front

Rosalia Card
  Class of '36, Waves, WWII
Ernie Bisio
  Class of '36, Air Corps, WWII, China, Burma, India
Miles Bubenick
  Class of '36, Navy, WWII, Seabees
Elia Bubenick
  Class of '36, WWII, Home Front
William Elder
  Class of '36, Coast Guard, WWII, South Pacific
Winston Bradshaw
  Class of '36, Air Corps, WWII, Glider Pilot, Europe
Dean Stanley
  Class of '36, Army, WWII, 41st Sunset Div., New Guinea
Robert Hatz
  Class of '37, Army, WWII, Battle of the Bulge
Kenneth Van Gordon
  Class of '37, Army, WWII
Ray Renfro
  Class of '37, Army, WWII, European Theater, South Pacific
Lynn Richardson
  Class of '37 or '39, Army, WWII, 41st Sunset Div.
Walt Timm
  Class of '37, Air Corps, WWII, B-29, South Pacific
Jean Kunz
  Class of '37, Army, WWII, 41st Sunset Div., New Guinea
William Horton
  Class of '37, Air Corps, WWII, Stateside
Tom Lattanzi
  Class of '38, Army, WWII, 41st Sunset Div., New Guinea
Emil Becker
  Class of '38, Marines, WWII, Guadalcanal, Bougainville
Marshall Dana
  Class of '38, Navy, WWII, South Pacific

Richard Birkemeier
    Class of '38, Air Corps, WWII, China, Burma, India
Colin Ackerson
    Class of '39, Brig. General, Army, WWII, Pacific Theater
Frank Driver
    Class of '39, Army, WWII, Corregidor, POW
Hans Juhr
    Class of '39, Navy, WWII
Violet Calhoun
    Class of '39, WWII, Home Front
John Howell
    Class of '39, Air Corps, WWII, P-51 Pilot, Air Force, Korea
Lawrence Secor
    Class of '39, Navy, WWII
Charles Seymour
    Class of '39, Marines, WWII, Palmyra Island
Richard Burns
    Class of '39, Army, WWII, European Theater
Don Foidel
    Class of '39, Navy, WWII, PT-103, South Pacific
Lewis Simpson
    Class of '39, Navy, WWII
Rose Howe
    Class of '39, WWII, Home Front
Melba Searle
    Class of '39, Aircraft Spotter, WWII
Dorothy Ueland
    Class of '39, Waves, WWII
Richard Short
    Class of '39, Army & Navy, WWII
David Parker
    Class of '39, Coast Guard, WWII, Philippines, Okinawa
William Cooley
    Class of '39, Army, WWII, 41st Sunset Div., New Guinea

Eldon Ulrich
    Class of '39, Navy, WWII, Hospital Corps
Edward Lind
    Class of '39, Army, WWII, 41st Sunset Div., New Guinea
Floyd Taylor
    Class of '40, Army, WWII, 41st Sunset Div., New Guinea
Irene Taylor
    Class of '40, WWII, Home Front
Charles Speer
    Class of '40, Army, WWII, South Pacific
Arthur Crino
    Class of '40, Navy, WWII, Sub Chaser, South Pacific
Richard Jamison
    Class of '40, Army, WWII, Normandy, European Theater
Jim Grizzell
    Class of '40, Navy, WWII, USS Lexington, Coral Sea
Jim Downs
    Class of '40, Air Corps, WWII, B-17, European Theater
Terry Metcalf
    Class of '40, Air Corps, WWII, B-26 Gunner, North Africa
Mary Spoelstra
    Class of '40, WWII, Homefront
Merrill Peterson
    Class of '40, Navy, WWII, Stateside
Elna Schmidt
    Class of '40, Women's Army Corps, WWII
Elaine Varker Minihan
    Class of '40, WWII, Stateside
Dick Salter
    Class of '41, Navy, WWII, USS Nevada, Pearl Harbor Survivor
Bill Woolford
    Class of '41, Air Corps, WWII, Air Force, Korea
Stanley Whipple
    Class of '41, Navy, WWII

Betty Doel
    Class of '41, WWII, Home Front
Bob Bunnett
    Class of '41, Air Corps, WWII, B-24, Search & Patrol,
    Air Force, Korea, B-29
James Schuld
    Class of '41, WWII, Korea
Leslie Peake
    Class of '41, Navy, WWII, South Pacific
Don Dolan
    Class of '41, Army, WWII, South Pacific
Jim Fleming
    Class of '41, Army, WWII, European Theater
Bob Egge
    Class of '41, Army, Engineers, European Theater
Barbara Nusbaum
    Class of '41, Waves, WWII
Floyd Aldridge
    Class of '41, Army, WWII, India
Bob Yoshitomi
    Class of '41 Army, Japanese American 442nd, Italy
Ann Yoshitomi
    Class of '41, WWII, Internment Camp
Art Crino
    Class of '42, Navy, WWII, Submarine Chaser, South Pacific
Ed Stauffer
    Class of '42, Marines, WWII, South Pacific
Don Allison
    Class of '42, Navy, WWII, USS Breton, South Pacific
Nilo Untenen
    Class of '42, WWII
William McDonald
    Class of '42, Army, WWII, Okinawa
George McEachran
    Class of '42, Air Corps, B-17, European Theater

Bill Carey
    Class of '42, Army, WWII, Signal Corps, South Pacific
Sid Hall
    Class of '42, Air Corps, WWII, B-29
Ina Hall
    Class of '42, WWII, Home Front
Richard Foltz
    Class of '42, Navy, Seabees
Coralie Hubbard
    Class of '42, SPARS, WWII
Stanley Johnston
    Class of '42, Air Corps, WWII, B-17, European Theater,
    Dutch Underground
Jim Juhr
    Class of '42, Navy, Seabees, WWII, New Guinea, Philippines
Boyd Gibson
    Class of '42, Navy, WWII, USS Tennessee, Pearl Harbor
Ralph Nortell
    Class of '42, Army, WWII, European Theater
Alden Loring
    Class of '42, Navy, Seabees, WWII, New Guinea, Philippines
Wayne Sawyer
    Class of '42, Marines, WWII, Saipan, Tarawa
Don Davis
    Class of '42, Air Corps, WWII, B-29, Stateside
Chuck Morrissey
    Class of '42, Air Corps, WWII, Parachute Rigger
Marvin Bischoff
    Class of '42, Marines, WWII, Iwo Jima
Hugh Mills
    Class of '42, Navy, WWII, South Pacific
Warren Fleming
    Class of '42, Navy, WWII, LCVP, Okinawa, Korea
Richard Clark
    Class of '42, Army, WWII, 38th Div., New Guinea, Philippines

Menter Peterson
    Class of '42, Air Corps, Crash Fireman, European Theater
Ottis Taylor
    Class of '42, Navy, WWII, Destroyer, South Pacific
Harold Elder
    Class of '43, Marines, WWII
Owen Street
    Class of '43, Navy, WWII, Tanker, Saipan, Okinawa
Calvin Howard
    Class of '43, Army, WWII, Iwo Jima
Urban Arbour
    Class of '43, Air Corps, WWII, Stateside
Rod Clayton,
    Class of '43, Air Corps, WWII, Stateside
Ed Neubauer
    Class of '43, Navy, WWII, LST, D-Day, Normandy, Okinawa,
    Korea, USS Epping Forest
Don Ives
    Class of '43, Air Corps, WWII, Burma, India
Joe Cartasegna
    Class of '43, Army, WWII, European Theater
Bill King
    Class of '43, Army, WWII, England
Clarence Lewis
    Class of '43, Navy, WWII
Don Graber
    Class of '43, Air Corps, WWII, Air Force, Korea
Lee Lucas
    Class of '44, Navy, WWII, Destroyer, Atlantic & South Pacific
Jack Sperr
    Class of '44, Air Corps, WWII, Stateside
Bob Wiley
    Class of '44, Navy, WWII, Armed Guard, South Pacific
Bill Farr
    Class of '44, Navy, WWII, South Pacific

Delmer Eisert
     Class of '44, Merchant Marines, WWII, South Pacific
Cliff Snider
     Class of '44, Army, WWII, European Theater
Ray Sawyer
     Class of '44, Marines, WWII, South Pacific
Bill Hanson
     Class of '44, Air Corps, WWII, Philippines
Bill Johnston
     Class of '44, Navy, WWII, Aircraft carrier
Cecil Dammen
     Class of '44, Navy, WWII, Stateside
Charles Parker
     Class of '44, Navy, GMSM, WWII
Bill Shultz
     Class of '44, Marines, WWII
Bob Palmer
     Class of '44, Army, WWII, Air Force
Mervin Foxworthy
     Class of '45, WWII, Army
Earl Wiseman
     Class of '45, Army, WWII
Jack Aldridge
     Class of '45, Army, 41st Sunset Div., WWII
Jim Orrell
     Class of '45, Navy, WWII, Philippines
George Scheider
     Class of '45, Air Corps, WWII, B-17, European Theater
George Crockett
     Class of '45, Navy, WWII, USS Tarawa, South Pacific
Don Marquardt
     Class of '45, Army, WWII, European Theater
Charlie Farnsworth
     Class of '45, Coast Guard, WWII, South Pacific

Dorthy Schultz
Class of '45, Marines, WWII, Korea
Don Link
Class of '45, Air Corps, WWII
Bill Heater
Class of '45, Navy, WWII
Glen Frey
Class of '45, Navy, WWII
Evan Winter
Should have graduated Milwaukie High but instead joined the Navy, Awarded belated diploma, WWII, South Pacific
Larry Dennis
Class of '43, Army, WWII, 17th Airborne Division, Battle of the Bulge, Invasion of Germany
Betty Lovelett King
Class of '46, WWII, Home Front
William Bader
Class of '46, Army, Korea
Don Ray
Class of '46, WWII
Peter Welzbacker
Class of '46, Navy, Korea
Ken Yates
Class of '47, Army, Korea
William Horton
Class of '47, Air Corps, WWII, Stateside
George Crocket
Class of '47, Navy, WWII, USS Tarawa
Orville Adams
Class of '47, Marines, Korea
Don Doersch
Class of '47, Navy, Korea
Bob Burke
Class of '47, Army, Korea

Bill Luchs
    Class of '47, Army, Korea
Robert Potts
    Class of '47, Army, MP, Korea
Dean Gotchall
    Class of '47, Marines, Korea
Doug Mclean
    Class of '48, Navy, Corpsman, Korea
Bill Lundell
    Class of '48, Navy, Korea
Don Glivinski
    Class of '48, Air Force, Korea
Richard Wonderly
    Class of '48, Army, Korea
Bob Welzbacker
    Class of '48, Navy, Korea
Ed Conroy
    Class of '48, Navy, Korea
Frank Fassold
    Class of '48, Navy, Korea
Martin Burke
    Class of '48, Army, Korea
Russ Ekstrom
    Class of '49, Navy, Vietnam
Bill Oetken
    Class of '49, Army, Korea
Bert Becker
    Class of '49, Navy, Korea
Keith Rislove
    Class of '49, Air Force, Korea
Charles Schol
    Class of '54, Air Force, Korea, Vietnam
Jay Lillie
    Class of '58, Marine Corps, Captain, Vietnam, Medal of Honor
    Jackson School for the Arts football coach

Don Chambers
  Class of '59, Navy, Vietnam, Submarine
Lloyd White
  Class of '59, Army, Vietnam
Roger Cherry
  Class of '60, Army, Vietnam, Special Forces
Bob Hill
  Class of '63, Army, Vietnam
Ron Koenig
  Class of '62, Air Force, Vietnam
Grant Angel
  Class of '64, Army, Vietnam, Special Forces,
  Nixon's Presidential Staff
Michael Gebbler
  Class of '64, Marines, Vietnam
Robert Hanson
  Class of '64, Army, Marines
Chris Thompson
  Class of '64, Army, Vietnam
Craig Neff
  Class of '64, Air Force, Vietnam
Bob Adams
  Class of '65, Army, Vietnam
Curtis Chapman
  Class of '66, Navy, Vietnam
Allen Matter
  Class of '67, Army, Vietnam
David Branham
  Awarded belated diploma at MHS LHD 2004, Army, Vietnam
Mike Harryman
  Class of '76, National Guard, Persian Gulf
Bert Darnielle
  Class of '79, Navy, Beirut, Grenada
Garth Didlick
  Class of '83, Air Force

Paul Henderson
    Class of '85, Navy, USS Enterprise, Operation Praying Mantis
Corey Hester
    Class of '97, Army, Hurricane Katrina
Tracy Hester
    Class of '97, Army, Guantanamo Bay, Cuba
Eric McPherson
    Class of 2000, Army, Airborne, Iraq, Afghanistan
Kyle Rovetto
    Class of 2001, Army, Iraq, Medic

FORMER MHS TEACHER VETERANS

John Checkis
    Art Teacher, Marines, WWII, Okinawa
Robert Yorkston
    Photography Teacher, Army, WWII, North Africa, Sicily, Italy
Richard Geer
    Drama Teacher, Army, Korea
Hank Cedros
    Social Studies Teacher, Army, Korea

MHS JAPANESE AMERICAN STUDENTS
INTERNED DURING WWII

Brig. General Colin Ackerson and members of the Class of '39 presented a beautiful plaque to MHS in the late 1990s. They felt very strongly that their fellow classmates should be remembered. Colin Ackerson stated, "We've always felt a terrible injustice was done to our classmates and their families of Japanese American descent. We did then and we still feel that way today. We want current and future MHS students to know that these MHS graduates of the WWII generation were patriotic American citizens of Japanese Ancestry, but they were interned from 1942 to 1944." Many of the boys volunteered to join the Army and served in the 442nd Regimental Combat Team, which was a segregated Regiment of Japanese Americans. They fought against the Germans in the European Theater in Italy and were one of the highest decorated regiments in all of WWII.

INTERNED JAPANESE AMERICAN MHS STUDENTS

Roy Yokata	George Furukawa	Utaka Morishita
Takeo Morishita	Kena Tanabe	Henry Tambara
Pearl Yamada	Sheen Morikawa	Shea Morishita
Tuu Yamada	Tae Yamada	George Morishita
Yoshi Morishita	Charles Yamada	Mecha Yamada
Rose Tambara	Jack Yoshitomi	Ayame Tamiyasa
Frank Morishita	May Tambara	Martha Tanabe
Tae Yoshitomi	James Yamada	Kio Kuribayshi
Chiyo Yamada	Mary Yoshitomi	Sakae Morikawa
Robert Yoshitomi	Masuo Kuribayshi	Saude Tamiyasu
Sam Sasaki	Hattie Yamada	Ruth Watanabe
Arthur Yoshizawa	Dutch Watanbe	Masako Hinatsu
	Yoshi Hosokawa	

The following list is all the names of Milwaukie High School Alumni who died while serving our country in the Armed Forces. They are honored every year at MHS during the 'Gold Star Assembly'. We know of no other high school in Oregon that does anything like this. We are missing important information for many of them. Hopefully, this will lead to collecting and updating this list.

Please go to Remembering America's Heroes Facebook homepage or the Remembering America's Heroes homepage to watch the video 'Gold Star Assembly 1932-1979 — Milwaukie High School'.

Lest We Forget

Talbot Bennett
> Class of '32, Marines, WWII, South Pacific

Richard Umphrey
> Class of '33, Navy, WWII, Fighter pilot shot down during 'Battle of Midway', Married high school sweetheart

Ted Fisch
> Class of '35, Student Body Secretary, Basketball, State Champion Swimmer, Air Corps, WWII, B-17 pilot shot down in Philippines

Jack Levy
> Class of '35, Basketball, Tennis, State Swimming Champion, Maroon Staff, Air Corps, WWII, B-17 pilot shot down at Solomon Islands

Johnny Stein
> Class of '35, Student Body Officer, Maroon and Milwaukian Staff, Air Corps, WWII, B-17 pilot shot down over Germany

Bobby Stein

    Class of '36, Student Body, Football manager, Class clown, Marines, WWII, Died during training at Camp Pendleton

Marvin Walker

    Class of '37, Navy, WWII, Fighter pilot shot down

Mark Estes

    Class of '39, Army, WWII, Died in airplane crash

Bob Landstrom

    Class of '39, Army, WWII

Gordon Carney

    Class of '39, Army, WWII

Robert Donald Russell

    Class of '39, Navy, WWII, USS Neville, Guadalcanal

Owen Bauserman

    Class of '40, Football manager, Navy, WWII, Pearl Harbor, USS Selfridge, Solomon Islands, South Pacific

Alfred Spor

    Class of '40, Army, WWII, 101st Airborne, France

Gene Foidel

    Class of '40, Football (Halfback), Army, WWII Era, Killed in automobile crash at Fort Lewis Army Base, Washington

Mickey Burke

    Class of '41, Football, State Boxing Champion, Baseball, Marines, WWII, Guadalcanal, Left fox-hole three times to rescue wounded Marines, rescued two Marines, never made it back on the third trip

Jim Sherwood

    Class of '41, Three sport star Football Basketball and Track, Student Body President, Navy, WWII, Corpsman attached to Marines in Saipan

Randall Townsley

    Class of '41, Football, Army, WWII, Philippines

Jack Jamison

    Class of '42, Football, Wrestling, Navy, WWII, USS Vincennes sunk at Battle of Savo Island, Guadalcanal

Wendal Schmidt
    Class of '42, Air Corps, WWII, Airplane shot down
Ralph Mosher
    Class of '42, Student Body President, Army, WWII
Bill Geil
    Class of '42, Band, Navy, WWII, Ship sunk in South Pacific
Robert 'Bob' M. Gribble
    Class of '43, WWII
Gordon Criteser
    Class of '43, Navy, WWII, USS Spence, Destroyer,
    8 Battle Stars, ship sunk during Typhoon Cobra at Okinawa
Louis Kearns
    Class of '43, Army, WWII, Died in non-hostile incident
Kenneth Wright
    Class of '43, Air Corps, WWII, shot down in Germany
George Dunigan
    Class of '46, Class President, Army, WWII
George Kerr
    Class of '43, Army, WWII
David Wright
    Class of '43, Navy, WWII, ship sunk in South Pacific
William N. Cromwell
    Class of '46, Army, Korea, Chosin Reservoir
Keith P. LaBarr
    Class of '47, Air Force, Korea
Wesley R. Wallace
    Class of '47, Korea
Louis Cavendish Honeyman Jr.
    Class of '48, Army, Korea
Clarence Ruben Berreth
    Class of '47, Army, Korea, Silver Star
Raymond McCoun
    Class unknown, Marines, Korea, Battle in South Korea
Gerald Timm
    Class of '57, Coast Guard, died of injuries from accident at sea

James 'Jim' P. Turney
    Class of '46, Army, Korea
Bud Smith
    Class of '59, Basketball, Baseball, Student Body President, Air Force, Vietnam, Fighter pilot, Jet shot down, Parents owned Candy Store on Main St.
Warner 'Craig' Jacobson
    Class of '60, Football, Tennis, Senior Class President, Army, Vietnam
David F. Popp
    Class of '61, Army, Vietnam, Airborne, Helicopter shot down, daughter Cynthia graduated from MHS in '84
Jere J. Nelson II
    Class of '62, Air Force, Vietnam, Missing in Action
Wayne Conrad Reinecke
    Class of '64, Navy, Vietnam, USS Bennington, Helicopter crashed at Gulf of Tonkin
Larry Iannetta
    Class of '64, Attended Central Catholic HS transferred to MHS Senior year to graduate with friends, Army, Vietnam, Helicopter shot down
Martin Dietrich
    Class of '64, Army, Vietnam
William Block
    Class of '65', Army, Vietnam
Keith Arnold
    Class of '65, Army, Vietnam, Helicopter pilot
Michael Greeley
    Class of '66, Loved working on cars, Marines, Vietnam
Donald Schafer
    Class of '66, Navy, Vietnam
Larry Dikeman
    Class of '67, Army, Vietnam
Daniel Irvin Mambretti
    Class of '69, Army, Vietnam

Cliff Redding

> Class of '79, Navy, Submarine, Murdered on leave

Tom Swanson

> MHS Chemistry teacher, football coach, Normandy, France

Dylan Carpenter

> Class of '05, Navy Corpsman, Afghanistan

Jordan DuBois

> Class of '09, Army, Iraq

The last two alumni veterans' names were added in 2012. Jordan and Dylan were added with controversy. There were some teachers and administration that felt that it was dishonorable to include the two alumni veterans to this impressive Gold Star Assembly because they both committed suicide. I decided to be proactive, so I asked for veterans' opinions on the issue at The 1st Marine Division's and The Chosin Few's monthly lunches. Most of the feedback cannot be printed due to the colorful language. They all stated they would personally visit MHS and demand that the two alumni veterans be added immediately. Well, that was not necessary as I met with the principal and told him how the veterans of both organizations felt about this issue. He agreed and both Jordan and Dylan were added. There was never any question for me that both young men's names should be on this memorial.

★

MILWAUKIE MUSTANG ALEX HUSSEY

Alex was a student of mine in weight training and an extremely hard worker. Since I started teaching weight training in 1982, I recognized the hardest worker in class every month and rewarded them with a T-shirt with the words 'STEEL WORKER' emblazoned on it. In between those two words was a picture of a man wearing a hard hat and pressing two heavy dumbbells overhead. It was a highly sought after shirt. I would always tell students it could not be bought but only earned. Alex and his training partners, brother Zach Hussey and best friend Dillion Floyd, all earned T-shirts. All three joined the Army after graduation. In 2012, on his first tour in Afghanistan with the 82nd Airborne Division, Alex stepped on an explosive device and lost both legs and three fingers on his left hand. For over two years, Alex endured many surgeries and therapy and was living in a military rehabilitation center in California. Early in 2014, I learned that he needed to buy a wheelchair accessible truck and the VA could only give $30,000 towards the truck and the truck would cost $50,000. I knew right then that I needed to organize a fundraiser. Around March, I was contacted by a former MHS classmate of mine, Bob Stull. Our MHS Class of 1972 did not have a 40th class reunion, so he had the idea of organizing the 42nd class reunion in conjunction with also raising money for The Wounded Warriors organization. I told him about MHS wounded alum Alex Hussey and asked him what he thought about raising money for Alex. Bob agreed. The VFW Post 4248 in Milwaukie donated their facility. Bob was very popular in high school and a talented musician. He formed an alumni rock band for entertainment, and I had some other talented professional performers sing also. The Milwaukie Police, Clackamas County Police, The Clackamas County Fire Department, and The Milwaukie Fire Department escorted Alex to the event. I came to the event with $9000 raised as I started a fundraiser on Facebook in June and challenged all MHS Alumni from every class to donate. The Mustangs of many classes rose to the occasion. After Alex arrived, we passed hats around the crowd and thirty minutes later we had just over $20,000. The MHS Class of 1972 led all fundraisers with $7,500. We were all shocked at the generosity of everyone and the success of the event. Alex and his wife Kim were very grateful.

List of Donations

Class of '72 -	$7,520	Total Mustangs Donations	$12,156
Class of '89 -	$1,021	Total Veterans Donations	$10,075
Class of '94 -	$830	Total Milwaukie Community	
Class of '84 -	$745	Friends & Family Donations	$3,494
Class of '88 -	$720	Total PSU Vikings	
Class of '49 -	$200	Football Alumni	$1,520

Class of '51 -	$175
Class of 2010 -	$140
Class of '34 -	$100
Class of '47 -	$100
Class of '57 -	$100
Others -	$505

GRAND TOTAL $27,245

Alex married his wife Kim the year before, and she was at his side for his two years of surgeries and rehabilitation. When Alex was in a coma, the doctors told her she needed to move on with her life as Alex was not going to make it and if he did, he would most likely be a vegetable for life. Kim refused to leave his side and ended up marrying Alex knowing that she would be a caregiver for Alex. What an amazing young lady.

MHS FLAGPOLE MEMORIAL

A memorial was built on the MHS campus for the MHS Gold Star Alumni veterans to be part of our school's flagpole. It was dedicated in the spring of 2009 with the driving force of Grant Angel and the help of the Class of '64. We fundraised for a beautiful flagpole memorial outdoors on the west side of campus. The sides were marble with the engraved names of all alumni who died while serving our country. Grant was able to convince North Clackamas School District to chip in to the fundraising efforts needed to build it. This beautiful memorial was dedicated with a ceremony in the spring of 2009.

HIGH COST OF FREEDOM DISPLAY

On Tuesday, September 11, 2001, I was working at school and glued to the classroom TV watching the live coverage of the destruction and shocking tragedy of the Terrorist attack on America. A student of mine was wearing a necklace she had made with pop tabs. Seeing it a thought came to me, what if we collected pop tabs and built a visual display that would illustrate the number of US Military Armed Forces members in all American wars, from the Revolutionary War to the recent conflicts. One tab would represent one military serviceman or servicewoman. None of us ever imagined that we would soon be adding pop tabs for the war in Afghanistan and then Iraq. My group of very loyal and extremely helpful students for our Living History Days started collecting the pop tabs. I then came up with the idea that we would string them on thin cable wire and attach them to sheets of plywood. While it was being put together, it was stored in my garage and students would work on the project in the evenings or Saturdays. All in all, it took over four years to complete. I should have tracked the hours spent working on it for it would be overwhelming. Many, many times, friends, neighbors, and relatives thought I was crazy. There were many times I agreed but when I thought about quitting and throwing it away, I would be overcome with tremendous guilt. I would imagine the many mothers and fathers whose lives were devastated from the news of losing their loved one to war. I am very grateful to West Coast Wire, Rope, & Rigging who very generously helped. As well as the Campfire and Boy Scouts who also helped in the completion of the project. I am also very grateful to Carl Loomis for taking care of the display and taking his own time to take it to various places and set it up. Also, thank you to all the others. When it was finally finished it was so emotional to see it displayed and observing people's reactions. The display consists of almost one and a half million pop tabs, and its length is over 75 yards long. It has been displayed at Milwaukie HS, Fort Vancouver, The Rose Festival Fun Center, The Oregon State Fair, the Traveling Vietnam War Wall at the Lincoln Memorial, and at a 4th of July Fireworks benefiting A Hero was Here, the Sgt. John 'Kyle' Daggett Foundation, and the Serving Those Who Sacrificed Serving Us stand in Vancouver, WA.

★

FACES OF THE FALLEN

Soon after we attacked Al Qaeda and Taliban forces in Afghanistan in 2001, the inevitable happened, US casualties started happening. The Washington Post started an on-line page posting the pictures and personal information of our soldiers who had fallen in combat. Seeing a face instead of just a name was visually powerful. I thought it would be very educational to download the pictures of every KIA, print them, and attach them to a large poster-size card stock paper. I approached my student assistant, Alicia Tallman, and asked her if she would like to create this display for her senior project. She was happy to do this. We also received a lot of help from MHS teacher Jeff Linman, to whom I am very grateful. We never imagined in our wildest dreams that this display would grow and grow, especially after we invaded Iraq. Working on this became emotionally draining for Alisha, as every day there were more names to add to the display. There were many days she worked on this with tears flowing. We named it 'The Faces of the Fallen' as a visual and educational tribute to each serviceman or woman killed in the conflicts in Iraq and Afghanistan. We set-up and displayed this display at high schools, Lincoln Memorial Cemetery, The Oregon State Fair, and The Rose Festival Fun Center. Public reactions to this display compared to reactions I have witnessed at The Vietnam Wall in DC, The Traveling Vietnam Wall, and The USS Arizona Memorial at Pearl Harbor, Hawaii was overwhelming and depressing. When Alicia Tallman graduated from Milwaukie High School, her sister, Kelly Tallman, assumed responsibility for taking over and updating the display. Over the years several students helped work on 'The Faces of the Fallen'. The display itself had 24 panels, measuring eight feet by three feet, with biographies and photos of the fallen on both sides. After I retired from teaching at MHS in 2009, InSpirit Marketing Inc. in Albany, Oregon asked to borrow the display and set it up at a mall for several weeks leading up to Veterans Day. InSpirit Marketing continued to display this every year until 2014 when Vets Helping Vets HQ of Albany took over taking care of it. They changed the name to 'The Wall of Honor' and they reprinted everything, purchased new panels, and updated the fallen to the present. Vets

Helping Vets HQ has taken the display around the state and has done an amazing job with this, and we are very grateful.

— ⋆ ★ ⋆ —

OREGON MILITARY HALL OF FAME

In 2006, my R.A.H. board chair, Jim Riggle read about an Annual Military Hall of Fame Banquet and Induction Ceremony in Oklahoma City, and I was then sent down to learn how we could start one here in Oregon. We held our 1st Oregon Military Hall of Fame in April of 2007.

2007 Inductees
Oregon Chapter of the Chosin Few
Roberta Leveaux
 RAF pilot, WWII,
Gordon Morgan
 Marines, WWII, Guadalcanal, Purple Heart
Kenneth Reusser
 Marines, WWII, Korea, Vietnam, 2 Navy Crosses, 5 Purple Hearts
Art Jackson
 Marines, WWII, Peleliu, Medal of Honor
Larry Dahl
 Army, Vietnam, KIA, Medal of Honor
David Kingsley
 Army Air Corps, WWII, KIA, Medal of Honor

2008 Inductees
Jerry Pero
 Marines, Vietnam
10th Mountain Division Oregon Chapter
41st 'Sunset' Division, 'Jungleers', Oregon Chapter
442nd Regimental Combat Team, Oregon Chapter

General Herbert B. Powell
  Army, WWII, Korea, Silver Star, Bronze Star, Purple Heart
General Marion Carl
  Marines, WWII, Korea, Vietnam, 2 Navy Crosses
Robert Maxwell
  Army, WWII, Medal of Honor
Maximo Yabes
  Army, KIA, Medal of Honor

2009 Inductees
Ernest Argo
  Marines, Korea
Edward C. Allworth
  Army, WWI, Medal of Honor
Rex T. Barber
  Army Air Corps, WWII, Navy Cross, 2 Silver Stars
John Noble Holcomb
  Army, Vietnam, Medal of Honor
Marc A. Lee
  Navy Seal, Iraq, KIA, Silver Star
Harry H. W. Niehoff
  Marines, WWII, Pearl Harbor, Guadalcanal, Tarawa, Saipan, Tinian,
  Silver Star
Stuart S. Stryker
  Army, WWII, KIA, Medal of Honor
Oregon Ex-POWs

I hope you will enjoy *Remembrance Volume II* with more WWII stories and the Korean War when it arrives in 2021 followed by *Remembrance Volume III Dear Vietnam Veterans, I'm So Sorry For How You Were Treated When You Came Home.*

In Flanders fields the poppies grow
Between the crosses, row on row,
That mark our place; and in the sky
The larks, still bravely singing, fly
Scarce heard amid the guns below.

We are the Dead. Short days ago
We lived, felt dawn, saw sunset glow,
Loved and were loved, and now we lie
In Flanders fields.

Take up our quarrel with the foe:
To you from failing hands we throw
The torch; be yours to hold it high.
If ye break faith with us who die
We shall not sleep, though poppies grow
In Flanders fields.

~ Lieutenant-Colonel John McCrae
"In Flanders Fields"

Made in the USA
Middletown, DE
08 October 2021